WAR BIRDS
The Diary of A Great War Pilot

WAR BIRDS

The Diary of A Great War Pilot

Elliott White Springs

Drawings by
Clayton Knight

Annotations by
Lieutenant Horace Fulford

Introduction by
Mark Hillier

Frontline Books

WAR BIRDS
The Diary of A Great War Pilot

First Printed as *War Birds: Diary of an Unknown Aviator* by John Hamilton Ltd.,
May 1927.
This edition published in 2016 by Frontline Books,
an imprint of Pen & Sword Books Ltd,
47 Church Street, Barnsley, S. Yorkshire, S70 2AS

Copyright © Elliott White Springs
Drawings © Clayton Knight
Annotations © Horace Fulford
Additional text and notes © Mark Hillier 2016

The right of Elliott White Springs to be identified as the author of this work has been asserted by him in accordance with the Copyright, Designs and Patents Act 1988.

ISBN: 978-1-47387-959-1

All rights reserved. No part of this publication may be reproduced, stored in or introduced into a retrieval system, or transmitted, in any form, or by any means (electronic, mechanical, photocopying, recording or otherwise) without the prior written permission of the publisher. Any person who does any unauthorized act in relation to this publication may be liable to criminal prosecution and civil claims for damages.

CIP data records for this title are available from the British Library

For more information on our books, please visit
www.frontline-books.com
email info@frontline-books.com
or write to us at the above address.

Printed and bound by CPI Group (UK) Ltd, Croydon, CR0 4YY
Typeset in 10.5/12.5 point Palatino

Contents

Introduction by Mark Hillier	vii
A Brief History of 85 Squadron	xix
Squadron Roll, Officers of 85 Squadron	xxv
Acknowledgements For New Edition	xxviii
List of Abbreviations	xxx
Foreword to the Original Edition	xxxiii
PART I **THE UK AND TRAINING** 20 September 1917 to 20 May 1917	1
PART II **THE WESTERN FRONT** 25 May 1917 and Beyond	93
Appendices	187
References and Notes	237
Select Bibliography and Source Information	257

Introduction to the New Extended Edition

The wind whistling through your hair, your eyes streaming with the cold, frostbite beginning to nibble at fingers and toes, temperatures below freezing and a lack of oxygen to boot. One could be writing about a polar explorer or a mountaineer; few would consider that this was the experience of the early aviators in the First World War.

Having flown open cockpit aircraft for many years I can safely say from experience that it provides an invasion of the senses that no-one can prepare you for. The noise, the smell of the exhaust, plus the cold and weather; you need to be suitably dressed, well prepared and mentally focused. Flying at just 4,000 feet for an hour in the winter chills the exposed aviator to the bone and, unless dressed adequately, the flyer's reactions and decision-making capabilities are quickly slowed and exhaustion soon becomes a noticeable factor. Then there are the operational factors to consider – trying to read a map with an 80mph wind whipping around the cockpit or changing an ammunition drum on a machine-gun.

I have the utmost respect for those early aviators who volunteered for service in the air arms, with little knowledge of what they were likely to face. They may have watched an early flying machine trundle overhead or, if very fortunate, had a quick 'flip' in some flimsy craft.

They approached aviation as a big adventure, as is so graphically portrayed in this new extended edition of *War Birds*, though, as the reader will discover, that adventure was a dangerous and deadly one.

Compared to those serving in the trenches for example, many were minor celebrities of their time, but they paid a high price. Not for nothing were they once referred to as 'the twenty minuters', this in turn being a reference to the life expectancy of a pilot or observer and made famous by the BBC's *Blackadder* television series.

The truth, as might be expected, is somewhat better, although the figures are still stark. Life expectancy in reality was more likely to be from three to ten weeks. As an example, statistics for 56 Squadron, provided by the historian Martin Middlebrook, suggest that 41% of those aircrew who started with the unit were dead within ten weeks. A further 16% were wounded and 28% were taken prisoner. This constitutes an 85% chance of death, injury or capture.[1]

What is also apparent is that many suffered with mental stresses and torment, now more commonly referred to and recognized as Post Traumatic Stress Disorder. Even after the war many committed suicide or were too ill to work.

In my mind the early pilots and observers were like explorers, pioneers blazing the trail for military aviation. What makes these men so special is that like the explorers they also had to battle the elements and exhaustion to fight, albeit over short periods of time, but with the added risks of aircraft and engine unreliability and, of course, the enemy shooting at them. On top of this was the unpleasant smell and taste of oil, which was flung in their faces from their aircraft's engine, whilst being tossed around by the air currents.

To master aerial warfare, the early pilots had to learn on the job, often testing and understanding the limits of their aircraft and developing their skills in the heat of battle. Indeed, anything other than simple manoeuvres was often frowned upon in training for fear of crashing the aircraft, at a time when the understanding of materials and the effects of stress on airframes were in their infancy. Many early aircraft which became overstressed simply broke up in flight. Duncan Grinnell-Milne, a First World War pilot, once quoted the words of a fellow aviator: 'In aviation, there is as much art as science, and with aeronautics, in its earlier stages, art often seemed to be marching ahead of science that was in its infancy and waiting for the pilots whose progressive discoveries, be it said, were frequently the result of accident.'[2]

It is sadly true that during training the risks were extremely high, the death toll amongst pilots and observers in training in the United Kingdom being around 8,000 by the end of the war. Prior to 1917, when a more formalised method of training was introduced, fatalities numbered six or seven a day. Observers received no formal training at all until 1917, often being introduced to the aircraft and flying by the pilot they were paired up with.

Early pilot training was carried out on very basic machines, with pilots sometimes receiving only two to three hours' dual instruction before being expected to go solo. Cecil Lewis was one such airmen, recalling: 'One and a half hours' dual stood to my credit. I had trundled round the aerodrome with Sergeant Yates my instructor, doing left hand circuits, and made a few indifferent landings.'[3] At this point his

INTRODUCTION TO THE NEW EXTENDED EDITION

instructor was happy to allow Lewis to go solo in the afternoon – if the wind was right!

The engines on many of the early machines were frequently described as 'cantankerous', and control over them rudimentary. To reduce lift, the pilot would simply kill the engine, either by using a fuel lever or blip switch, and put the aircraft into a glide. Later rotary engines did have a throttle but the pilot also had to tune the fuel-air mixture with a 'fine adjustment' lever and a blip switch was still used for landing. The rotary engines on some aircraft also made them more difficult to operate due to the gyroscopic forces produced.

Some pilots were sent to the front to face the enemy with less than fifteen hours' flying time to their credit. A letter written on 22 July 1917 by the Commanding Officer of 7 Squadron, and which appears on one pilot's service records, states: 'He came out here with about 23 hours flying, only ½ hour of which was on R.E.8s. On his first flight out here he wrecked the machine owing to a bad "take off" and the next time he put up a very bad exhibition of flying, and he will not be fit to take up an observer for a long time. He has lost his confidence temporarily, and I strongly recommend that he should be sent home for further instruction, after which he should be alright.'[4]

Even though formal training programmes had been introduced during 1917, a survey of training accidents in May 1918 involving only four aircraft types – Sopwith Camels, R.E.8s, S.E.5as and D.H.4s – revealed that in the course of one month no fewer than forty-one aircraft had been lost to what was known as 'the dreaded spin'. This spin normally started from a stall, which meant the aircraft departed from normal flight into a nose-down rotating, yawing and pitching movement. The temptation for the pilot was to pull the stick back to recover the nose to the horizon but his was ineffective as the wing was stalled. To recover, pilots had to push the control column forwards to recover the air flow over the wing, use rudder to stop the yaw, before recovering from the nose down attitude. Many pilots lacked understanding of this phenomenon and were unable to regain control.[5]

The statistics regarding losses make grim reading. By the end of the war, a total of 14,166 aircrew had been killed, of whom more than half, as previously mentioned, had died during training.[6]

The situation had become so bad that a parliamentary question was raised on 27 June 1918 asking for an explanation. Mr William Joynson-Hicks, the MP for Brentford, 'asked the Undersecretary of State to the Air Ministry what proportion the fatal casualties in flying in his country bore to those at the front for the year 1917 and for the first five months of this year?'

INTRODUCTION TO THE NEW EXTENDED EDITION

The response by Major Baird was that, 'The proportionate figures asked for in this question would be entirely misleading in the absence of a comparative statement as to the number of pilots under instruction, standards of training, and number of hours flown. Considerations of public interest do not allow this information to be made public.'[7]

As well as inadequate flying training, another factor that contributed to the huge operational losses was the lack of tactical training. This was recalled by Lieutenant William MacLanachan of 40 Squadron: 'The real omission in the training curriculum was on the subject of the psychology and tactics of fighting much more than in the technicalities of flying or even formation flying. It was a notorious fact that the majority of the really trained fliers, being filled with the aggressive spirit, thought aerial fighting was merely a matter of shooting and stunting. What they failed to realise and no one could blame them, was that it takes several weeks if not months, of "flirting" with death, to key the senses up to the alertness that formed the bulwark round experienced fighters.'[8]

Action in the air was fierce and frantic, the risk of collision extreme as the combatants wheeled and dived to gain the advantage over their foe. The aircraft, made of wood and fabric, although fairly sturdy, were prone to damage under fire, and no armour plating meant the crew were out in the open and susceptible to shrapnel from anti-aircraft fire or hot zipping bullets, ripping into the fabric and onwards into unprotected flesh. These crews were not even allowed the luxury of a parachute to bail out if their machine was spinning out of control and on fire. Many pilots and Observers chose to carry small arms in the cockpit with the idea of taking their own lives, as Major Mick Mannock did, rather than face the prospect of being burnt to death.

One can only imagine the pressures that these young aviators were subjected too; the constant fear of death, and witnessing comrades being shot down in flames. The mental anguish took its toll on some, as Elliott White Springs eloquently reveals in *War Birds*. Likewise, the following quote from a letter written by a medical officer to the Royal Flying Corps' headquarters, about one of the pilots serving on 21 Squadron, gives some indication of the effects of aerial combat:

> This officer joined the infantry at the beginning of the war, being then 16 years old. He served in the ranks until June 1915 when he got a commission in the North Staffords. He came to France on September 1st 1916, was through the Beaumont Hamel fighting and in the trenches until December 1916. He then came straight to the

RFC as Observer on probation, without any course at home, and was with No. 46 Squadron until March 1917, when he came to No.21 Squadron.

Until five weeks ago he felt perfectly fit, but then began to be troubled with Insomnia and bad dreams, and to feel generally tired and depressed. He went on leave a week later which he spent quietly at home and was beginning to feel better, but on his return the old symptoms recurred. He further began to avoid the society of his brother officers, and to make a practice of keeping a flask of whisky by his bed, with the hope of getting some rest at night by that means. On one occasion he apparently disgraced himself when under the influence of alcohol.

On examination he presents the signs of one who is generally tired and depressed. His pulse rate is increased above the normal at rest, his heart being in that 'imitable' state frequently found amongst those suffering from the strain of service. As regards the connection of alcohol with his case, I consider that it is not responsible for his condition, but may have aggravated his previous symptoms. I think that he needs a good rest under supervision, but should completely recover with care. At present he is temporarily unfit for service.[9]

These pilots and observers were brave men which makes their first-hand accounts even more precious. Some of the best books written by pilots and observers have been re-printed many times over the years, such as *Sagittarius Rising* by Cecil Lewis and *Wind in the Wires* by Duncan Grinnell-Milne, amongst others. This particular book, *War Birds: Diary of an Unknown Aviator*, written by Elliott White Springs, was first published in May 1926, and proved to be both popular and controversial, for reasons that will become apparent.

Springs and his best friend, John McGavock Grider, were two young Americans who enlisted in the United States Air Service. Following their country's entry into the war in 1917, both were posted to the United Kingdom. There, along with other Americans, they continued their training with the Royal Flying Corps, being sent to Oxford College for initial training – a process which many of the pilots had already endured, having spent time on the Curtiss JN4 in the United States.

Having stayed together through this training, Springs and Grider were then hand-picked by Major William Avery Bishop V.C., D.S.O., M.C., in March 1918, to fly with the newly-formed 85 Squadron at Hounslow Heath Aerodrome. Both flew to France with this unit, along with another American by the name of Lawrence Kingsley Callahan, the trio becoming known as the 'three musketeers'. Grider was to be killed in action only a month after the squadron arrived on the Western Front.

On 18 June 1918, Springs and Grider were on a sortie together and had just shot down one German aircraft when the latter's aircraft went missing. A few days after his loss a German pilot dropped a message describing his burial. His body was not recovered until after the war.

Springs continued to fly with 85 Squadron until he was shot down by *Leutnant* Josef Raesch of *Jasta* 43, suffering a bad facial injury in the crash that resulted. He was subsequently posted to the 148th Aero Squadron of the Unites States Air Service.[10]

When first released, *War Birds* soon made an impact. One reviewer stated that 'it may be recommended to all whose taste for war literature has been spoiled by satiety, since it is possible that no more remarkable product of war has appeared in black and white … The life – and what a life – of the flying man in war is all here with the names of the real people punctuating its vivid effects. There is surely no more attesting document of the breathless career of the aviator during the greatest war.'[11]

A much more expansive review appeared in the pages of *The Western Morning News and Mercury* on 31 August 1927, under the title 'Young America in the War'. It is perhaps worth quoting the review in full:

> Of all the elements that made up the fighting forces of the world's armies during the Great War none gathered unto itself greater glory nor showed a nicer appreciation of military etiquette – chivalry, if that much-abused term be preferred – than the Air Force, whose combats revealed in modern warfare many of the characteristics of the old-time hand-to-hand encounter in which courtesy to one's opponent meant as much as, if not more than, the actual business of killing. By that we do not mean to imply that chivalry was the peculiar possession of airmen, but the fact that the combatants were, in many cases, known to each other – that they often ignored the presence of other enemies, who ignored them, in order to engage the attention of a well-known "ace" – meant a revival of the spirit of personal contact that was a feature of the battles of the Middle Ages. Hence, many of the reminiscences of members of the Air Force have a personal touch that is lacking in the official histories of the war, and they possess an added attraction in the naïve manner in which they are written.
>
> After all, the Air Force was essentially the unit of Youth – gallant, reckless, confident Youth, thinking and living for the day only,

careless of self, knowing only the joy of combat, the thrill of speed, the sudden spectacular death. It is no disparagement to those who fought on land and sea to say these boys made a very special appeal to those who were unable to participate in the grim five years' struggle. Let us be frank and say at once that it was because of their youth and their daring – the exotic nature of their calling – that thrilled the hearts of those who read of their deeds.

A REVEALING BOOK
That is one of the reasons why "War Birds," written, as the publishers assure us, by a young American aviator, who was killed in 1918, will be in tremendous demand. It is an extremely frank record which could have been written only by a very young man – and an aviator. None other could have penned a book that, with all its careless phrasing and lack of literacy style, burns its way into the very soul of the reader, for within its pages are lined the thoughts and hopes, the aspirations and bitter cynicism, the follies and the gay courage of youth in time of war and as a participator in its grim game.

This anonymous diary is, too, or real and lasting value as revealing the psychology of one who may with justice be called a typical young American of the war period. He commences his narrative on September 20, 1917, when he was three days out of New York, bound – though he did not know it then – for England. Full of the task before him, slightly scornful of Britain and British achievements, arrogant, keen, and efficient, the author came gradually to a realization of what the war meant.

He learned his first lesson in, perhaps, the best place for a person of his kidney – Oxford, where he and his fellow cadets were in training; then he acquired a greater knowledge in London, where he plunged headlong into the hectic follies that seemed to thrive on the war fever. His last and greatest lesson he learned only too well – in France, and after the first flush of victory over opponents as young and brave and as full of the joy of living as himself, the utter futility of all wars was revealed to him in a series of tragic episodes, not the least being the knowledge that it was only a question of time – maybe a few weeks – before he, too, went the way of so many of his comrades.

FOLLY OF WARFARE
From a light-hearted boy he became a grim, disillusioned man – carrying on from a sense of duty and by reason of his own grit, but

INTRODUCTION TO THE NEW EXTENDED EDITION

sick at heart and utterly and unspeakably weary of it all. And at length he met his death 20 miles behind the German lines, where he was given the funeral which the airmen of both sides accorded a hero.

"War Birds" is not an attractive book; it is finer and greater than that. In its stark realism, its brutality, its lapses into sheer vulgarity, it possess a strength and forcefulness that no mere literary talent and beauty of writing could achieve. It does, also, reveal the influence which British breeding and tradition has on those who come within its sphere. Slowly the young American sheds his prejudices, his slang, his sense of superiority, until, before his death, he has become more English than the English themselves. It is certainly a book to be read – it is a human document in the truest sense of the word.

Such reviews aside, *War Birds* has been subject of some controversy over the years, for several reasons. One of these is that when it was produced, Springs initially made no mention of the fact that the publication was based on the diary and letters of his best friend, John McGavock Grider. Apparently both had agreed that they would publish each other's memoirs in the event of the other's death. Springs eluded to this in the introduction to the second and subsequent re-printings.

As Springs explains in his foreword, the first edition was privately published, with only 210 copies being printed. *Liberty* magazine then obtained a copy and published it serially, and eventually it was mass-produced with numerous editions. In its time it was a best seller, the post-war audiences lapping up the stories of mixing with high society, action and death. It was also applauded by a number of other flying veterans such as Sholto Douglas who considered it to be 'a splendid and heart-warming story'.[12] R.R. Money, who was another RFC pilot, called the book 'one of the finest books of the war in the air'.[13]

Doubts, however, began to be raised about its accuracy, when it was realised that the diary could not be all Grider's, due to the date of his death being 18 June 1918 – the book runs on to 27 August. Springs himself later explained that the account was an amalgam of both his own recollections (and extracts from his letters home) and Griders' diaries. Springs did also contact some of his old squadron colleagues to solicit their views and comments on the text and that they approved it before release.

Of great relevance to this subject is the book entitled *Letters from a War Bird: The World War I Correspondence of Elliott White Springs*. Edited by David K. Vaughan, this publication not only sets out all of Springs' letters, notes and extracts from his log book, but analyses the structure of *War Birds* and how extracts from the letters were incorporated into

INTRODUCTION TO THE NEW EXTENDED EDITION

the text. It reveals that one of Springs' letters states that *War Birds* was 'based largely on my letters, my diary and my combat reports. I also used [Eugene] Barksdale's diary and supplementary matters given to me by [Robert] Kelly and [Larry] Callahan.'[14]

Also of interest is the fact that Springs is quoted as saying that the diary 'became the actual history' of the 210 [total] US Air Service cadets who went over to the UK and served with the RFC or USAS under RFC control, which implies that its purpose was more of a representation of the experiences of all of them rather than a tribute to one.

For some time, I had wanted to obtain a copy *War Birds* to see how much it reflected the true events of 85 Squadron during the First World War. It arrived in very poor condition, with pages falling out and no jacket. My disappointment at the condition of this obviously well-thumbed copy soon vanished when it became apparent that I had stumbled across something quite unique.

I discovered that this particular copy contained numerous handwritten annotations in the margins and had many original and captioned photographs inserted through its pages. A clue to the original owner was the name Wing Commander Horace Fulford, purportedly of 85 Squadron, written on the title page. Was this a copy once owned by one of the squadron's pilots? Just who was Fulford?

Thanks to the many clues the previous owner had littered throughout the book, a period of research soon provided the answers that I craved. Horace Frederick Fulford hailed from Pitsmoor, Sheffield – and he was indeed a member of 85 Squadron.

Born on 10 November 1890, Fulford had gone on to study music before the war, at which point he was aged twenty-four. He soon enlisted in the Royal Engineers and, with the rank of Corporal, was employed as a motorcyclist. He arrived in France during 1914.

It was not until 1916 that Fulford volunteered for service with the Royal Flying Corps. It is clear that his intention was to fly, and he was initially sent to No.1 School of Military Aeronautics at Reading on 12 August 1916. This was followed by postings to 41 Training Squadron RFC at Doncaster, where he learned to fly the Caudron GIII. His next posting was to 15 Training Squadron, again at Doncaster, to fly the B.E.2 and R.E.8. He returned to 41 Training Squadron, only to be declared unfit for duties as a pilot or observer in June 1917.[15] The reason for this has not been established – was it the result of an accident or did a medical condition render him unsuitable for a pilot or aircrew role? What is certain, however, is that he was, at some stage, awarded his wings as photographs of him in the book indicate.

INTRODUCTION TO THE NEW EXTENDED EDITION

Even though he was unable to fly, Fulford remained in the RFC and became an assistant instructor in gunnery. From this role he eventually became the armaments officer on 85 Squadron (with the initial rank of lieutenant), a post he took up with effect from 2 April 1918. By the end of hostilities, Fulford had achieved the rank of wing commander.

In 1939, Fulford re-joined the RAF. He was posted to No.939 (West Riding) Squadron of the Auxiliary Air Force, being commissioned as a Pilot Officer in the Balloon Branch with effect from 7 May that year.[16] Both of his two sons followed in their father's footsteps and volunteered for the RAF. David served as a fighter pilot during the Battle of Britain, whilst John flew in Bomber Command. Sadly, both were killed in action.[17]

Having read the book and the additional notes by Fulford, it became apparent that the stories within it are factual, despite the previous discounting by some as being partly historical fiction – though admittedly in some instances they are an amalgam of events. What is clear, however, is that some of the dates may be inaccurate.

Springs, for example, was shot down and injured on 27 June 1918, and upon his recovery was attached to the 148th Aero Squadron from 3 August 1918.[18] Yet the diary continues on as if he or Grider were still at 85 Squadron until the end of August. That said, what David Vaughan makes clear in *Letters from a War Bird* is that Springs was still close to, and fraternising with, a number of pilots at the squadron, and so was able to hear many stories concerning his old unit.

There are other dates in Springs' diary which do not correspond with known facts, such as the death of Mick Mannock. Springs wrote that Mannock met his demise on 20 July, when in actual fact the loss of Mannock occurred on 26 July.[19]

Another factor to note is that *War Birds* is referenced in other accounts written about contemporary squadron members such as *Macs Memoirs: The Flying Life of Squadron Leader McGregor*, which was written by G.H. Cunningham. It is worth including some of the comments by Cunningham:

> On June 26th [sic] the squadron suffered the loss of Lieutenant Springs, one of the two remaining Americans. He was shot down on the British side of the lines, and after he left hospital, was transferred to No.148 American Aero Squadron.
>
> *War Birds*, which purports to be a record of the doings of 'Eighty-Five' fall off in accuracy thereafter, as it was necessarily written by Springs from hearsay. In mid-July the remaining American,

xvi

INTRODUCTION TO THE NEW EXTENDED EDITION

Lieutenant Callahan, was also transferred to this unit.

The squadron was sorry to lose its Yanks; for they were highly regarded and, if the truth must be told considered as part of the entertainments for which No 85 Squadron was famed.[20]

What is clear is that Fulford clearly felt that *War Birds* was a record of the service of 85 Squadron – making a comment to that effect on the title page of his copy – and also that historically some of the facts were correct if not entirely chronologically accurate.

As well as his photographs, I have also retained Fulford's original annotations throughout. At the same time, I have added facts to this book in the form of endnotes to help set the scene and bring in additional background information. This includes daily events in the life of 85 Squadron garnered from other contemporary sources and combat reports. I have also added further details on personnel mentioned in the book.

What is beyond doubt is that *War Birds* is a fascinating and descriptive text written by a pilot who experienced the dangers and realities of the air war at first-hand. It is therefore not only a valuable reference source, but a fitting tribute to the contribution made by the American pilots to the RFC and RAF during the First World War.

Mark Hillier,
Fontwell, West Sussex,
June, 2016.

'The Flying Foxes':
A Brief History of 85 Squadron

Albeit a late comer to the First World War, 85 Squadron was formed around a nucleus of experienced aerial combat practitioners who had already been blooded on the Western Front. During its brief history in France in 1918, the unit claimed a significant number of victories, ninety-nine in total over a six-month period.[21]

It was on 1 August 1917 that 85 Squadron was formed at the Central Flying School at Upavon in Wiltshire. Shortly afterwards, the squadron moved to Mousehold Heath near Norwich, under the command of Major R.A. Archer. At that time it was equipped with the Sopwith Dolphin.

During November 1917, the squadron transferred to Hounslow Heath Aerodrome in Essex, and in March 1918 Major William Avery 'Billy' Bishop V.C., D.S.O., M.C., took command and carried out his orders to prepare and train his personnel for front line duties in France. The new CO had previously been flying with 60 Squadron on a Nieuport 17 and the Royal Aircraft Factory S.E.5a, amassing forty-seven claimed victories.[22] At Hounslow the squadron, especially its new American recruits, enjoyed the high life, often socialising with high society in London.

It was whilst based at Hounslow that the unit was to receive its mascot, a flying fox presented to it by Princess Marie Louise. On 1 April 1918, the squadron was transferred into the newly-formed Royal Air Force. Following this period of training the squadron deployed to France during May 1918, having also swapped its Sopwith Dolphins for the S.E.5a.

On 22 May 1918, 85 Squadron departed Hounslow, heading for its new home at Petite-Synthe, an airfield near Dunkirk, for acclimatisation. Although it was a fair distance from the front and the pilots were supposed to be getting used to the terrain and carrying out familiarisation flights, the old hands on the squadron got the 'itch' and went looking for trouble.

The location of the initial airfield at Petite-Synthe soon proved unpopular with some of more experienced pilots, as Malcolm Charles McGregor, a New Zealander who was known as 'Mac' by his colleagues, revealed in a letter home: 'This is a rotten part of the line, and the sooner we shift the better. The Huns around here take more stalking than an old stag. You cannot get within miles of them. For instance, last night (June 7th) went 20 miles into Hunland, and still they went further in.'[23]

Despite the problems encountered in engaging the enemy, some successes did result. Billy Bishop was the first to claim a victory on 27 May, notching up his forty-eighth victim. He subsequently made eleven further claims before the unit moved closer to the front.

Another successful pilot during 85's time at Petite-Synthe was 'Mac' McGregor. He had previously opened his account with 54 Squadron over Cambrai during June 1917.[24] He claimed a further three victims before the unit's next move.

It was on 11 June that the squadron moved to St Omer, the majority of claims there again being made by Billy Bishop who filed a further thirteen. There has been much controversy about the actual number of 'kills' made by Bishop, a situation exacerbated by the fact that the majority of his victories were not confirmed by other witnesses – this being the result of his 'lone wolf' tactics.

This was, however, not always the case. One of Bishop's combat reports, that dated 1 June 1918, reveals that on this occasion he was leading a patrol of three S.E.5as near La Gorgue, north of Arras, when they came across six enemy aircraft. Bishop's subsequent report states: 'While on practice patrol, I led patrol consisting of Captain Horn, Lieut. McGregor, Lieut. Springs, diving on six enemy E.A [Enemy Aircraft] zoomed and dived again on to the leaders tail fired 30 rounds from 50 yards, E.A went down in a straight dive, then spun and crashed near La Gorgue. During fight I saw Lieut. McGregor shoot down E.A., which fell completely out of control a long way and another E.A. fell completely out of control from above me. This must have been shot down by Lieut. Springs, I saw it still out of control quite low down. Lieut. McGregor also shot down another E.A. out of control. Lieut. Springs confirms the E.A. I shot down.'[25]

Regardless of the controversy surrounding his tactics and claims, William Bishop was, at the end of the war, officially recognised as the British Empire's highest scoring Ace with seventy-two victories, twenty-five of which were when he was with 85 Squadron.

Bishop returned to the UK on 20 June 1918. What one pilot thought of him and his tactics, is best summarised in a letter Elliott White

Springs sent to his mother on 20 June 1918: 'Three days the order came. They think he's too valuable a man to fight the Huns in person. Perhaps they are right – I'll bet the Huns think so too. But he certainly showed what kind of stuff he was made of. First he raised unshirted hell about it but it was no good. Then he went up and shot down two Hun machines. The next day he got his orders and ticket. And he went up and shot down three Huns. So today he was to leave at noon and everybody felt pretty bad about it. But he went up at ten o'clock and attacked five Huns. One of them got away by going into the clouds. Then on the way home he saw a two seater and shot it down in flames.' On reflecting about Bishop, Springs wrote: 'So our Major is gone but if ever a C.O had the respect, admiration, and love of his unit 'twas him.'[26]

On 18 June 1918, there was a change of command when the new CO, Major Edward 'Mick' Mannock D.S.O., M.C., was officially posted in but he did not arrive on the unit to 3 July, temporary command being given to Captain Baker. Mannock was welcomed by the pilots who had made it clear they wanted him as CO; his reputation preceded him and the men were not disappointed. Mannock's training methods encouraged fighting as a unit rather than as individuals which had been the more common methodology under Bishop. On arrival at the unit Mannock already had fifty-two claims to his name, achieved whilst he was flying with Nos. 40 and 74 squadrons.[27]

One of Mannock's old 40 Squadron colleagues summed up his ability as a pilot and leader: 'Mick's quick intelligence had grasped the essential features of aerial warfare; the psychology, tactics and spirit that were demanded from those who wished to make themselves efficient in their jobs. He knew that our aerial supremacy had been maintained not by superior numbers, for these could be, to a greater extent, discounted because of the inferiority of our machines, but by the spirit, determination and intelligence of the pilots. He therefore enlightened the pilots on the psychological reactions they were likely to feel, the types of enemy they would encounter, and the tactics they should employ. Above all he tried to imbue his listeners with the spirit that would turn them into fighters.'[28]

The squadron went from strength to strength under Mannock's command. He would often lead patrols over the lines, acting as a decoy to attract the German aircraft. Then when they engaged, the rest of the squadron could swoop down and hope to get easy claims using their height advantage. A dogfight that took place on 7 July near Le Doulieu alludes to the tactics used, although on this occasion without the hoped-for results. Mannock was flying at 7,000 feet and his report states: 'Observed combat taking place over me at locality above mentioned.

Fight descended to 7,000 feet and S.E was attacked by a red-bodied E.A which dived and lost height. Followed the E.A down, firing when the opportunity presented itself. This E.A. went vertically into the ground at approximately a mile East of Doulieu. Height at termination of engagement 1,500 feet. Climbed for about 1,000 feet and observed second S.E being engaged by two E.A [probably Lieutenant Longton] took one which was on S.E's tail and engaged same. Fired approximately 30 rounds from each gun when E.A. went into a spin at about 1,000 feet and I lost sight of it almost at once. I am sure that this E.A. crashed. Lieut. Longton saw the first E.A. go down.'[29]

Whilst this was happening, the main patrol flying above Mannock was being led by Captain Spencer Bertram Horn at 16,000 feet. A seasoned veteran of the Royal Flying Corps, having flown with 60 Squadron in Nieuport Scouts, he had six victories and an award of a Military Cross to his name before he joined 85 Squadron.[30] His combat report gives the bigger picture in that he states: 'When leading the patrol, I saw 7 E.A. at 18000 feet above us. [Even though Mannock was below as bait, the Germans were above the main patrol] I climbed towards the lines, the E.A. following. The front two dived, I then turned into the E.A. formation, and two of them were on Lieut Longton's tail. I shot one off which went down completely out of control and watched it down for about 4,000 feet. I then got on the tail of a second E.A. which I followed down to 6,000 feet, the planes eventually coming off and machine crashing near Steenwerck. I then saw a fight going on west of me, I dived towards it and saw Lieut Longton shoot an E.A down which crashed at Sheet 36A.F.14.'[31]

This first combat under the command of Mannock was a success, with no less than four Fokker D.VIIs claimed. This was a much needed boost to the squadron who had recently seen the loss of a number of popular pilots such as Elliott White Springs and Grider.

Mannock was clearly a fine leader and he would often take up younger pilots to show them the ropes, as detailed by Lieutenant C.B.R. MacDonald, a Canadian who served with 85 Squadron: 'He would select one of the young pilots to fly with him in order to give him instruction, and together they would hunt about the sky at about 15,000 feet, whilst the rest of the Squadron would be about three-quarters of a mile away flying at a higher altitude awaiting his signal, a red very light, that he was about to attack. Then the war would commence in earnest – The Hun would be seen tumbling in flames or pieces or diving helter skelter for the ground.'[32]

Mannock had told many of his pilots of the 'foolishness' of following victims down to low level and not breaking off until they had run out of ammunition or the victim had crashed. Unfortunately, for some reason his downfall was due to that very tactic.

It was during a patrol on 26 July 1918, accompanying Lieutenant D.C. Inglis (a New Zealander) over the front line, that Mannock met his fate. Inglis up to this point had not claimed any victories and again Mannock was acting in his role as mentor.

One account provides this description of what happened: 'After shooting down an enemy LVG two-seater behind the German front-line, Mannock is believed to have dived to the crash site to view the wreckage, seemingly breaking one of the unwritten rules of fellow pilots. In consequence, while crossing the trenches the fighters were met with a massive volley of ground-fire. The engine of Mannock's aircraft was hit and immediately caught fire, and shortly after the plane crashed behind German lines. Mannock's body is believed to have been found, though this is unproven, about 250 yards from the wreck of his machine, perhaps thrown, perhaps jumped. The body showed no gunshot wounds; Mannock always promised to shoot himself if he was ever going down.'

Inglis himself wrote: 'Falling in behind Mick again we made a couple of circles around the burning wreck and then made for home. I saw Mick start to kick his rudder, then I saw a flame come out of his machine; it grew bigger and bigger. Mick was no longer kicking his rudder. His nose dropped slightly and he went into a slow right-hand turn, and hit the ground in a burst of flame. I circled at about twenty feet but could not see him, and as things were getting hot, made for home and managed to reach our outposts with a punctured fuel tank.'

Of the loss of 85 Squadron's leader. 'Mac' McGregor wrote: 'We have lost our Squadron Commander. Went down in flames after getting 70 Huns [sic], and so the Royal Air Force has lost the best leader of patrols, and the best Hun getter it has had. In another month he would have had over 100. However unlike other stars, he left behind all the knowledge he had, so it is up to the fellows he taught, to carry on. I was with him a few days ago when he shot down what turned out to be one of the crack Hun Airmen. It all happened 25 miles across the lines, over a Hun aerodrome; it was a pretty sight to see the way the Bosche handled his triplane, pretty little thing, all black with a white tail. Although he put up a good fight he had somebody better after him, and it was not long before the Major got his position for a few seconds and, with both guns going, shot off his tail.'[33] On 18 July 1919, one year after his death, Major Mannock was awarded a posthumous Victoria Cross.

After Mannock's loss, the squadron's new Commanding Officer was Captain Arthur Clunie Randall. An experienced flyer with five victories at the time of his appointment, Randall would go on to score a total of ten as well as be awarded a DFC.

Randall duly made way for Major J. Blackwood, though the latter's command was short-lived as Major Cyril Marconi Crowe took over on the 28 August, remaining in post for the remainder of the war. Crowe was an experienced S.E.5a pilot with fourteen victories to his credit prior to his arrival, although he only claimed one further victim with 85 Squadron, being awarded a D.F.C. for his work.

During its stay at St Omer the squadron claimed at least fifty-eight aerial victories (including one kite balloon) for the loss of nine pilots killed, injured or taken prisoner. In the last few months of the war the squadron moved airfield four times. The first of these changes came on 13 August 1918, when the men left St Omer for Bertangles. The subsequent bases were Estrées-en-Chaussée and Escaucourt in October and November respectively, followed by Phalempin and finally Ascq in November and December 1918.

By the time of the Armistice, 85 Squadron's tally stood at ninety-nine victories. Besides Bishop and Mannock, and the other individuals already mentioned, the squadron had a number of notable Aces, men such as Spencer B. Horn with thirteen victories, Malcolm C. McGregor with a score of eleven, Walter H. Longton also with eleven, Arthur Clunie Randall with ten, John Warner with eight victories, Edwin Louis Benbow with eight, Alec Cunningham-Reid with seven, and Lawrence Callahan, an American with five. Elliott White Springs himself claimed four whilst at 85 Squadron, totalling sixteen by the end of hostilities, some of these claims being shared or out of control and not claimed destroyed.

The squadron returned from France in February 1919, being sent to RAF Lopcombe Corner in Wiltshire. It was disbanded on 3 July 1919.

Squadron Roll
Officers of 85 Squadron

This list of 85 Squadron's officers is based on one complied by Lieutenant H.C. Fulford, the Armaments Officer. Founding members are marked (F).

Commanding Officers
Captain George B.A. Baker MC; Bishop's second in command and temporary CO whilst awaiting the arrival of Mannock (F).
Major William Avery 'Billy' Bishop VC, DSO, MC (F).
Major J. Blackwood.
Wing Commander Cyril Marconi Crowe MC, DFC.
Major Edward Corringhame 'Mick' Mannock VC, DSO & Two Bars, MC & Bar; shot down and killed 26 July 1918.
Major James Thomas Byford McCudden VC, DSO & Bar, MC & Bar, MM; Fulford states in his notes that McCudden came to 85 Squadron for seven days as CO.
Captain Arthur Clunie Randall DFC; originally the 'B' Flight commander.

Flight Commanders
Captain Edwin Louis Benbow MC; shot down and killed 30 May 1918 (F).
Captain George Clapham Dixon; Canadian (F).
Lieutenant Colonel Spencer Bertram Horn MC; the first officer to be asked to join 85 Squadron by Bishop and who commanded 'C' Flight (F).
Captain Malcolm Charles McGregor DFC; a New Zealander (F).

Officers
Lieutenant Colin Frank Abbot (F).
Lieutenant G.M. Baldwin.

SQUADRON ROLL OFFICERS OF 85 SQUADRON

Captain Gordon David Brewster MC; arrived mid-June 1918.
Lieutenant Edward Cecil Brown; killed in action 18 October 1918.
Lieutenant Lawrence Kingsley Callahan DFC; American (F).
Lieutenant John Davis Canning; a New Zealander.
Captain Douglas Carruthers; Canadian (F).
Lieutenant Alec Stratford 'Bobby' Cunningham-Reid DFC (F).
Lieutenant William E.W. Cushing; the Recording Officer.
Lieutenant Paul Desire D'Albenas; Canadian, killed in action 11 October 1918.
Lieutenant Arthur Hector Ross Daniel; South African, killed in action 29 August 1918.
Lieutenant Charles William Davison; Canadian, killed in action 4 October 1918.
Lieutenant E. Dawson; prisoner of war 21 July 1918.
Lieutenant Dickson.
Lieutenant John Dymond (F).
Lieutenant Stuart C. Elliot.
Lieutenant Horace Frederick Fulford; Armament Officer (F).
Lieutenant John McGavock Grider; American, shot down and killed 18 June 1918.
Lieutenant C. Roy Hall; Canadian, prisoner of war 13 June 1918 (F).
Lieutenant Herbert.
Lieutenant Donald C. Inglis DCM; New Zealander (F).
Lieutenant Kelly; as appears on Fulford's list, though no further information can be found detailing this individual.
Second Lieutenant Frank Lindon Le Lievre; killed in action 4 October 1918.
Second Lieutenant Robert Aubrey Hastings Lloyd, died of wounds 10 October 1918.
Captain Walter Hunt 'Scruffy' Longton DFC & Two Bars, AFC (F).
Lieutenant Charles Beverly Robinson MacDonald; Canadian (F).
Second Lieutenant Nelson H. Marshall; confirmed as a prisoner of war 17 July 1918.
Lieutenant Thomas Cranston Martin; killed in action 12 August 1918.
Captain E.F. Nichol.
Lieutenant Orville Alfred Ralston DSC; American.
Lieutenant Elliot Gavin Robertson; killed in action 27 September 1918.
Lieutenant William Scott Robertson; killed in action 13 July 1918.
Lieutenant J.C. Rorison; American, joined June 1918.
Lieutenant Peter Rosie; Engineering Officer (F).
Lieutenant Smith (F).
Captain Elliott White Springs; American (F).

SQUADRON ROLL OFFICERS OF 85 SQUADRON

Lieutenant John Randolph Stacey; Canadian, killed whilst flying 8 April 1918 (F).
Lieutenant Herbert Ernest Thomson (named as Thompson by Springs and Bishop); prisoner of war 16 June 1918 (F).
Lieutenant Donovan Joseph Trapp; Canadian, killed in action 19 July 1918.
Lieutenant John Weston Warner DFC; shot down and killed 4 October 1918 (F).

Original members of 85 Squadron
(as far as can be remembered)

C.O.   Major   W A Bishop V.C. DSO. MC.
          Capt   Benton
            "   Horn   (Ex Dragoon Guards)
            "   Baker
          Lt   Warner
            "   McGregor
            "   Inglis
            "   Smith
            "   Hall
            "   Longton
            "   Didmond
            "   McGrider
            "   Springs
            "   Callahan
            "   Kelly
            "   McDonald (Ex RE)
            "   Abbott
            "   Thompson
            "   Carruthers
            "   Cuningham-Reid
            "   Dixon
            "   Rose   (Equip:)
            "   Cushing (Adjt)
            "   Fulford (Ex RE)
                          (armament)

Other C O's. Major McCudden VC DSO.
                " Mannock VC DSO.
                " C. Crowe DSO MC.

Lieutenant Horace Fulford's handwritten list of the original members of 85 Squadron. (Mark Hillier)

Acknowledgements

Thanks go to the Springs Close Family for allowing publication of this new, extended edition and for access to their archive of photographs (in particular, thanks go to Ann Yarborough Evans from the Springs Close Family Archive who worked so hard in her support of this edition); the Clayton Knight family for permission to reproduce the original drawings; and Mark Taylor who helped bring the project to fruition.

Abbreviations

AEF	American Expeditionary Force
AFC	Air Force Cross
ASC	Army Service Corps
AW	Armstrong Whitworth
Bde	Brigade
BEF	British Expeditionary Force
CB	Companion of The Most Honourable Order of the Bath
CCS	Casualty Clearing Station
CO	Commanding Officer
Col.	Colonel
DCM	Distinguished Conduct Medal
DFC	Distinguished Flying Cross
Div	Division or Divisional
DSC	Distinguished Service Cross
DSM	Distinguished Service Medal
DSO	Distinguished Service Order
GCB	Knight Grand Cross of The Most Honourable Order of the Bath
GCIE	Knight Grand Commander of The Most Eminent Order of the Indian Empire
GCSI	Knight Grand Commander of The Most Exalted Order of the Star of India
GCVO	Knight Grand Cross of The Royal Victorian Order
GHQ	General Headquarters
GOC	General Officer Commanding

HA	Heavy Artillery
HE	High Explosive
HQ	Headquarters
Lt	Lieutenant
Lt Col	Lieutenant Colonel
MC	Military Cross
MM	Military Medal
MO	Medical Officer
NC	North Carolina
NCO	Non-Commissioned Officer
PoW	Prisoner of War
Pte	Private
RA	Royal Artillery
RAF	Royal Air Force
RAMC	Royal Army Medical Corps
RFA	Royal Field Artillery
RFC	Royal Flying Corps
RNAS	Royal Naval Air Service
Sec Lt, 2/Lt	Second Lieutenant
USAS	United States Air Service
VC	Victoria Cross

Foreword to the Original Edition

Mention American aviators during the war and the infantry will express its contempt. All artillerymen proclaim that they never saw an American plane near the front. They overlook the fact that in addition to the planes of the American Air Service, hundreds of French, British and Italian planes were flown by Americans, in American uniforms, who were attached to their armies.

In the summer of 1917, two hundred and ten young university men, who had joined the Air Service at the declaration of war, volunteered for immediate service abroad. They were sent to England, just as others were sent to France, Italy and Canada, to be trained by our Allies and to fight with them until our army could supply them with fighting planes.

One of these men kept a diary which has been published as *War Birds*. He was one of two hundred and ten, neither the best nor the worst, but because he was the closest to me in life, I have undertaken to publish the story of his career in the A.E.F. Before he was killed, he gave me his diary and told me how he would like to have his deeds reported in case I survived him. He was very definite in his ideas and I agreed to respect them. He promised to do the same for me in case I should go first. I have discharged this trust faithfully.

Though *War Birds* is an individual diary, intended only to refresh the mind of the writer in later years, it became the actual history of those two hundred and ten men. It tells, for the first time, of their lives and deaths, their successes and their failures. Though it gives the opinions and prejudices of one individual, these same opinions and prejudices were shared by us all. Whatever errors he made, were made by us all. If he committed any transgressions, so did we all. It could have been the diary of any of the two hundred and ten.

As such, his entries concerning his loved ones at home had no place in a public document. With no thought to change his character, such references were omitted. His identity was of no public concern, so it was not divulged. He is not a candidate for public honor. With no thought of concealing anything, his diary was published as *The Diary of the Unknown Aviator*. Would you dig up the Unknown Soldier and identify him to satisfy curiosity?

When *War Birds* was prepared for publication, it was financed privately and only two hundred and ten copies were to be printed. Through a strange circumstance a copy of the manuscript reached an editor of *Liberty* and due to the interest of Capt. Patterson it was published serially in that magazine. The original edition of two hundred and ten copies was published and distributed to those intimately concerned. Later a public edition was printed. Instead of the book being a financial burden, it is now the means of bringing to the family of the dead writer a considerable sum.

Of the two hundred and ten men who landed in England and trained with the Royal Flying Corps, fifty-one were killed, thirty were wounded, fourteen were prisoners of war and twenty became mentally unfit for flying before they finished their training. When the Armistice was signed the survivors found themselves on the American front, under the American high command. Through jealousy or stupidity their experience and ability were not recognized and their services not utilized. They wandered home by various channels – a sort of lost battalion – disillusioned and discouraged. They returned home only to meet the derision of the infantry, who confused them with the thousands of aviators who had spent the war in Paris, London and New York. They were told by the men who had not volunteered for service abroad when they had the chance, that the best aviators were kept in Texas as instructors and only the worthless ones sent to the front to fight. They were without rank or medals and they suffered by comparison with the much decorated pilots from the American front who returned with rank and headlines. It was for these survivors that the publication of *War Birds* was intended. They will attest its authenticity. And they will understand it.

War Birds is not an attempt to prove any contention. It is not an attempt to make heroes of any group of men. It is the actual story of one man and his friends, first as guests of an ally in a strange land and then under the stress of battle.

There are many things I could have done with the diary. Except for his instructions and a strange impulse, it would probably still be at the bottom of my old army trunk. But on the seventh anniversary of his death, I brought out the diary and began to type it.

FOREWORD TO THE ORIGINAL EDITION

Two of the greatest literary men in America read it. One told me that it was too sensational to be published. The other told me it was not sensational enough. Many suggestions for revising it were made to me but I rejected them all. Both *Liberty* and Mr. George H. Doran kindly agreed to publish it without making any changes.

The ten men whose names appear in it most prominently read it and compared it with their own diaries and records. They gave their endorsement to it without asking for a single deletion or change. Their only stipulation was that if I was responsible for the publication of their private histories, I must not take out my own name. My name and Callahan's appear oftener than any others. I have no apologies to make for that since we three were constantly together for nearly a year. None of the books I have read about the war mention the fact that any one beside the writer thereof did any fighting at all.

I do not like the title *War Birds*. It was given to the diary by *Liberty* and stuck so closely that it was necessary to use it on the book.

But to me it will always be *The Diary of the Unknown Aviator*.

His body lies at Houplines, near Armentières. His spirit still haunts the pages of his diary. Let the critics rage! I have carried out his orders.

Elliott White Springs,
Fort Mill, South Carolina,
July, 1927.

PART I
THE UK AND TRAINING

20 September 1917 to 20 May 1918

A group photograph of 'The Three Musketeers' – Larry Callahan, Elliott White Springs and John McGavock Grider – which was believed to have been taken in London in April or May 1918. Note how Springs is wearing RFC wings (no doubt soon to be changed to RAF wings), the other two have US Air Service wings.
(Courtesy, The Springs Close Family Archives, Fort Mill, SC)

War Birds

September 20th, 1917
Aboard R.M.S. *Carmania*[34] in the harbor of Halifax.
Well, here I am aboard ship and three days out of New York, waiting for a convoy at Halifax. This seems to be a fitting place to start a diary. I am leaving my continent as well as my country and am going forth in search of adventure, which I hope to find in Italy, for that is where we are headed. We are a hundred and fifty aviators in embryo commanded by Major MacDill,[35] who is an officer and a gentleman in fact as well as by Act of Congress. We are traveling first class, thanks to him, tho we are really only privates, and every infantry officer on board hates our guts because we have the same privileges they do. Capt. Swan, an old Philippine soldier, is supply officer.

This morning when we steamed into harbor, which is a wonderful place, we found five or six transports already here. The soldiers on them, all that could, got into the boats and came over to see us. They rowed around and around our boat and cheered and sang. They were from New Zealand and a fine husky bunch they were. One song went:

> 'Onward, conscript soldiers, marching as to war,
> You would not be conscripts, had you gone before.'

This is a beautiful place. I expect my opinion is largely due to my frame of mind, but it really is pretty. Low jagged hills form the horizon and on the south side of the river as we came up, is solid rock with a little dirt over it in spots but the rock sticking thru everywhere like bones thru a poor horse.

We went thru two submarine nets stretched across the mouth of the harbor. I wish I had words to describe the feeling I had when all the soldiers in the harbor came over to tell us howdy. One New Zealander,

I think he was a non-com, stood up in the back of the boat and said, 'You fellows don't look very happy.' And I guess our boys don't at that – the doughboys, I mean. We've got over two thousand of them on board of the 9th Infantry Regiment of the regular army. Anyway, New Zealand beat us cheering with their full throated, 'Hip Hurrah Hip Hurrah Hip Hurrah!' But they said they were five weeks out and knew each other pretty well, while our boys aren't acquainted yet.

I have a stateroom with Lawrence Callahan[36] from Chicago, who roomed with me at Ground School, where we suffered together under Major Kraft and had a lot of fun from time to time in spite of him. We almost got separated at New York as he was going to France with another detachment over at Governor's Island. I got Elliott Springs,[37] our top sergeant, to get the Major to have him transferred to us. We had a good crowd over at Mineola and I saw him in town and he told me he was in a rotten bunch over there. I was a sergeant as Springs had me promoted because I took a squad out and unloaded a carload of canned tomatoes after two others had fallen down on the job. We got him transferred all right and then he got mad as fury at Springs because he made him peel potatoes for four days for chewing gum in ranks.

On the fourth day Cal told Springs how much trouble he had taken to join his outfit and that he hadn't come prepared to be a perpetual kitchen police. Springs said he was very glad to have him but if he wanted to chew gum in ranks he'd have to peel potatoes the rest of the day every time he did it. Cal said he'd already been assigned to the job for four days. Springs said he knew it but that so far he hadn't peeled a single potato and he was going to get one day's work out of him if he had to chain him to the stove to do it. Cal won tho, because Springs was too busy to watch him and he never did finish one pan of spuds.

I've got to go to boat drill now. We practice abandoning ship every day.

That's over. My platoon is assigned to the top deck and Captain La Guardia[38] is in charge of our boat. He is a congressman from New York City and learned to fly last year. He is an Italian so was sent over with us. He managed to bring along two of his Italian ward bosses as cooks. One of them owns a big Italian restaurant and yet here he is as a cook. And he can't cook!

I probably won't write much in this thing. I never have done anything constantly except the wrong thing, but I want a few recollections jotted down in case I don't get killed.

I am going to make two resolutions and stick to them. I am not going to lose my temper any more – I fight too much. And I am going to be

PART ONE: THE UK AND TRAINING

WAR BIRDS

Above: Ground school for the recruits on aircraft construction at Princetown University. Springs can be seen sat on a trestle at the rear of the room in the light shirt. This picture was taken in April or May 1917. (Courtesy, The Springs Close Family Archives, Fort Mill, SC)

Below: A pair of Curtiss JN-4 'Jenny' training aircraft outside the hangars at Princetown University's flying field in June 1917. (Courtesy, The Springs Close Family Archives, Fort Mill, SC)

PART ONE: THE UK AND TRAINING

Above: Students 'hanging out' at Princetown University's flying school. (Courtesy, The Springs Close Family Archives, Fort Mill, SC)

Below: Aviation students in front of a Curtiss JN-4 'Jenny' at Princetown University's flying school. Springs can be seen second from the right, in the second row. The picture was taken in June or July 1917. (Courtesy, The Springs Close Family Archives, Fort Mill, SC)

Above: Aviation cadets washing a Curtiss JN-4 'Jenny' at Princetown University's flying school. (Courtesy, The Springs Close Family Archives, Fort Mill, SC)

Opposite: Elliott White Springs in the cockpit of Curtiss JN-4 'Jenny' at Princetown University's flying school, May or June 1917. (Courtesy, The Springs Close Family Archives, Fort Mill, SC)

---

very careful and take care of myself. I am not going to take any unnecessary chances. I want to die well and not be killed in some accident or die of sickness – that would be terrible, a tragic anti-climax. I haven't lived very well but I am determined to die well. I don't want to be a hero – too often they are all clay from the feet up, but I want to die as a man should. Thank God, I am going to have the opportunity to die as every brave man should wish to die – fighting – and fighting for my country as well. That would retrieve my wasted years and neglected opportunities.

But if I don't get killed, I want to be able to jog my memory in my declining years so I can say, 'Back in 1917 when I was an aviator, I used to –!' I'll probably not write any more for a week, or perhaps no more at all.

PART ONE: THE UK AND TRAINING

September 21st
We left Halifax in a haze just as the sun, blood red, broke through the clouds for an instant before it set behind those rock-ribbed hills. It was a wonderful sight seen from our ship, one of a convoy of fourteen strung out, as we left the harbor in a stately majestic procession. All hail to Mars, the Kaiser's godfather!

As we came thru from the inner basin down the river south to the sea, we passed the British battle cruisers, their bands all playing the *Star Spangled Banner* and their crews cheering with their well-organized 'Hip Hurrah,' the 'Hip' being given by an officer thru a megaphone. As we were coming out of the inner basin, one of our convoy steamed past us with one lone bugler playing our national anthem and everyone on board standing rigidly at attention. I never had quite such a thrill from the old tune before and I am really beginning to love it. The bugler played, 'God Save the King,' too, and not a sound was made on either ship as the clear, sweet, almost plaintive notes stole out over the water. I am sure every man on board was affected no matter how hardboiled he was.

There is a cottage to the right of the river going up where only three women live. I am sure no men are there and they must be Americans for they had a big U.S. flag. When we passed they dipped their flag on the house and one of them wigwagged, 'Good-by, good luck, God bless you!'

September 22nd
We haven't done much to-day except watch the other ships. They changed their formation every little while during the morning and finally settled down in three lines of four ships each with one ship leading and the *Carmania* bringing up the rear. That makes fourteen in the convoy not counting our escort. It rained all morning but held up this evening. It remained cloudy and the wind blew. Everyone thought we were going to have some rough weather to-night. I was just on deck and the stars were peeping thru the clouds and they were as bright as diamonds. I never saw sky more beautiful. I tried to count the other thirteen ships but could not. I was arrested by the guard for smoking on deck. He saw my wrist watch. No lights, no matter how faint, can be shown except the red and green navigating lights on the masts. A British Commander told us that one ship was torpedoed because someone carelessly struck a match on the deck.

There is never an intermission of cards in the smoker. We shoot crap in our staterooms and I am gradually collecting all kinds of money, – Italian, French, English and best of all, a little American. We don't know what all this foreign money is worth so we have to shoot it by the color, – green against green, and yellow against yellow. The coins rank by size. I guess it's all even in the end.

September 24th
I wrote nothing yesterday. Nothing happened except I saw a fight on the lower deck from above and heard a quartet and a speech down below. Quite a sea has been running to-day, or so it seems to me, and several of the boys have been sick. Especially Leach from Tuscaloosa, who is awfully low. They put a sign on him as he lay in his chair on the deck: 'I want peace and quiet.'

We spend two hours a day studying Italian. La Guardia and the two cooks and Gaipa are the instructors. I am way behind and will never catch up. I am discouraged about it. I learned all sorts of queer things at Ground School without much trouble so guess I can catch up but I sure hate to think of the hard work I have to do.

There's a full moon to-night and the sea is beautiful. Oh, for words to describe it! It makes me sad and makes me ache inside for something, I don't know what. I guess it's a little loving I need. There are twenty nurses on board but they are all dated up for the rest of the voyage. They certainly ought to get all the attention they need.

The wind is rising and whining thru the rigging of the ship. We can hear it crying down here in our staterooms. I am going on deck to see what goes on. It's a wonderful night, as clear as a bell and this big old ship rising and falling, sloughing its way thru the sea. This must be a wonderful life at sea. I shall always carry the picture in my mind of the damp decks and masts rearing along under the stars with the white foam spreading from both sides every time she dips. I wish I could soak it all up and keep it.

God, I am young, life is before me, and if I have wonderful memories, when I get old I will be happy. I have spent all my life so far in harsh surroundings and had so much hard work that I think some good time is coming to me. And I have always longed for better things but didn't know how to go about getting them. But now Fate has tossed me this opportunity. I must make the best of it! All I have to pay for it is my life! I must make it worth the bargain! I am always feeling sorry for myself, a poor habit and one I am going to cut out. Well, I'll try this thrice accursed Italian for a few minutes now.

September 25th
Something queer went on this evening. The Painted Lady, as we call the camouflaged cruiser that is escorting us, turned around and circled be-

hind us and fired a few shots. We don't know what she was firing at. She sure is a queer-looking boat. She's painted all different colors in lines and squares and you can't tell which way she is going or what she is until you get close to her. Another boat in our convoy is painted the color of the ocean and then has a smaller ship painted over it going the other way. From any distance it is very deceptive. Another ship has the same arrangement except the deception is in the angle of her course.

We went below, Cal and I, to hear the Steerage Quartet, as they call themselves. Enlisted men they are and natural born entertainers. One boy sang 'I ain't got nobody' wonderfully well. Spalding played one of his own compositions for us. One day at Mineola, Springs was looking about as usual for some kitchen police. He put the first six men to work peeling potatoes. While they were manicuring the spuds he checked up their service records.

One record caught his eye. The name on it was Albert Spalding[39] and he gave his profession as musician. He was sent to our detachment as an Italian interpreter. Springs went out to the kitchen and asked him if he was the guy that played the fiddle. Spalding allowed as how he was. Springs asked him where his pet instrument was. He said he'd left it in town. So Springs pardoned him from the peeling and sent him back to town after it. He isn't a cadet but an enlisted man and isn't eligible for a commission as we are. I hear that he lost a $35,000 a year contract. I guess he will be figured into a commission somehow, tho. He should be. They put him down in the steerage and won't allow him up in the first class with us. Springs and MacDill are trying to get him up but the regular army colonel of this regiment won't hear of it. But he plays for the enlisted men every night down below.

I feel safe from seasickness now and would enjoy myself immensely if it were not for this Italian. I never will learn it unless I do some work so here goes! I thought my troubles were over when I got rid of that wireless.

September 26th
Nothing much doing. We have to do submarine watch after to-morrow and I am sergeant of the second relief. At last I will get a chance to go up on that little trick platform on the front of the ship and also on the bridge.

September 29th
I haven't written anything for the past two days. Nothing really of noteworthy importance has happened until this evening. I was sergeant of the guard yesterday or rather of the submarine watch. We had a

watch posted at five points on the ship. Each man had a certain arc that he was to keep his eye on. No man was to take anything to drink for twelve hours before he was to go on watch. We were supposed to look out for gulls which they say usually follow in the wake of a sub.

Everybody has to take their turn at it except Springs, who is sort of perpetual officer of the day and runs the show. We did have a guard mount at five in the afternoon but MacDill and Springs and Deetjen[40] are the only ones that know how to do it so we had to abandon that after the first day. No periscopes have been sighted yet tho one boy got all excited over a big piece of timber that was sticking up. The signal for take to the boats is five whistles and yesterday while our company barber was shaving one of the boys, it blew three times. It scared the barber so bad that he couldn't finish the shave.

Nervousness has been growing for the last few days about subs. There has been a kind of tension barely noticeable. No one is actually scared but we all feel a little nervous about it. We have had to wear our life preservers all the time since yesterday morning. They are very uncomfortable and are a great nuisance but the order is strictly enforced. We wear them to meals and put them beside our chairs while we eat. No refuse of any kind is thrown overboard except at night when it is all thrown over at one time. That's to prevent leaving any trace.

Everybody felt funny about the thing until four this afternoon, right after Italian. I went up on deck and the sea was swarming with submarine chasers. Lord, how happy every one was at the sight of them! They are the prettiest little ships I ever saw, about a hundred and twenty feet over all, I would say. They cut thru the water instead of riding the waves but there were no waves today. You can't feel the motion of the ship at all. They say we have three American chasers with us but we couldn't tell which they were. Lord, those little boats are fast; they fairly fly thru the water and cleave it so clear and clean. I would give a leg to own one. They are all run by steam. I thought there would be gas boats, but I guess we are too far out for them.

I never slept as much in my life as I have on this ship. Must be the salt air.

I hear we will sight the coast of Ireland to-morrow about twelve o'clock and be in Liverpool Monday. It can't be too soon for me, I'm sick to death of this Italian.

Everybody on board makes fun of my laughing. I never knew before I joined the army that there was anything unusual about it, but it seems to waken every one on this side of the ship. Poor McCook, the ugliest man alive, is worried to death about subs. The boys, Curtis and McCurry, have kidded him until he sleeps in his clothes including his puttees and shoes. Curtis says he'll be mad as hell if the ship isn't sunk.

We have an ex-cowboy with us named Bird, who has been having a terrible time behaving himself. Bob Kelly was a cowboy out in Arizona for a while when he was trying to shake off the con and every time they get together the storm clouds gather. They are good friends of Springs's and whenever they get started he joins them and tries to quiet things down. One night last week Bird got tired of this paternal supervision in the bar and went down below. Then he started giving his cowboy yell and the matter was reported to the Major. The Major said he didn't want to be hard on anybody but he couldn't overlook it, so he left the punishment to Springs. Springs put him on the wagon for a week. Since then he has been sitting around the table in the bar drinking ginger ale and looking at Springs in a pleading tone of voice so he let him off to-night in honor of the prospects of seeing land to-morrow. We had a big crap game later in our staterooms. First Jake Stanley took all the money and then Springs took it all from him and finally Stokes ended up with it all. I don't know how much it was but there were a couple of handfuls of assorted paper.

How I hate those Italian lessons. They finally got Spalding up in the first class on the excuse that he has to be there for private instructions. All he does is play bridge with Springs, Cal and the Major. They say that he is the fastest bridge player in the world, whatever that means. Crap is my game but the Major outlawed that. We can gamble at bridge and drink all we want as long as we don't get drunk. Now isn't that a fine distinction! I don't know how to play bridge and I like to get drunk.

October 1st

To-morrow we will wake in Merrie England. Oh, boy! This voyage is nearly over. I am sorry in one way and glad in another. I am growing restless and want a change. This ship is too monotonous.

We left the other ships about nine-thirty last night and steamed off at full speed. We are making nineteen knots now and it seems high speed after the snail's pace we have had. We picked up a lighthouse shortly after leaving the convoy and Cal and I fancied we saw land by the light of the moon away off on the starboard. The sea is as green as grass and has been all day. It's beautiful, and the foam from our wake is as white as snow. We have only one chaser with us and it is streaking along in front. I found out that they are not as small as they look. They are nearly three hundred feet long. I am rather excited about arriving in Liverpool tomorrow and going across England by train to London. I know it will be a peach of a trip.

PART ONE: THE UK AND TRAINING

October 3rd
So this is England. We landed yesterday morning and took a train right at the dock for Oxford. We aren't going to Italy after all. We've got to go to Ground School all over again. Our orders got all bawled up in Paris and MacDill, La Guardia, the doctors, the enlisted men and Spalding have gone on to France. MacDill said he would go on to Paris and get the orders straightened out and come back for us.

Somebody had made a mistake. All our mail is in Italy, all our money is in lira and our letters of credit are drawn on banks in Rome and we've wasted two weeks studying Italian and two months going to Ground School learning nonsense for now we've got to go thru this British Ground School here. And we hear that everything that we were taught at home is all wrong. Gosh, I hope some day I get a chance to tell Major Kraft that. We left all our baggage and equipment at Liverpool because we couldn't wait until it was unloaded. Springs left Kelly in charge of it and he picked Bird and Adams and Kerk to stay with him to help. I'll bet they don't show up for a month. They are fools if they do.

We came thru the most beautiful country I ever saw. It made me think of Grimm's Fairy Tales. The greenest fields imaginable and no fences, just hedges and occasionally a stone wall. We did see some fences too, but very few and they were board, no wire. I think the biggest field I saw was about sixty acres and they ranged down to about one and a half acres. Most of the fields were pasture lands or seemed so. They were covered with this intensely green grass. I saw a good many hay stacks, so I guess they must cut this grass and cure it. There was never a frame house, all the houses were the softest red brick, I mean the color, and all pretty too, or I should say, picturesque, and never an inch of ground wasted even on the railroad right-of-way, which was all in grass except where it was planted in vegetables.

I am living at Christ Church College in a room with Callahan, Jim Stokes and Springs. Stokes and Springs had a stateroom together on board ship. Our barracks are a million years old, I know, because it took it that long to cool off to this temperature. The stone is crumbling away and the whole place is very ancient and has all that charm and dignity that only antiquity can give. Cardinal Wolsey and Henry VIII built it or had something to do with it. I haven't found out whether they got fired from it or gave money to it. Either one makes a man famous. Our mess hall is like a chapel, with stained glass windows and the most wonderful paintings all around the walls. The ceiling is very high and is beamed. It's an inverted V and has the old black wood inside with the cross fancy work showing on it.

We have champagne with our meals at $2.10 a bottle! We get the vintage of 1904. This is indeed the life! I am full of it now and that's why I can't write very well. Every one over here is so damn polite. I know now why they always think of us as savages. This is the most charming country I ever dreamed of. Cal and I went canoeing on the Thames this evening and saw some sights. I tell you this is the home of the brave and the land of free love.

Most of the boys are pretty mad. We all came over as volunteers and we volunteered for service in Italy and not in England. There seems to be a good deal of prejudice against the British.

This is Sunday. I don't know the date but I am sober so it must be Sunday. The description of this country is so far beyond me that I will have to leave it to a better pen than I wield. It suits me!

Yesterday the old fellow, the dean of Christ Church College, took us all thru the church and showed us the interesting things there. The newest part of the church is only about four hundred years old but it is built on the ruins of an old Norman church and one of its present walls was built in 700 A.D. being then a part of the priory of St. Frideswide. This quadrangle where we live is called Peckwater Quad and where the mess hall is, Tom Quad. The architecture over there is Moorish and is the work of Sir Christopher Wren.

I would love to know all the old English gentlemen who spent, or misspent their youth here at Oxford and slept in this very room. I'll bet they love the wasted part of their youth best.

I hear to-day that we will only be here five weeks. I think that will be long enough but I won't mind as long as the champagne holds out. Fry, Curtis, Cal, Brown, and I took a bicycle ride over to the Duke of Marlborough's palace at Woodstock. It is a beautiful place and was given to the old Duke by Queen Anne, I think, for winning a battle. It fulfils my idea of what a palace ought to be. It's on a hill overlooking a beautiful lake with little islands in it and a most imposing picturesque bridge across it. He has erected the statue of Victory or some such idea on the far side of the bridge to commemorate his victory. The Duchess is an American girl.

It's a ten mile ride from Oxford and about every two miles there is the most delightful wayside inn where you get this English ale and Scotch whiskey and cheese and bread. We made all the stops going and coming and I never saw such quaint places or quaint people. We stopped in Woodstock and had a bottle of port and lunch. The woman who ran the place could hardly understand our American way of talking.

I went to the barber shop yesterday and asked for a hair cut. I got a hair cut, shampoo, singe and a big revolving brush run over my head

PART ONE: THE UK AND TRAINING

for the equivalent of fifty cents. They don't have any regular barber chairs over here. They sit you down in a regular office chair, and they never heard of a hot towel.

Everything over here is dirt cheap. The English don't run up the price on anything just because it's scarce. I think there're some laws on the subject. There's no candy for sale except in small lots at a few places, yet the price is the same as if it were plentiful. I tried to buy all the chocolate they had at one little shop. They told me they couldn't sell but one piece to a customer and when that was gone they couldn't get any more. I told them I would buy it all and they could close up and go on a vacation. But they couldn't see it that way and all I got was one piece.

We met a private last night in the Carlton Bar who seemed to resent the presence of American troops in Oxford. He was Irish and seemed to be looking for trouble. I was all for helping him find it. He wanted to know where we had been for the last three years. I wonder how much of that feeling there is. Every one else has seemed more than glad to see us and is more than cordial. I wonder if some of the boys have been going around bragging. No one gives a damn, but I had rather these people would think well of us and feel kindly towards us for after all, we are their cousins. The British cadets are as nice as can be and go out of their way to help us when they have the opportunity.

I am going over to the library and read some old books. The last time troops were quartered here was in Oliver Cromwell's time.

We have no commissioned officer here so do about as we please. Springs is a good hard worker and does the best he can to keep order but he hasn't the proper authority to back it up. Everybody realizes that if we don't obey him we'll catch hell from somebody else later. But there are a few rough-necks in every outfit that will cause trouble and get the whole bunch in wrong. I've got my eye on one of that sort and the first break he makes is going to be his last. I can't put him in the guard house, but I can put him in the hospital. Springs is only a sergeant so can't legally discipline any one and according to the Constitution no officer of a foreign army can discipline an American soldier, so if anything goes wrong they'd have to send to London for an American officer. Stokes was a lawyer before he took wing and keeps finding all sorts of trouble. He may have had a law office but I'll bet he made his living shooting crap. He cleaned out the whole crowd last night.

Some of the boys are getting reconciled to England but there's still a lot of cussing about it and a lot of them are looking for trouble.

October 8th
Cal, Stokes, Springs and I went to supper and a show to-night. Dismal failure. This has been our first day of real work. I believe the course will be easy as we've had it all once except the Vickers machine gun and rotary motors. Both of these are used extensively by the Royal Flying Corps.

I hear that the Germans have the goods in airplanes and A.A. guns. I guess it's the North and South over again. Of course, no one doubts our winning out in the end but it will be a long hard fight and few of us will be left to enjoy the fruits of our victory. I surely am lucky not to be in the trenches. Some, in fact, most of the cadets have been out and they say it's hell. 'Only we young chaps we can stand it,' they say. Most of these English cadets are kids and the instructors themselves wouldn't average over twenty-two. Our machine gun instructor has a bullet hole thru the flap of his ear. He says he's going to get one in the other ear so he can wear earrings.

Kelly and his squad arrived to-day with our baggage. They look like they had a good time. Bird was telling some story about their driving a coach until Kelly fell thru the top of it.

The only thing that confuses us is this English alphabet. Instead of saying: A, Bee, Cee, Dee, they have a different way of designating the letters. They say: Ak, Beer, Cee, Don, E, F, G, Haiches, I, J, K, Ella, Emma, N, O, Pip, Q, R, Esses, Toc, U, Vic, W, X, Y, Zed. And as they call everything by initials, it's very confusing.

They also drive on the left-hand side of the street. If there was any traffic we'd all be run over.

October 16th
I am neglecting this important volume lately, I am afraid. The last few days have been crowded with events. A regular army West Point army came over from Paris to look us over Sunday and straffed hell out of us in front of the British Colonel and his staff.

Besides the hundred and fifty of us, there are sixty more American cadets over at Queen's College that came here two weeks before we did. They have a sergeant named Oliver in charge of them. He is a son of Senator Oliver and is only five feet high. When he marches along beside the first squad it's an awfully funny sight because none of them are less than six feet five. All the Englishmen like him and cheer every time they see him marching the detachment around.

This major had a parade of both outfits and inspected us and then got us in the mess hall and pitched into us as if we were convicts. He said he had heard that we were grousing because we had to go to Ground School again and hadn't gotten our commissions as we had been promised. He said if any of us didn't like it, he would send us over to France and send us up to the trenches as privates. He said he could do what he pleased to us in time of war and would. He said he had heard that there was some objection to having the Colonel discipline us but that we were going to take it and going to like it. He said he'd asked the Colonel as a special favor to him, to give us all the discipline that his own cadets got. He certainly did despise us in public with a loud voice.

He didn't like our uniforms. He said they were all right at home but they wouldn't do over here where everybody has to be smart. So we've got to buy tailor-made uniforms and pay for them ourselves. If we haven't got money enough, we've got to borrow it and any man who refuses to buy one of these special uniforms, is to be sent to France for discipline.

Springs has a big letter of credit and has offered to lend it to us as far as it will go. And we've got to wear these funny little monkey hats and R.F.C. belts. Our detachment will be the funniest thing when they blossom forth in their bastard British-American get-up. Springs was the first to adopt the monkey hat and we all nearly died laughing when he showed up. Our belts were issued today and they look awfully funny with these short blouses.

We don't like the idea of adopting the British uniform and looking as much like an Englishman as possible. But that's what the major was after. We will sure look funny as the devil as every man has designed his own uniform and picked different material and colors. These tailors ought to give that major a commission. I hope some day I meet him again. He's one man that ought to have his face shoved down his throat. If we ever meet as equals I'm going to break my resolve about keeping my temper. He'll always retain possession of my goat and as an American, I'm as ashamed of him as he was of us. I'll bet he never does any fighting! He got hightoned by the Colonel and lost his head and indulged himself in an orgy of bootlicking. That was the reason for the whole thing.

If he wants us to look like officers, why doesn't he get us our commissions? They were promised to us. If we have to obey army rules and regulations, why doesn't he? If he has authority to violate the Constitution, why hasn't he authority enough to give us our commissions and pay? How can he make enlisted men buy their own uniforms? By calling us cadets. The cadets are the mulattoes of the army.

They get the privileges of neither enlisted men nor officers and get all the trouble coming to both. MacDill dressed us as we are; what business is it of his if the Colonel wants to doll us up like Englishmen?

October 19th

A British major with the D.S.O. and the M.C. talked to us the other day. He said as I remember it, 'You men are starting on a long trip. It's a hard trip and will require a lot of courage. You'll all be frightened many times but most of you will be able to conquer your fear and carry on. But if you find that fear has gotten the best of you and you can't stick it and you are beyond bucking up, don't go on and cause the death of brave men thru your failure. Quit where you are and try something else. Courage is needed above all else. If five of you meet five Huns and one of you is yellow and doesn't do his part and lets the others down, the four others will be killed thru the failure of the one and maybe that one himself.

'This individual hero stuff is all tommy rot. It's devotion to duty and concerted effort and disciplined team work that will win the war. War is cruel, war is senseless and war is a plague, but we've got to win it and there's no better use of your life than to give it to help stop this eternal slaughter. It's a war of men – strong determined men and weaklings have no part in it.'

He looked just like he talked.

None of the men I've talked to curse the Hun particularly. So far, I've met no eye witnesses of atrocities and not much is said of them.

I hope I can stick it thru. I know I'm not afraid to die. I'm pretty young to be ready for it and I'm not. Why, I'm just beginning to live! And after going to all this trouble to help make history, I want to live a little while to be able to tell about it. If we make the world safe for democracy, as some salesman remarked, brandishing a Liberty Bond in one hand and a flag in the other, what price salvation if we are not here to be democratic? Glory is hardly a passport to paradise. I can't imagine a man with a lot of rank and a lot of medals and a lot of dog, getting through the eye of a needle any easier than a camel. I'll have to consult Springs on the matter. He was an honor man in philosophy at college and is the authority on heaven, hell and hard licker.

I was talking to a little English cadet who had on an old battered Sam Browne and I asked him was he trying to look like a veteran. He smiled and said, 'My brother wore it two years. He was killed by Richthofen.' There seem to be a lot of them after that bird. Wonder how long before somebody sneaks up behind him and drops him. It will take a good man from all I've heard. There's no price on his head but I'll bet the fellow who gets him gets a lot of decorations.

Above: American flying students receiving their post during the 'Mail Call' at Oxford University, an image probably taken in October 1917. The individual in the centre handing out the letters is Elliott White Springs. (Courtesy, The Springs Close Family Archives, Fort Mill, SC)

Below: American aviation cadets marching to ground school classes during their training at Oxford University, a photograph possibly taken in October 1917. Elliott White Springs can be seen on the far left marching alongside the squad. (Courtesy, The Springs Close Family Archives, Fort Mill, SC)

Kelly and Bird got started again. We were all over in the R.F.C. Club doing a little quiet drinking, – Cal, Stokes, Jake and myself. Kelly and Bird came in with a good start. Bird said he couldn't enjoy his drinking unless he had Springs to watch him and tell him when he had enough. Kelly said that in that case the best thing to do was to send for Springs. They wanted to know where he was so we told them he was over in the room writing some letters. They found some one who was going back to the college and sent word to him to come right over or Bird would start giving his cowboy yell and keep it up until he got there.

By the time Springs got there they were well oiled. They are both six feet three and would rather fight than eat. I had visions of them both being sent to Leavenworth in chains. They nearly killed Springs with an affectionate greeting and he had to do some fast thinking. Bird said he supposed he was going to be put on the wagon for another week and he wanted his portrait painted doing it. Springs ordered a round of double brandies. Then Kelly, who always has to pay for more than anybody else, ordered triple whiskies. Then Bird called for some port and they started a round again. It was a good battle while it lasted. We had to put Springs in a cold tub before he could call the roll for dinner and Kelly and Bird never raised their voices again until the next morning. They are on the wagon all right and it didn't require any orders either.

We met a French officer from Chicago to-night who came over from France to see his brother Paul Winslow,[41] who's over at Queen's College with the first outfit. He's in the French Air Service and says the Hun has the supremacy of the air on the French front without a doubt. It seems that we will be the goats as France has about shot her wad. He says we are lucky to be here as all the cadets in France are having a terrible time. They haven't done any flying but live in tents and do manual labor. They help build the flying fields and have to do the same work as the German prisoners and get the same food. Their letters are censored and they aren't allowed to write home how they are being treated. They had a German spy in command of them for a while. He says he expects to hear of a mutiny any time.

October 22nd

We have moved to Exeter College. And why? Thereby hangs a tale. Bim Oliver and his crew had finished their course and made the highest marks in the examinations on record. So the officer in charge of Queen's gave them all passes Saturday night to go out to dinner and celebrate. That was also Jake Stanley's birthday and he gave a party at Buol's that night to celebrate it. It was a right good party. He had a private room on the third floor and there were present: Cal, Springs, Stokes, Paul

Winslow and his brother Alan[42], Hash Gile, Dud Mudge, an English staff officer and myself. Dwyer and a bunch of others came in later. Everybody was all teed up before they got there and then we had cocktails by the quart and champagne and then each man got a half gallon pitcher of ale.

We sang that old song and made everybody do bottoms-up by turn. Jake had a cake and he kept announcing that he was going to 'tut the twake.' When he did cut it, Hash Gile insisted on helping Springs to eat it and got most of it down his neck and in his ears. I never laughed so much in my life.

When the party broke up and we were all getting out, the English officer and the French officer were assisting each other home. The Colonel came up with a flashlight and tried to stop a bunch of them. The English officer gave the Colonel a push and ran and the Colonel made a flying tackle at him but missed and grabbed Winslow. The Colonel insisted on knowing who it was that ran and when Winslow refused to tell him, he went down to Queen's and ordered a formation of all of Bim's detachment. They say it was the greatest sight that Oxford ever witnessed, – sixty American soldiers in all sorts of costumes, in all stages of drunkenness, trying to get into line and stay there, in a dark and ancient courtyard, hallowed by the scholars of the ages, with a British colonel dashing about with a flashlight and bellowing like a bull at each man as he came in, 'Are you the man that pushed me and ran?' The first sergeant that tried to call the roll passed out cold in the middle of it and had to be carried off. The second one got the British and American commands mixed up and was led away babbling something that sounded like a cavalry drill.

The Colonel tried to question them but all one man would say was: 'I wasn't on the third floor, I was on the second floor.' No matter what the Colonel would ask him, that was all he would say. Another one asked the Colonel, 'What do you mean run, sir? How fast is a run?' Finally the Colonel had to give it up but he made the French officer leave the college and he wants to make a complaint to the French Ambassador. It certainly was an international mess.

Bim and his crew left the next day to go to Stamford to learn to fly and the Colonel moved us over here to Exeter where we can't corrupt any of his cadets and turned the place over to us. We have the whole college to ourselves. There are a million rumors flying around about what is going to happen to us. The Colonel sent over one of his staff officers to help Springs. And who did he send but the very same officer that pushed him and ran! You can't laugh that off. He and big Shoemaker, who used to drive a dogteam in Alaska, are great friends and I foresee trouble.

PART ONE: THE UK AND TRAINING

Ten of us went to a dance Saturday night at Miss Cannon's. She's a real English girl and wears a monocle. I'm going riding with her Wednesday afternoon. Oxford isn't such a bad place after all. Stokes came to the dance illuminated and did an Indian war dance in the middle of the floor. He nearly passed away next day over the kidding he got. We have a way of getting in late at night by climbing over a high wall with the assistance of a limb of a tree that hangs over from the inside. Fulford and I were coming in by that route and we heard a plaintive call for help. It was Brownie and he had tried to get over at the wrong place and had got hung by the seat of his trousers on a nail. We had a time getting him down and putting him to bed.

We brought four boiled lobsters back with us and a couple of bottles of port. We woke Springs up and he was as mad as hell. He said if the rest of the crowd got on to the fact that he was letting us come in when we pleased, he wouldn't be able to control anybody. We told him that everybody was out anyway and to go back to sleep and forget it. So we ate the lobsters and drank the port ourselves. About that time Kelly and Bird came in with Capt. Swan. He had come up from London to pay us off and they had run into him and brought him on over the wall with them. He told us some funny stories of the Philippines. Kelly and Bird were all lit up and had a bottle of whisky which they had brought to Springs. He wouldn't take it so they drank it themselves with Capt. Swan.

We finished the lobster and put the shells in a big bucket outside the door. Bird saw it and decided it was a football and took a terrific kick at it and scattered it all over the courtyard outside. Springs got up steaming like a scalded hog and told Bird that he had to get a flashlight and go out and pick up every piece or he'd have to put him under arrest in the morning for it. Bird thought it was a joke at first but Springs made him do it. It sure was a funny sight, that big cowboy out in the court with a flashlight, down on his knees looking for lobster claws. We all went out and helped him.

Sunday morning we were all just as sick as we could be from that lobster. Cal, Stokes and I couldn't get out of bed and couldn't get to drill. Springs was raging. Along about noon we got up and managed to stagger in to lunch. Then Springs informed us that we were under arrest and couldn't leave the college. And the damn fool made us stay in all the afternoon and evening too. He said if we were too sick to drill we were too sick to go out and get drunk again. I'll get even with him. He says he is going to demote all three of us. He's just mad because he's missing all the fun. Kelly and Bird go out every night and take off their white hat bands and say that they are mechanics from this squadron outside of town. They throw a big party and then come in and wake

Springs up to tell him about it because they say they don't want to do anything behind his back that they wouldn't tell him about to his face. Some morning this detachment is going to wake up and find they haven't got any sergeants.

We had a boxing tournament last week. Springs and I went in and won our first bouts, but got knocked out in the second round. Pudrith and Jake Stanley each won in their classes and got a trip to London over the week-end as prizes.

October 24th
We had mail from home to-day which seemed to sadden the boys more than cheer them up. It sort of made us realize how far away we are. Springs certainly had a funny collection. He ought to save them for publication some day when people get their senses of humor back.

November 6th
Harroby Camp, Grantham, Lincolnshire.[43]

I wish I could have stayed at Oxford for the horseback ride with Miss Cannon but we were all suddenly sent up here to Grantham to the machine gun school. All except Springs and twenty who have gone to Stamford to learn to fly. Springs had to pick the twenty and naturally every one wanted to go. He picked those who'd done the most flying already. He took only those who were ready to go solo and Deetjen, Garver and Dietz because they have done a lot of hard clerical work for the detachment. I couldn't see why he wouldn't take Cal and me and I told him so. What's the use of having friends if you don't stick by them and do things for them? And what's the use of having authority if you can't use it to help your friends?

I'm a Jackson democrat and I believe the victim is entitled to what is spoiled. And when I fight, I fight to win. I don't want to know anything about the Marquis of Queensberry's ideas. When I fight I only hit a man once and the first thing he knows about it is when he reads about it in the papers. And when I swing, somebody gets 199 of my 200 pounds where they least expect it.

Mit wanted to go to Stamford and he kicked up an awful row. He claims that he is a friend of General Wood's and he wanted to call up the American Ambassador when Springs wouldn't let him go. He stood out in the court and cussed for half an hour because he said there was a conspiracy against him. Finally I went over and told him that he was about to be crowned and that if there was any partiality in it I would be going to Stamford myself. He says he's going to spend the rest of his life getting even with Springs.

We all chipped in to buy Springs a parting gift. We couldn't see wasting $75 on a cup that he couldn't use so we bought him a big silver flask.

We had to leave poor Jim Stokes behind. He was operated on for appendicitis the day we left. He got thru it all right.

We were met at the station here by a band and escorted to our barracks. The English rank us as officers now and we don't have to salute anything under majors. Some of us are rather embarrassed because we are treated as officers when we really aren't, tho it isn't our fault. We just aren't nephews of the right people in Washington. Mit is in his glory. He has blossomed out in boots and swaggers about in the bottom half of a Sam Browne belt and cusses his batman. We have a regular servant who cleans our hut and shines our shoes. We have our own mess – a regular officers' mess. The classes are terribly boring and take all the daylight hours but we do as we please in the evening and don't have to be in until twelve o'clock.

Cal, Schlotzhauer, Leach and I went over to Nottingham Sunday and had supper. Believe me, it is some town. There have never been any troops quartered in Nottingham and there are no camps near it and all the men have been gone for three years. I never knew there was such a place. The women clustered around us all the time and talked to us as if we were a new species.

Stillman is in charge now and I am a platoon commander still. When Springs was trying to decide whom to appoint in his place, every one wanted Bird as top sergeant. Springs likes Bird but isn't so particularly keen about Stillman but he said he was afraid of Bird so he put Stillman in as top and made Bird second in command. I guess it's just as well. Somebody has got to hold this crowd down and Bird has been in too much devilment already to be effective on his own responsibility. Stillman is a fine fellow and certainly looks the part. He's six feet seven and a half and weighs over 200. He used to play end on Yale.

McCurry came in to-night and begged me with tears in his eyes to go with him and cut off Ken's mustache. He sure was tanked. He ran into the barbed wire between this hut and the next one and nearly tore his brand new uniform off.

I miss Kelly and Springs and Jim. This is the first split and I guess there will be many more.

November 7th

We have Raftery in our hut. He is going to bed now, putting his money belt on over his pajamas and wearing a knitted helmet. He's the funniest thing I ever saw.

I heard that Jim is getting on all right.

November 8th
I got four letters from home to-day and they seem to have traveled a little bit further than the others. Poor old Fat Payden hasn't gotten even a postal since he left the States. His eyes are inflamed and he doesn't go to classes but sits in here all day and gossips with Fry and our batman. He laughs at everything any one says, no matter how stale it is. I just found out to-day that he is just twenty.

Cal, Herbert, Fulford and Fry are sitting around the table now drinking port out of their canteens and writing home. Every one is fed up. I don't see how we are going to stand three more weeks of this. Aren't we ever going to fly? There was some talk of making ground officers of some of us. Some of the married men decided they wanted to be ground officers but nobody else would consent. An English general made us a talk and said this war was no great adventure: you were either scared to death or bored to death all the time.

This camp is sort of a pretty place. When I look down at Grantham nestling between these pretty checkered hills with the sky all colored up by the setting sun and the clouds so low you can hang your hat on them, it kind of gets up in my neck and I think this old world is a damn fine place to live in. The hill on the other side of town we see from here is checkered up with little fields – every one a different color and it's very pretty. If the sky wasn't filled with aeroplanes all day, you'd never think of war. I hope I never see another machine gun. I came over here to fight – not to sit around and talk about it forever.

November 9th
Lord, I have the blues, the worried blues. Anderson was in here playing his steel guitar. How that boy can play! A couple of the English instructors have been going to see a couple of girls and not making much progress. So they took Andy along with them and put him in the next room and made him play soft Hawaiian music to keep them in the proper frame of mind.

Morrison came in to-night with a beautiful bun and a new pair of boots. They were tight too and it took four of us to pull them off.

I've got the blues so bad I think I'll get drunk to-morrow and see if that will help things.

November 10th
One of the boys came in the other night after midnight without his Sam Browne belt. He was last seen walking down the street with a girl and he had it on then. So everybody got to kidding him about bushwhacking. He couldn't remember where they had gone but he had

PART ONE: THE UK AND TRAINING

to have a belt and was broke so he decided he'd go back and ask the girl where he left it. But when he went back he woke up the girl's father and he came out and chased him down the street. But he had his belt back the next day so I guess love found a way.

November 13th
Well, the old man is himself again. Jack Fulford, Cal, Morrison, Leach and I went to Nottingham over the week-end. We didn't get very drunk.
  Springs flew up from Stamford to see us while we were away.
  Last night was guest night in our mess and we had all the English staff over. These Englishmen sure have a funny idea of a party. They want to smash everything. Fulford got the idea that he was a baseball pitcher and he knocked the end out of our hut throwing whisky bottles at it. We caught Ken and cut his mustache off at last.

November 18th
Cal and I went down to Stamford to spend the day and nearly died laughing. Our stomachs are still sore. Springs and Kelly are rooming together over a millinery shop. They spend all their time at a club there.
  There was a sort of straff going on that day. They had a new C.O. and he was an ex-Guards officer and had a grudge against the Huns and

A photograph of a crashed Royal Aircraft Factory F.E.2b taken in 1917, almost certainly whilst Lieutenant Fulford was at Hounslow. (Mark Hillier)

Above: A Royal Aircraft Factory R.E.8 built by Daimler which, with the serial number A3618, crashed on landing in a cross wind in 1917 – also a picture that was obtained by Fulford whilst he was at Hounslow. At the time the aircraft was being operated by 19 Reserve Squadron, which had formed at Hounslow. It was repaired and went on to serve with 3 Squadron on the Western Front, being shot down whilst being flown by Lieutenant J.L.M. Sandy and Sergeant H.F. Hughes during a combat against Albatross aircraft of Jasta 29 on 17 December 1917. (Mark Hillier)

Below: The fate of one Royal Aircraft Factory B.E.2 in a picture dated 1917, one of a number of photographs collected by Fulford and which he entitled 'Comedies and Tragedies'. It is unlikely the pilot survived this crash. (Mark Hillier) wanted to get on with the war. There were a lot of young English kids that had been there some time swinging the lead and he sent for them all and lined them up. He told them that there was a war on and that pilots were needed badly at the front and that they were all going solo that afternoon. They nearly fainted. Some of them had had less than two hours of air work and none of them had had more than five.

We all went out to the airdrome to see the fun. I guess there were about thirty of them in all. The squadron was equipped with D.H. Sixes[44] which are something like our Curtiss planes except they are slower and won't spin no matter what you do to them.

The first one to take off was a bit uneasy and an instructor had to taxi out for him. He ran all the way across the field, and it was a big one, and then pulled the stick right back into his stomach. The Six went straight up nose first and stalled and hung on its propeller. Then it did a tail slide right back into the ground.

The next one did better. He got off and zigzagged a bit but instead of making a circuit he kept straight on. His instructor remarked that he would probably land in Scotland, because he didn't know how to turn.

Another one got off fairly well and came around for his landing. He leveled off and made a beautiful landing – a hundred feet above the ground. He pancaked beautifully and shoved his wheels up thru the lower wings. But the plane had a four-bladed prop on it and it broke off even all around. So the pupil was able to taxi on into the hangar as both wheels had come up the same distance. He was very much pleased with himself and cut off the engine and took off his goggles and stood up and started to jump down to the ground which he thought was about five feet below him. Then he looked down and saw the ground right under his seat. He certainly was shocked.

Another took off fine but he had never been taught to land and he was a bit uncertain about that operation. He had the general idea all right but he forgot to cut off his motor. He did a continuous series of dives and zooms. A couple of instructors sang a dirge for him:

> The young aviator lay dying, and as 'neath the wreckage he lay
> To the Ak Emmas [ground crew] around him assembled, these last parting words did he say:
> 'Take the cylinder out of my kidney, the connecting rod out of my brain,
> From the small of my back take the crankshaft, and assemble the engine again!'

There were a lot more verses but I can't remember them.

WAR BIRDS

Above: This particular crashed Royal Aircraft Factory B.E.2, serial number 2563, was one of a batch of 100 constructed by Wolseley Motors. (Mark Hillier)

Opposite: A Royal Aircraft Factory B.E.2e which came to grief in the grounds of a private residence! The image is dated 1917. (Mark Hillier)

Below: Another tragedy at a Royal Flying Corps Reserve Squadron. (Mark Hillier)

PART ONE: THE UK AND TRAINING

We thought sure he was gone but he got out of it all right and made a fairly decent landing but not where he had expected.

The next one didn't know much about landing either. He came in too fast and didn't make the slightest attempt to level off. The result was a tremendous bounce that sent him up a hundred feet. He used his head and put his motor on and went around again. He did that eight times and finally smashed the undercarriage so that next time he couldn't bounce. Then he turned over on his back. The C.O. congratulated him and told him he would probably make a good observer.

They finally all got off and not a one of them got killed. I don't see why not tho. Only one of them got hurt and that was when one landed on top of the other one. The one in the bottom plane got a broken arm. I got quite a thrill out of that.

A flying field is not at all what I expected it would be like. They all seem to do pretty much as they please, go where they please and fly when they please. The chief occupation seems to be passing the flowing cup.

There is a cemetery right in the middle of the town and since the Americans came the ghosts walk about it all night. Kelly has a joke on Springs about it. I saw Horn, Knox, Taber, Roth, Neely, Watts and a couple of others.

November 17th
Cal, Curtis, Brown, Fry and I are ordered to Thetford[45] to learn to fly at last. This is the final bust-up of the Italian Detachment. I am lucky to get a good gang.

I had Ken but I swapped him for Curtis. Fry said it was just like swapping horses.

November 18th
I went to Stokes Castle this afternoon for lunch and stayed for tea. I think this has been the best day I have spent in England. I met a Mrs. Chapin out there from Louisiana. She is a sure-enough Southern aristocrat and I am proud of her. She reminded me of Gramma. She dominated the whole table at dinner and was so interesting and made every one feel at home. She took me to her room and showed me the picture of her old home in Louisiana.

It was an old Italian villa on the banks of the Mississippi. I certainly enjoyed talking to her. It was like a visit home. I wonder if I will ever see the Mississippi again. It flows thru another world like the River Styx that Springs talks about.

PART ONE: THE UK AND TRAINING

Above: A B.E.2e photographed after having crashed into a hedge, circa 1917.
(Mark Hillier)

Below: With the serial number B1735, this Sopwith Pup was one of a batch of 150 built by Standard Motors. (Mark Hillier)

33

Above: A Royal Aircraft Factory B.E.2, an Armstrong Whitworth-built example with the serial number 2028, pictured after a taxiing accident. One of an order of twenty-nine, this particular aircraft was unique in that it was armoured. (Mark Hillier)

Opposite: This Curtiss JN-4, serial number A5168, was one of nine ordered by the RNAS only to be subsequently taken over by the RFC/RAF. This aircraft appears to have stalled or spun in to this building. (Mark Hillier)

The castle was a wonder, too. It was full of old paintings and relics – some of them a thousand years old. There was a picture of a woman kissing Christ's feet by Rubens. The library was about forty by eight and lined with books and relics. The best part of the place was the grounds, about three acres, I guess.

We leave for Thetford to-morrow at eight-thirty and at last I am really going to learn to fly. It's over six months since I enlisted to fly and I am not sorry they are past.

November 20th
Arrived at Thetford via Peterborough and Ely. We had about four hours at Peterborough and went to see the Cathedral. It's the most magnificent thing I have seen so far. I saw where Mary, Queen of Scots, was buried before she was moved to Westminster.

Thetford is not much. We are going to start on Rumptys as these Henry Farman planes[46] are called. They say that you test the rigging by putting a bird between the two wings. If the bird gets out, there's a wire gone somewhere. They are so unstable that they never go up

PART ONE: THE UK AND TRAINING

Above: A recovery vehicle is pictured alongside this crashed Curtiss JN-4. With the serial number B1935, it was another from an ex-RNAS contract. (Mark Hillier)

Below: A Martinsyde G.100 Elephant, serial number 7263, which at some stage served with 27 Squadron on the Western Front. (Mark Hillier)

Bottom: Another stricken Curtiss JN-4 'Jenny', B1933 was one of fifty from an ex-RNAS contract. (Mark Hillier)

PART ONE: THE UK AND TRAINING

Above: One can only wonder at the fate of the pilot of the B.E.2e that crashed in this hedge row. (Mark Hillier)

Below: This particular Spad 7, tipped upside down during a landing, has the serial number A8795, telling us that it was built by the Air Navigation Company. (Mark Hillier) except when the air is very smooth. No one flew to-day except Roberts.

These old short-horn Farmans are awful looking buses. I am surprised they fly at all. We have the same sort of wild kids here for instructors that we had at Oxford, only more so, – wilder and younger.

I was told that they kill off more instructors in the R.F.C. than pupils and from what I've seen, I can well believe it. I have a Captain Harrison for an instructor. He seems to be a mere kid. He's about nineteen and is trying hard to grow a mustache. Classes are a joke.

This is real country here. The fields are bigger and rougher. I like it better too. This is Norfolk – I wonder if the jacket originated here.

Cal and I are posted for early flying to-morrow. He just came in and said in a shaky voice, 'Well, let's get ready for our last sleep.' The fool plays bridge all the time for the good of his soul. While he's playing I usually do my writing on this thing. Fry is in the same room with us and is terribly funny.

November 25th
Just returned from my first leave. I went down to London to get my teeth fixed. It cost me forty pounds. These teeth of mine certainly are expensive, my sweet tooth being the worst. London is a town after my own heart. I stopped at the Savoy. I tell you it is a wonderful sight to sit in the dining room and see all the women in evening gowns – all the soldiers on leave, airmen, observers, artillerymen, infantrymen, sailors and marines. It's a wonderful sight. Think of the sacrifice laid at the feet of the God of War!

To-day I saw my first scout machine, a Sopwith Pup. It's the prettiest little thing I ever laid my eyes on. I am going to fly one if I live long enough. They aren't as big as a minute and are as pretty and slick as a thoroughbred horse. Tiny little things just tag enough for one man and a machine gun.

It snowed to-day and it's as cold as a nun's lips. The wind is rattling the stove pipe. I guess I'd better turn in.

December 6th
I have been flying for three days and Capt. Harrison says I can solo to-morrow if it's calm. I tell you it's a great life. I am absolutely ruined for anything else. I wish I could describe it. The thing most surprising to me is the feeling of absolute safety. I have put in two hours and twenty minutes in the air and I would have soloed this evening if it had been calm enough.

I have been to London again. I went to Murray's night club with the Chinless Wonder. Cal and Fry joined us at the Court later where we had a suite. Then I took the Wonder to a dance we heard about at the Grafton Galleries.[47]

I saw Jake Stanley, who was down from Stamford. He told me a funny story. Springs and Kelly went to a dance after a party the staff officers gave to the Americans. Kelly didn't want to go home and threw a bicycle at Springs which missed him. Then Kelly sat down on the side of a ditch and said, 'If you want me to go home, let's see you take me.' Every time Springs would try to pick him up Kelly would push him in the ditch. Kelly would make two of Springs and can push him all over the place. About that time Jake came by and Springs called for help. They decided that the best thing to do was to knock Kelly out and then carry him home peacefully. So Jake got behind him and put his hands under his arms and lifted him up on his feet. Then Springs got in front of him and tilted Kelly's head back and adjusted his jaw to just the proper angle and hawled off and took a terrific swing. Just as he swung, Kelly's feet slipped and instead of landing on the jaw, Springs hit Jake on the nose and they all went over in the ditch. May Dorsey was going home with a big package of his own and saw Springs hit Jake and thought there was a fight on and jumped on Springs.

Before he knew what was happening Springs had a black eye and Dorsey was working on the other one. Then Springs got on top of Dorsey and nearly killed him. He was bumping his head on a piece of cement when they pried him loose.

A couple of Bobbies came up and helped Springs get Kelly over his shoulder and then he carried him home quietly.

I met Dora at Murray's and had lunch with her the next day. She is very pretty and witty and smart. She came up to Thetford and brought another girl with her. Fry called her the Long Lean Lanky Devil. We had dinner and they caught the eleven-thirty train back to London. The landlady at the Bell Hotel refused to take them in at the indecent hour of ten-thirty.

January 1st, 1918
London Colney, Hertfordshire.[48]
This is New Year's Day. I haven't written up this diary for quite a long time – nearly a month, and many things have happened.

I have done my four hours solo on Rumptys and am done with them forever, thank God. I have done two hours on Avros[49]. They are entirely different and I have to learn to fly all over again. We had our days' leave in London before we left Thetford. Cal and I finished the same day and came to London together. Cal rolled into a Roman dugout on his last landing and I thought sure he was killed. Fry wrote off a bus by pancaking from two hundred feet.

We met Jim in London and had a wild party. Jim is living there now and is attached to Headquarters. After the show we had Beatrice Lillie[50] and the entire cast of *Cheap* up in our suite at the Court and they brought along Lord Somebody or other. Cal salaamed before him and shook hands and said, 'Hello, God.' He was much shocked. That was the first lord I ever met. They all got to fraternizing among themselves so we split up. Cal has fallen in love with a sweet little thing called Peggy. She is very pretty but that's the best I can say for her.

We have been posted to London Colney, which is the greatest place yet. It is only twenty miles from London and they have Pups and Spads and Avros.[51] There's no discipline or wind-up at all. One class a day in machine guns and one in wireless but we know more than the instructors and nobody cares whether we go or not. We go to London when we please. There are only two Avros for about thirty of us so we will be here for some time. Americans are not popular with the C.O. and adjutant. I guess they've got a good reason to dislike us.

It seems that the U.S. Army has bought a lot of Curtisses at home for primary training planes and they are building a lot of planes like Sopwith Pups but they don't want to build any Avros if they can help it. So they sent orders over to take the best men that finish on Curtisses[52] and put them on Pups without letting them go up in Avros. Springs and DeGamo were the first two to finish on Curtisses so they sent them down here to London Colney to be used as experiments.

The C.O. and adjutant said it would be plain murder and refused to let them have Pups. There was a U.S. Lieut here named Gaines and he forbade them to try it. The London Headquarters called up and told them to go ahead anyway. The C.O. ordered them off the tarmac and said he was fed up on funerals and the U.S. Army would have to conduct its own executions. A British general came over and backed up the C.O. so they compromised by sending Springs and DeGamo back to Stamford for further instructions.

The C.O. at Stamford got sore as a boil and said there was nothing more he could teach them on Curtisses and that they were ready for anything.

The adjutant at London Colney tried to put it off on the two of them so Springs and DeGamo wrote a letter and said they were always willing to do it and were ready at any time and had been ordered off the tarmac at London Colney but they were still ready to try it. There was a big row over it and the adjutant caught hell for not carrying out orders. Then the Paris Headquarters sent over orders that they were to loop and spin Curtisses and then be put on Pups anyway – the worst that could happen would be two funerals. Don't these non-flyers love us! What are a couple of aviators, more or less?

Up at Stamford, Springs and DeGamo were duly ordered to go up and loop and spin those ancient crates. They couldn't get any of the instructors to go up and show them how to do it. They knew better! Besides the orders came from American Headquarters and the British didn't approve of them. But up they went and looped and spun anyway. Springs did ten loops in succession and landed. Ainsworth went up later in the same machine and was coming over the top of his loop when the wings fell off. He was killed instantly.[53] He's the first of the American cadets to go. I'm afraid there'll be many more before the Kaiser is pushed over backwards.

The C.O. at Stamford refused to permit any further foolishness and Paris backed down and sent orders over for DeGamo and Springs to stop all flying until it could be decided what form the experiment would take. So they had to sit around for a month doing nothing while everybody else was going on. DeGamo is instructing on Sixties and Springs is ferrying. A great system we have. Everything we have had to do so far has been messed up.

I'll guarantee our noble commanders will kill more Americans than Germans before it is over. But what can you expect when they promote the jackasses on seniority and put men in charge of important technical affairs just because they have spent their lives doing infantry drill in the Philippines and transferred to the aviation section a week ago to get a soft berth and more pay? Why should they worry about mistakes? They aren't the ones that get killed. An order from the adjutant general can't make a pilot out of a quartermaster.

Last night Cal and I and four English officers went to a dance at an Insane Asylum. Cal became fascinated with a charming young Welch nurse.

January 3rd
There's a U.S. Lieut here that certainly is looking for trouble. He enlisted the same time we did, but he did his flying first and got out of going to Ground School and got his commission right away. He's quite impressed with his exalted rank and makes us all salute him continuously just because the government hasn't kept its promise to us and we are still cadets.

The English can't see any difference between us and it makes him foam at the mouth. He was an instructor at home and has done two hundred hours on Curtisses. But he's no good on Avros. Two instructors turned him down and he's got to have a lot of dual. I wish they'd send him up in a Pup as an experiment!

Machine gun class is awfully boring. Kent Curtis draws pictures of everything in his notebook. One of the lecture headlines is, 'The tripping of the lock.' Instead of taking down the lecture, Curtis drew a picture of it. The next paragraph is headed, 'The depression of the seer.' He drew a picture of an old soothsayer looking into a crystal ball and biting his nails.

Then he drew a picture entitled 'The care of the piece,' and another, 'The return of the fusee.' The sergeant caught him at it and got mad and reported him to the C.O. The C.O. had him up on the carpet and made him bring the notebook. He nearly died laughing. So for punishment he made him draw the same pictures on the walls of the office. Now every time a general comes over to inspect they get in the office and get to laughing and there's no inspection.

January 12th
Springs and DeGamo showed up to-day. They were as welcome as the measles. The adjutant will probably file their flying wires. The experiment is all off and they are to fly Avros if they ever get a turn. Springs looks bad and says Kelly has been getting his revenge for that party in Stamford. Joe Sharpe[54] was killed over at Waddington on a D.H.6. There was a fine fellow for you.

January 14th
Yesterday was washout day so we all went into town and threw a party at the Court. The traveling is so congested over the week-end that the flying corps takes its holiday during the week and works on Sundays.

Dud Mudge had a funny crash over at Northholt. He was up on his first solo in a Rumpty and lost his head coming in and flew right into the side of a hangar. The nacelle came on thru and pitched Dud on the floor. A mechanic was at work in there and was smoking and he was so frightened at being caught smoking in a hangar that all he could do was to stammer and make excuses while poor Dud lay on the floor with a broken arm. The engine was full on outside and the throttle was on the inside and before anybody could get to it, the Rumpty slowly pushed the side of the hangar in and the roof fell on top of it. No one could get to the throttle then and it ran until the cylinders overheated and froze up. It must have been a funny sight to see that boxkite pushing madly at that hangar and then jump on top of it.

Hash Gile cracked up a Curtiss but didn't get hurt. His instructor had bawled him out for not getting his tail up when he was taking off, so the next time he started off he pushed the stick forward up against the dash and held it there. His tail came up and kept on coming. It got higher and higher and still Hash kept the stick forward. The poor old Curtiss did the best it could and turned a forward somersault. When they fished Hash out of the wreckage he was still holding the stick forward. I also hear that Al Rothwell distinguished himself by spiralling into the ground.

January 20th
We all went into town and tore off a real raspasass party at the Court. Everybody was there for dinner. Springs's beauty nearly broke up the party. She got mad when he started drinking and then got insulted when some other girls came in to join us. She said she couldn't be seen with such girls – they were not respectable. I told her that there was only one place in London she could go to a party and that was Buckingham Palace and I wasn't sure about that. She referred to us as 'your uncouth friends,' and made Springs take her home.

January 24th
I'm feeling pretty much at home in the air now. But after doing very many vertical banks I feel rather sick and dizzy. If to-morrow is a good day, I am going up to ten thousand and shut off and spin down and see what happens. I am quite good at spinning but it makes me a little sick. I guess I'll get over that, tho, and I think a lot of it is due to the castor oil from the motor.

Springs, DeGamo, Nathan and Barry have all finished Avros and gone on Pups. Barry and Springs crashed the first time but got away with the second try.

Dora and another girl, who was so big that Fry called her a Handley-Page, came up and had dinner with us at the Peahen Inn at St. Albans. They went back on the eleven-thirty train. There was a snow storm and we had to walk back the five miles. Fulford and Fry insisted they were going to sleep in the snow so we left them in a big drift.

I am afraid that this diary will not be of any value as an historical document. I don't write it the way I date it always. Sometimes I don't get a chance to write in it for a week or so, and then I take a couple of hours off when Cal is playing bridge or it's raining, and then I go back and write it up properly. I'm getting so I really enjoy writing in here. It makes me realize how lucky I am. And some day it will be my greatest pleasure to read it over. Maybe some day I'll read parts of it to my grandchildren and tell them all about the war.

We went into London again last night, Capt. Pentland[55], the wild Australian, Fry, Cal, Springs and myself.

We went down to Jim's hotel for dinner. Then we all went to the Flying Corps dance at the Grafton Galleries. The whole flying corps was there, with a good sprinkling of our crowd. All the American cadets manage to cluster themselves around London. We spent the night at Jim's hotel and caught the seven-thirty train back.

Jerry Pentland and Springs stepped into the St. Pancras Hotel opposite the station for something to eat. They couldn't get any service so Jerry put Springs in the dumbwaiter where he promptly went to sleep. Some maid on the top floor pressed the button and up went the waiter. Jerry got scared and started up the stairs and climbed six flights. The maid started to put some dishes in and saw Springs and let out a yell and pressed the down button just as Jerry burst in. Down went Springs with Jerry in hot pursuit. The dumbwaiter got stuck in the basement and they had a time getting Springs out of it. The manager wanted to turn him over to the military police, but Jerry swore that he was Russian and Springs quoted a little Latin and the manager saw all the eagles on his buttons and believed it and let them catch the train without any further argument. I saw little Halley and Newt Bevin[56] and Matthiesen at the Savoy.

January 28th
I took my altitude test to-day. I went up thru thick clouds to nine thousand five hundred feet and damn near froze. The bus was covered with ice where it had been touched by the clouds coming up. The sky up there was the bluest I ever saw, absolutely glassy blue with just a few cirrus clouds about five miles up, snow white, and this beautiful snow white plain of clouds beneath me. I felt awfully lonely. I could see, I know, at least a hundred miles. I saw another plane about ten miles away and I thought it was a bird at first but it started spinning and I knew it was a plane.

I spun down and came out of the spin in the clouds. It was the nastiest sensation I ever had. I didn't know whether I was upside down or not. At last I got into a straight dive and came out of the clouds at a hundred and fifty miles an hour right over the airdrome.

There's a little captain here with the M.C. and a bar named Keller[57], just back from the front, who loves to stunt close to the ground. He seems to be daring the ground to come up and hit him. He took me up with him in an Avro and for thirty minutes we never got above fifty feet and only then to clear the trees. His specialty is flying under bridges.

The other day one of his friends was getting married in the center of London and he flew down in a Pup and broke up the wedding procession by diving on them. He was looping and rolling between the church spires. Some general was a guest and got excited and put in a complaint about it so the wing sent around orders for us to stay away from London below five hundred feet. That boy has been knocking on the golden gate for sometime and if he isn't careful as well as lucky, he's going to push too hard and get in. He and MacIntaggart chased each other all over the country for an hour at an altitude of fourteen inches. Scared me to death to watch them.

Roy Garver[58] was killed on an Avro day before yesterday.

January 29th
A girl who is a friend of Springs's in New York wrote over to some people that live near St. Albans and they called him up and invited him to dinner and told him to bring along a couple of others. So Cal and I went along with him to dinner last night.

They have a beautiful place about three miles north of St. Albans. Their name is Drake and they are direct descendants of Sir Francis Drake, who did something famous, either discovered the North Pole or licked the Spaniards. I've forgotten which.

There were three Drake brothers there, back from the front on leave, and their wives. A fine looking trio they were, two captains and a major, two M.C.s and one D.S.O., three years in the trenches. Another brother was killed.

Dinner was a very formal highbrow affair. A lot of dog but very little food. They asked us the usual questions: How do you like England? Do you get enough to eat? Don't you miss the sugar? Do you ever get frightened when you are up in the air? We answered yes to all of them.

Food is getting very scarce in this country and even the rich can't get what they need. That poor hostess didn't have enough to go around.

After dinner was over the atmosphere underwent a decided change. The ladies withdrew and our host brought out a bottle of real pre-war whisky that had the kick of Brown's mule. Then we all got to acting natural.

Later Cal got at a piano and the poor thing was nearly shocked off its legs. How that boy can play!! He can make 'Nearer My God to Thee' sound like 'Georgia Camp Meeting' The ladies wanted to learn the latest dance steps, so Springs and I tried to teach them how to do them. It's a long jump from the Boston and the hesitation to the giant swing, but we had them all fox-trotting in no time.

The party was concluded by the three Drake brothers putting on a pukka drill with some of Sir Francis's own muskets. Gosh, it was great and those men certainly could drill. They were in blue dress uniforms and looked snappy as the devil. I wish we could strut a little.

We had to walk all the way back – eight miles. We stopped at the Peahen in St. Albans long enough to get a warm drink and give Cal time enough to kiss his Peggy good-night.

Springs went back this morning to pay his party call in a Pup. He chased the children around the yard and nearly scared them to death running his wheels on the front driveway. I don't guess we'll be invited back again.

An Australian Lieutenant was killed this morning flying a Pup.

January 31st
We put on a real circus at the Court night before last. Kelly and his instructor, Capt. Bell-Irving,[59] came down from Harling Road for the occasion. Cal, Springs, Tommy Herbert, Capt. Morton and myself went in from here and Budge Weir and Atkinson, two Scots, came down from Thetford. Anderson and Jim and three Englishmen and a U.S. Lieut named Fuller, a friend of Cal's from Chicago joined us later.

We got under a full head of steam at tea. We had the whole chorus from the Shaftsbury theater up in the suite. Kelly and Springs got caught out one night last week in a bomb raid, – the same night they dropped a bomb on the front entrance to Jim's hotel about fifteen minutes after they had all been standing there watching the searchlights. They were walking down the street and a bomb fell about a block away from them and they jumped for shelter. They got in the stage entrance and went behind the scenes in the Shaftsbury theater. The show was over but the actors hadn't gotten out and the chorus was all huddled over in one corner of the wings scared to death. Kelly and Springs got some one to play the piano and started a dance and before long they were having a regular party. They got them after the matinee to-day and brought them up to the Court for tea and early dinner.

The Chinless Wonder and Dora and Peggy were all there, – passing nasty remarks backwards and forward, and a couple of Sheilas. All the girls in London are named Peggy or Sheila.

Cal played the piano and we had a big dance later. We had four suites on the same floor and everybody kept running from one to the other. Next morning we were too near dead to get out of bed before eleven. We had a big champagne breakfast in our suite and didn't get back to the squadron until after two.

The C.O. sent for us at once. He and Capt. Horn[60], our new flight commander, were all set for a big straff because we were supposed to be back at nine.

The three of us lined up in the orderly room.

'Why are you so late in getting back to-day?' the C.O. asked us.

'To tell you the honest truth, sir,' I said as he was looking at me, 'we had such a hang-over this morning we couldn't have gotten out of bed before nine if our lives had depended on it.'

'That's at least original,' Capt. Horn remarked, 'usually it's a bomb raid or a sick aunt. Where were you last night?'

'In the Court,' I told him.

'What suite?' he asked.

'Oh, 103, 111, 115 and some other odd ones,' I told him.

'Well, you certainly made a lot of noise,' said Capt. Horn. 'I was in 104 myself.'

'You weren't exactly quiet on your side of the fence,' Springs chirps up. 'I thought some one was making boilers in there for a while.'

The C.O. got to laughing and said he guessed he'd have to pardon us this time for telling the truth. Capt. Horn says he wants to go in with us the next time we throw a party.

February 5th
Yesterday was washout day so we all went into town again.

Springs had a big suite in the Court and was giving a private party for his girl.

They had a big dinner and were just beginning to start to argue when the Huns came over and dropped a bomb on the Court bar. Springs said he heard the bomb go whistling by his window and when it exploded two stories below the poor girl was scared stiff. She was so badly scared that she made Springs take her home as soon as the raid was over and he joined us in disgust later.

February 9th
I got off in a Pup yesterday. Gosh, what a thrill! They are not so different, but they are so quick and sensitive that they will crash taking off or landing before you know what they are going to do. I didn't bust anything but I pancaked like the devil landing. I hate to think what would have happened to DeGamo and Springs if they had been allowed to go up that day. I doubt if they would have gotten off the ground. If they try to take them from Curtisses to Pups back home, the undertakers will sure do some tittering.

A horrible thing happened to-day. We were all out on the tarmac having our pictures taken for posterity when somebody yelled and pointed up. Two Avros collided right over the airdrome at about three thousand feet. God, it was a horrible sight. We didn't know who was in either one of them. I was glad I was sitting next to Cal. They came down in a slow spin with their wings locked together and both of them in flames. Fred Stillman was in one machine and got out alive but badly burned and Doug Ellis[61] was in the other one and was burned to a cinder.

I sat there watching. I kept trying to imagine what those poor devils were thinking about as they went spinning down into hell. It made me right sick at my stomach to watch. We all went up later and felt better after a little flying.

We went into town for a party with Capt. Horn. He had a girl with him from Georgia named Halley Whatley and it sure did my heart good to hear her talk. He couldn't understand her and Springs and myself when we dropped into the vernacular. Springs made a julep for her and she positively cried when she tasted it.

We all had dinner together and went down to Murray's. When it closed we went to a dance at the Grafton Galleries. Dora and Sousa and Peggy and the L.L.L.D. were all there. I met a sweet little thing with bobbed hair named Lily and we went to another dance at a private place for a while. She is a wonderful dancer and seems to know everybody that ever left the ground.

Hash was there and he and Springs had their weekly Princeton reunion. They drank toasts to old Nassau in enough champagne to float a battleship.

It was a right good party. Wonderful music and I'd rather dance than eat. The British officers were either in evening dress or wearing their blue dress uniforms, and looking very smart in their snappy jackets with bright colored wings and decorations. We looked like hell in our little khaki jackets. Our army isn't worth a damn for anything but fighting but I guess we can hold our end up when it comes to the cool of the evening. But these American women over here get away with murder. There was a girl there last night from St. Louis that sure was the belle of the ball.

I have always heard that the English were a tactless blunt people. That's all wrong. Here is an example of what I call tact. The other evening up in the room one of the girls took off her ring to wash her hands and forgot about it and left it on the shelf. She called me up the next morning and told me about it and said it was a very valuable diamond solitaire and asked me please to try and find it. I called up the manager of the hotel and asked him about it. When I was in yesterday I stopped in to see him and he told me it had been found and if I could identify it, I could have it. I identified it and he gave it to me in an envelope and on the envelope was marked, 'Found in Main Dining Room.' That's what I call tact. Try and laugh that off!

An Englishman spun an Avro into the ground this morning and got out of it alive but broke both legs.

PART ONE: THE UK AND TRAINING

February 10th
Big straff around here. One of our bright young cadets who is little Lord Fauntleroy in his home town, got to cussing in the bar the other night after he got a snoutful and the barmaid objected to his language and made a complaint. This brought on real trouble. The C.O. had to report it to the U.S. Headquarters. The cadet got thirty days' confinement and this American Lieut is put in charge of us. He takes his duties very seriously and is going to have roll call morning and night.

You can cuss before any lady in England and she will probably cuss back at you, but if you let your tongue slip before a barmaid, woe be unto you! They tell the world they are ladies and allow no liberties – during business hours. I always heard they were good at repartee but all I've seen so far have acted Lady Godiva holding on to her hair in a breeze.

Twelve of us were up in our suite at the Court having dinner last night and we decided we ought to have some girls. So after dinner we all went out in different directions to round up the girls after the theater. As we needed so many we thought that everybody should get as many as possible in case the others had no success.

By twelve o'clock we had twenty-two girls in the suite! Everybody was successful! Then they all got to fighting among themselves and each one said that the others were not ladies and it ended up by all of them leaving. By that time we were glad to see them go.

February 12th
I've done five hours on Pups and am ready for Spads as soon as they get one in commission.

This Lieut is a prime ass net. It was raining this morning and no one got up to answer his roll call. So he had us all in his room after lunch to bawl us out. He announced last week that no one could leave the squadron without permission from him. I don't know where he got the idea that it was any business of his because there are no restrictions anywhere else. He wanted to sit at the head table with the instructors but the major wouldn't let him and he hates to eat with us. Capt. Morton bawled the life out of him the other day and stood him easy. In spite of all his time on Curtisses, he's still on Avros, while Nathan, Barry, DeGamo and Springs are all thru with Pups and Spads and they started after he did. He also thinks he should have the preference of machines but he doesn't get it.

He told us that we were not taking the discipline seriously. He told Springs that he had been to London twice without permission from him and that he was going to punish him. Springs said he had finished his course in flying and was ready to go to the front. He said that made no difference. Springs said he thought that an aviator was supposed to fly and that what he did when the weather was unsuitable was his own business. As a matter of fact, Springs got in all his time by flying in bad weather when no one else wanted the planes and has put in more hours in the air than any other cadet. And he would go without lunch to get a plane while the rest were eating. He asked what the charges against him were. The Lieut said A.W.O.L. Springs said he wanted a court martial because he knew the Lieut didn't know how to hold one. They argued half an hour over the technicalities and Springs bluffed him out of it by quoting imaginary regulations. He tried to confine the rest of us to quarters and we all demanded court martials. He's postponed judgment until he can go into London and find out just what he can do.

February 15th
Flew a Spad to-day. Easy to fly but dangerous as hell. Just like flying the famous barn door that Beachy used to talk about. And it has the gliding angle of a brick. I've always laughed at the regulars wearing spurs to fly in but I needed a pair in this Spad. It bucked just like a bronco.

PART ONE: THE UK AND TRAINING

Above: Lieutenant H.C. Fulford in front of an R.E.8 during his pilot training with 15 Training Squadron at Doncaster. (Mark Hillier)

Above and Below: A Martinsyde G.3 pictured by Fulford at RAF Hounslow. (Mark Hillier)

The Lieut went into London and Dwyer told him to shut up and mind his own business and do a little flying himself. So Milnor told Cal.

Springs and Nathan and Barry are thru and went to Scotland at midnight last night to the machine gun school. Springs went hog wild yesterday afternoon. He and a little English kid named Rogers were raising hell all over the place in Spads. They were running their wheels on the ground and then pulling up just in time to try and run them on the hangar roofs. It was a great exhibition of damn foolishness. Then Springs got a Pup and began chasing a machine gun class in and out of the firing pit. He'd dive in the pit and chase them out and then run along the ground and chase them back in. In the midst of the party he lost his pressure and before he could pump it up his engine conked and he pancaked in a flower garden between a windmill and a summer house. The C.O. called him in the office and told him they needed fools like that in France and to pack and get going. Then MacIntaggart made him go over and fly the Pup out.

February 16th
DeGamo was killed to-day.[62] Nobody knows how it happened. He was up in a Spad and it was found about five miles from here in a small field over near Ratlett [Radlett]. It wasn't crashed badly but his neck was broken.

I've done five hours on Spads now and I feel I can fly them.

Tommy Herbert took us up to Bedford to a really nice dance with some friends of his. We had a fine time and he met a sort of vamp. Tommy asked us to go up there to dinner with him last night and we thought we were going to his nice friend's house. Imagine our surprise when we walked into the vamp's house. We all got lit and had a hell of a time. Cal took up with one Helen who could dance. Tommy amused the vamp and I was alone except for one Alice, who was the mistress of a general in private life. She had to go home early.

February 19th
We were getting dressed for DeGamo's funeral when the Lieut came in and bawled us out for being late. Cal looked up at him sheepishly and held out a box of candy. 'Have a piece of candy,' he said.

The Lieut looked like he was going to bust. 'Have you no sense of propriety?' he asked.

'Maybe not, Lieutenant,' I said, fixing a puttee, 'but I can at least thank God for a sense of humor!'

He glared at us and slammed the door as he went out. I hear he was once an All-American football player.

February 20th
Bulkley and Carlton have been killed. Two good men gone West. Bulkley was flying a Pup over at Hounslow and ran into an Avro.[63] The landing skid on the Avro tore his center section out and the plane came to pieces in the air. Carlton spun an R.E.8 into the ground at Spiddlegate.[64]

Cal had a forced landing with a Spad to-day. His elevator controls jammed and he had to do some quick thinking. He was flying around the insane asylum trying to see his nurse. He used his head and managed to flop down on a golf course. Some old duck was mad as hell when his game was interrupted. He got behind a bunker when he saw the Spad coming and Cal hit it and the Spad went over on its back. He said that when the Spad settled down he was looking right into this fellow's face and it was awful red.

Cal and I went into town again with Capt. Horn. Cal got mad at Peggy after dinner and she went off to a dance with a Canadian colonel and he started back for the squadron. But there was a bomb raid on and the Huns dropped three bombs on the station so Cal had to come back.

February 22nd
Fred Stillman died after a gallant struggle.[65] They thought he was going to pull thru but poisoning set in. A fine fellow! Also Montgomery was killed. Montgomery was killed when the pilot fell out of the front seat in an Ak. W. in a loop.[66] Montgomery was in the back seat and crawled up into the front cockpit and just had his hands on the controls when it crashed.[67] Think of watching the ground coming up at you for two or three minutes while you wiggle up the fuselage. Makes my blood run cold!

March 3rd
Here we are at Turnberry in Scotland. It's on the coast and is cold as hell. We go to machine gun classes for ten hours a day for ten days. They run us to death and we freeze and starve. There's a bunch of Americans up here and a few of them have gotten their commissions. I wonder what's happened to ours. Tipton got his and they had to close the bar for three days afterwards.

Nichol[68] was killed at Stamford on his first solo.

March 5th
No time to write. They work us too hard. I'm starved. Nothing to eat here but Brussels sprouts and vegetable marrow.

We went down to Girvan for a party. The Woman's Army Auxiliary Corps has a training school there. We watched them drill. Gosh, it was funny. A Barbados sergeant major was giving them close order drill and he was absolutely speechless with rage. He was used to flaying a company with his tongue mercilessly and there was nothing he could say to this crowd. There were no words in his vocabulary he could use. He just stood there and sputtered like a wet wick. He had a hundred and fifty Waacs of all sizes and contours and he was trying to line them up and couldn't because he didn't know what part of their anatomy to line on. He had my sympathy. It had taken him twenty years to acquire his drill vocabulary and now he could not use it. But why try to drill women anyway? I don't see the idea at all. They pay them the same as Tommies and give them the same discipline. A Waac officer can't walk out with a Tommy any more than an army officer can be seen with a Waac private. There weren't enough officers to go around with us so we took privates anyway.

March 10th
Heard to-day that Ludwig[69] was killed flying an S.E. He got into a spin close to the ground.

March 12th
Thank God that's over. We are now at Ayr at the school of Aerial Fighting. The pilots' pool is also here. When pilots are ready to go to the front they are sent here and then sent out when needed. We are quartered at Wellington House. Springs, Nathan, Barry, Landis, Zistell, Oliver, Capt. Morton, Hash Gile, Hammer[70], Winslow, Whiting, Tipton, Kissel[71], Mathews[72], Ortmeyer, Frost, Evans, Mortimer[73], Armstrong, and Clay are all here. Most of them have finished and are waiting for commissions before being posted overseas. We hear a lot of rumors about how we are going out. The British won't take us unless we are commissioned and we hear that Pershing has recommended that pilots be sergeants and not officers and that flying pay be abolished. He has stopped it in the A.E.F.

Springs, Oliver and Winslow got Second Lieutenancies and refused to accept them and asked for their discharges instead.

Everybody here wants to get out of the U.S. Army and join the R.F.C. where they'll get a square deal. We certainly have gotten a rotten deal from the U.S.A. and the British couldn't have treated their own Field Marshals any better. We owe the British a lot and have a lot to get even with our own army for.

MacDill and Jeff Dwyer are the only two officers that have made any effort to treat us decently. Jeff is sure our friend.

There's a big party going on here in spite of the wholesale funerals. Six American Naval pilots were sent over from France to take the course here. They thought that Camels were as easy to fly as the Hanriots[74] they had been flying in France and they wouldn't listen to any advice from the instructors here. Three of them were washed out one week.

Then Ortmeyer[75], who had three hundred hours on Curtisses at home as an instructor, spun a Camel into the ground and killed himself. Dealy spun into the ground the next day and before they got him buried, two Englishmen killed themselves. All in Camels and all doing right hand spins.

Col. Rees is in charge here and he tried to put pep in the boys by giving a stunting exhibition below five hundred feet. He certainly did fight the tree tops and he wouldn't come out of a spin above fifty feet. Then he made all the instructors go up in Camels and do the same thing. It was a wonderful exhibition and then he made us a little speech and told us there was nothing to worry about, to go to it. Several of the boys were so encouraged that they took off in Camels and tried to do the same thing. Only one was killed.

March 16th
Everybody had gone crazy over eggnog. Springs and Oliver found a dairy where they got some cream and they made some eggnog. Everybody demanded more. The next day they made five gallons and it lasted ten minutes. Then we got a big dairy vat and put all the Waacs to work beating eggs. All the cooks and maids up here are Waacs. Springs's father sent him ten pounds of sugar and we had three cases of brandy. It must have made fifteen or twenty gallons. Everybody from the Colonel down came over to drink it. By lunch time every officer in Ayr was full of eggnog.

We all went out to the airdrome after lunch and tried to fly. They are short of magnetoes and the only way they can get more is to steal them off crashes. There were three Spads so Capt. Foggin[76] asked for Spad pilots. He sent Springs up in one hoping he would crash it. He had a quart bottle of eggnog and he took it up with him to drink. The motor conked all right, but he made a nice landing in the field with a dead stick without crashing so Foggin sent him up in another one.

Springs decided he'd steeplechase. The field is in an old race course so he came down wide open and ran his wheels on the track. He tried to bank with the track for a turn but they had put up some heavy wires and his top wing caught them. He went straight up three hundred feet and stalled and fell out of the stall right into the middle of the field. God certainly took over the controls. He wasn't hurt but the Spad was a write-off and Foggin got one mag.

Springs was mad as a hornet because he had the bottle of eggnog in his pocket and when he saw he was going to crash he threw it out to keep from cutting himself up.

The Colonel sent for Springs to bawl him out. 'Ah, listen here,' said the Colonel, 'I really have enough trouble running this school without you youngsters interrupting my telephone connections. Don't do it! By the way is there any of your priceless concoction left?'

March 20th
Cush Nathan[77] killed. He was flying an S.E. and the wings came off at five thousand feet. He went into the roof of a three-story house and they dug him out of the basement. A real fine fellow. I liked him. So did everybody. He and Springs have been rooming together and that's the second roommate he's lost in two weeks. He doesn't want to ask anybody else to room with him but Reed Landis said he's not superstitious and moved in.

March 22nd
Last night one of the boys had a date with a staff officer's wife and couldn't get rid of him so brought him around to Wellington and asked us to get him tight and pass him out.

Springs and I took him on. We would each mix a drink by turn. When it came to my drink he did bottoms up and got nasty about it. He said American drinks were all too weak and he picked up a glass of it and threw it into the fire! It exploded! About a half hour later he went out on a shutter. That Scotsman was so tight he couldn't hoot no more than a dead owl.

Armstrong, the wild Australian, came in and said he had two lassies outside and needed help. Springs went out with him. The girl he drew was only sixteen and was sweet and innocent so he bawled her out and gave her a lecture on the perils of folly and the danger of trusting any man after dark. Then he took her home.

Armstrong came back tight and got into the Waacs' quarters by mistake. There was a straff over it this morning. The Waacs saved the day by not complaining officially. They have several rooms in the basement.

Cush's funeral was this morning. The staff officer who went out last night feet first was supposed to have been in charge of it but he couldn't make the grade. There was a long delay and then Springs took charge and somehow we got thru with it. One of the escort planes had a forced landing and one of the firing party got nervous and fired too soon and scared every one to death.

March 24th
For three weeks before Cush was killed, he and Springs had been going to a Scot dentist here to have their teeth reworked. We went to see him to-day to pay Cush's bill. We told him about the crash and do you know, that Scot wouldn't accept a penny! We explained that we had been directed by the court of inquiry to pay his bills but still he wouldn't take anything. He said he couldn't take money from a man who'd died for his country. Yet they crack jokes about the Scots loving money above all else. I'm glad that my blood is Scotch. If they don't hurry up and send us on out to the front a lot of German-Americans are going to have their veins full of Scotch too.

Springs said he'd pay his own bill right then as he might get killed too and didn't want to cheat him.

'But, mon,' says the dentist, 'I'm na thru wi' yer.'

'Oh, yes, you are,' says Springs, 'whether you know it or not. I'm not going to all the trouble and expense of having my teeth fixed when I'm this close to Lethe's waters. Every morning when I wake up I reach out to shake hands with Charon.'

'And dinna ye take na thought for yer soul when day draws nigh to return it to its maker?"'

'I've been to the kirk with you every Sunday since I've been here,' said Springs, 'and I'm helping to support a couple of distilleries. What more can I do for my immortal soul in Scotland?'

'Hoot, mon,' says he, 'Americans must be heathens. Ye dinna ken where to find the text in the Bible.'

Springs told me later that the dentist wouldn't work on his teeth unless he'd go to church with him. Then he shocked the dentist by pretending to look for Matthew in the Old Testament.

These Scots may be canny but they are a trusting lot. Any of the banks here will cash checks without asking for any identification. Yet down in England they won't even accept money for deposit until they've got a picture of you and know why your grandfather had to marry the girl.

Pansy hasn't taken a step since he's been here. He rides out to the field and back in the only taxi in town. He hasn't paid a penny to the driver yet and that poor fellow is going to get an awful jolt some day when he tries to collect.

This town is full of statues of Bobby Burns and bars. That's the principal industry. The barmaids are the belles of the town. I looked around at the show the other night and there were our three leading social lights, all escorting barmaids. The one down at the station hotel is the favorite. She takes a personal interest in each drink and every drinker. The other night Springs went down to the station to see Gile and Hammer off and she thought he was going too. She came out from behind the bar and threw her arms around his neck and cried over him. We've been kidding her about it and she's as mad as a hornet.

Ayr is really a beautiful spot and I'd like to stay here a while but they kill off pilots too fast for any one to linger very long. Springs says he's been to twelve funerals. One more coming to-morrow. All the flying here is stunting and we have service machines. Every time we go up, we are supposed to find another machine and have a dogfight with it. The Colonel stays up in the air a lot and is about the best at scrapping, – he and Foggin and Atkinson. Foggin is a wonderful pilot and only has one eye.

March 26th

Springs and Oliver got their commissions as 1st Lieutenants yesterday. It was Bim's birthday so they decided to give a party and invited every one to a dinner. It was a nice dinner party but our hosts never appeared until it was all over. They were back in the bar with the Waac barmaid experimenting with a new drink they had just invented. Every now and then they would send us in a sample by Minnie. It was a potent beverage, judging by the results, tho it tasted harmless enough. It had benedictine, cognac, champagne, vermouth and pineapple juice. They called it 'The Queen's Favor.'

Later on the adjutant's wife and sister came over with Alec to call. Bim came up to speak to them. He came in the door and bowed. Then he reached out to close the door. He reached short by about four feet. You could have knocked his eyes off with a spoon. Cal plays bridge all the time. Curtis says he is suffering from the Woofits, that dread disease that comes from overeating and under-drinking.

George Vaughn cracked up an S.E. in splendid style.[78] The engine conked with him over the town and he pancaked in a vacant lot and climbed up on top of a building. Later on, somebody wanted a picture of the crash and wanted him in it. He got back in the seat and the fuselage collapsed and the whole thing toppled over. He got his arm skinned up then, tho he hadn't gotten hurt in the original crash.

Pansy run into a chimney with a Camel and scored one complete write-off. Practically every one that has been killed in a Camel has done it from a right hand spin.

Hagood Bostick[79] came down here from Turnberry looking like the Queen of Sheba's favorite husband. He had on everything but the monocle to make him Hinglish. He had pale pink breeches, light tan tunic with skirts down to his knees and boots and gloves and cane to match. He comes from Charleston, S.C, so doesn't have to cultivate the accent. Plucky little kid, he's only nineteen. He and Pansy are our sartorial stars. Pansy really looks more dashing, due to his saber mustache. He talks too much about his yacht and his flunkeys.

Thank God we are thru with wireless forever. And just think of the valuable time we've wasted learning that damn code! Eight words a minute! Bah! An hour a day for eight months! Da-da-da diddy da! Bah some more! I knew I was going to be a scout pilot all the time!

March 27th

I am ordered to France on Spads even tho I haven't got my commission. I leave to-morrow. Hoorah! Hoorah!

The Lieut from London Colney blew into Wellington last night. He was all lit up like a new saloon. He asked for Springs and me. We weren't too cordial. He told us that he had come to see us and he realized we thought he was an ass and that he wanted to show us that he was a regular fellow. He said he wanted to give us a party and prove what a good sport he really was. We slapped him on the back a few

PART ONE: THE UK AND TRAINING

Above: A portrait of Major W.A. 'Billy' Bishop V.C., D.S.O. & Bar, M.C, D.F.C. (Courtesy of Andy Thomas) times and carried him home after he passed out. He's learning some of the values of this life, but a sense of humor is a divine heritage and can't be cultivated.

Springs's little girl came back for further instructions so this time I undertook her education. I took her down on the beach and gave her a short lecture. She's young and innocent all right, – but ambitious.

March 30th
I came down to London and was told that Spads are being washed out at the front and replaced with Dolphins so I am ordered to Hounslow to learn to fly them.

Springs came down from Ayr with me. Captain Horn is a flight commander out there in the squadron that the great Major Bishop V.C, D.S.O., M.C.[80] is organizing to take overseas. He wants the three of us to go out with him.[81]

They are letting Bishop pick his own pilots and he went with us to the U.S. Headquarters to try and arrange it. Col. Morrow said it couldn't be done. The whole staff nearly lost their eyes staring at us when we strolled out, arm and arm with the great Bishop.

He has a very pretty chauffeur and I made a date to take her to a dance Saturday night. All the cars in England are driven by girls.

The Lieut came down from Ayr and gave his party at Murray's. Gawd, it was terrible! He wouldn't have anything but individual bottles of everything. He was certainly determined to be a good fellow and everybody obliged him by getting soused to the eyeballs. He ended up the night sitting on Lillian's doorstep singing love songs thru the keyhole.

I went to a big dance and managed to collect a redhead. She gave every indication of being ready to burn my fingers so I left while the door was still open. I had lunch with her the next day and she sure is a goodlooking woman. But my grandfather told me never to get mixed up with a redheaded woman who wears black underwear.

Springs went back to Ayr after a very unsatisfactory conference with a major at headquarters, who is an officer all right but even an act of Congress couldn't make him a gentleman.

I hear that Nial and Lavelle and Jake Stahl[82] are in the hospital pretty badly smashed up.

April 2nd
Springs came back down last night and has orders to go overseas to an S.E. squadron. I got Bishop and we went into London and he arranged to have him sent out to Hounslow when he reports to the Yard.

PART ONE: THE UK AND TRAINING

I have taken an apartment at the Piccadilly Mansions and am quite hot these days.

April 6th

The dirty deed is done. Springs came out here mad as a hornet because they told him at the Yard that he was no good and would have to have some more instructions before he could go overseas. He didn't tumble at all and insisted that he was a damn good pilot and offered to prove it. But they had a report on him that was unsatisfactory so sent him out here. He didn't find out until he got to Hounslow that Bishop had had that report sent in. Now to grab off Cal as he passes thru.

April 7th

Sanford[83], Kissel, Zistell[84], Whiting[85], Frost, Tipton[86], Campbell and Hamilton are going out on Camels to regular British squadrons just as if they were R.F.C. pilots. The Hun has played hell with the troops in France and they need help. So we are to be commissioned at once and sent out to the R.F.C. as they need us. I got my commission to-day and Cal's is here too.

Everybody is discouraged over the continued bad news that comes thru. It's clear now that the war will be won or lost in the next two months. You certainly have to hand it to the British for keeping a stiff upper lip.

Cal arrived this morning from Ayr and we had everything fixed at the Yard like a greased chute.

We arrived at Hounslow in triumph and a one lung taxi. Bishop says he doesn't care where we stay, – so we are going to get some place in town and spend our last days on this earth in peace and comfort. Halley says she can get a house for us for less than one suite at the Court. That would be warm.

April 8th

We have a house! You can't laugh that off! Halley had a friend, a Lordship, who had a four-story house in Berkeley Square that he was willing to rent to us for ten pounds a week. We also have a cook and butler. Gangway!

We moved in and gave a big party on Saturday. Major Bishop, 'Nigger' Horn, MacGregor[87], MacDonald[88], Capt. Benbow[89] and Capt. Baker[90] came in from Hounslow for dinner and Col. Hastings[91] and Col. Hepburn of the Canadian General Staff.

We found out too late that we couldn't get any meat without meat coupons. And there was little else we could buy. We got around the food

Above: New Zealander Malcolm Charles McGregor pictured at RAF Upavon, Wiltshire, prior to his posting to 54 Squadron, from which he moved to 85 Squadron. Whilst at Upavon, he completed twenty-one hours flying including time on the Sopwith Scout. He gained his wings and his Upavon Central Flying School Certificate, No.2891, on 7 April 1917. (Mark Hillier) problem easily. All we had cooked was soup and fish. Then we made a big tub full of eggnog and a couple of big pitchers of mint julep. To make sure that no one got beyond the fish course, we shook up cocktails too.

Our guests arrived about six and we started doing bottoms-up in rotation. It was a riot.

Springs was at the head of the table and served. Everybody had a bottle of port and a bottle of champagne. The butler brought in a big platter of fish and Springs served them by picking them up by the tail and tossing one to each guest as if they were seals. At the end of the fish course, I was alone at the table. The rest were chasing each other all over the place.

His Lordship has a wonderful collection of ancient war weapons. Before going to the theater, where we had a box, all these ruffians armed themselves with swords, machetes, shillelaghes, maces, clubs, bayonets, sabers, pikes, flintlock pistols and various daggers and dirks. They looked like an arsenal. It's a wonder they weren't all arrested. Cal dropped a club on the bass drum in the middle of the show and Benbow nearly fell out of the box. Springs and Vic Hastings and I improved the idle hours by taking a Turkish bath and joining the rest of them later back at the house, as fresh as a spring morning.

April 11th
Springs has given birth to another idea. It may be all right. Some of his are good and some are awful bad. Information has been received that the Germans have developed a parachute that can be used from an aeroplane. Springs got all excited about it and went to see Calthorpe[92] the inventor of the Guardian Angel parachute that all the balloon-itics use. Calthorpe is working on the idea. Springs offered him two thousand dollars if he would make one for him according to his idea. Calthorpe said he couldn't do it as the War Office wouldn't let him work for individuals, but that he would be glad to have any assistance or ideas. Springs offered to test out Calthorpe's and take it to the front for further tests and they are working on the same idea.

Calthorpe's idea is to have the parachute arranged in the trailing edge of the wing like an aileron.

The trouble with that is that it is liable to foul on the tail and it would take some time for the pilot to get out of his seat and get the straps on. And he would have to get out in a spin or a steep dive. Calthorpe is developing it primarily for the big planes where there is a crew and all of them could possibly get out except the pilot.

Springs wants one made to fit on an S.E. where the steamline for the pilot's head is on the top of the fuselage. Then the pilot could wear the harness all the time and all he would have to do would be to unfasten his safety belt and jump. The objection to that again is the possibility of fouling. He figures on having a long cord between the parachute and the plane so that it would be free of the plane before it started to open. As the pilot fell away from the plane the cord would open the parachute and then the pilot could cut loose. It might be very difficult for the pilot to cut loose and Calthorpe figures on doing it with a series of rubber bands or an unraveling device.

I like the idea. It would certainly help at the front. Most pilots are killed by structural defects or by having the plane catch fire in the air. It would also be a great device for testing.

Springs tried to get permission from the U.S. Headquarters to go ahead with it but they said nothing doing.

We also hear rumors of a new machine gun invented by a Russian which uses larger bullets than the present ones and they are little shrapnel shells. This war is getting more dangerous every day. There is only one other American at Hounslow, Loghran from North Carolina.

April 12th
We've all been up in Dolphins[93] and they aren't so hard to fly but are very tricky. They have the two hundred and twenty horse power Hispano motors and the prop is geared which reverses the torque. They don't turn as well as an S.E. but better than a Spad. There's one great danger with them. They have twenty-four inches of back stagger and the top wing is very low. They have no center section and your head comes up thru the top wing where the center section ought to be. If anything goes wrong and it turns over, the whole weight of the plane will rest on your head. If you crash, the gas tank is right at your back like in a Camel and your legs are up under the motor. There's not much hope for the pilot. Capt. White was landing last week and a tire busted and the wheel gave way and he turned over. The plane caught fire and he was nearly burned to death before we could get him out. They spin very easily from a left-hand turn. Cal gives me the willies by always taking off in a left-hand climbing turn.

I heard a funny story about Tracy Bird. Two old maids got frightened at the air raids in London and moved out to the country. The third day they were there Tracy crashes into their roof in an Ak. W. [an Armstrong Whitworth design] and lands in their room. They were so frightened they moved back to London. Tracy wasn't hurt.

April 13th
Roberts and Al came around to the house last night after Murray's closed. Sheila and Peggy and the Queen Bee and the Brainless Wonder

PART ONE: THE UK AND TRAINING

Above: The cockpit of a S.E.5a, the type used by 85 Squadron during 1918.
(Courtesy of Andy Thomas)

Below: A view of the top gun mount on a S.E.5a, showing the Lewis machine-gun on a Foster sliding rail mount. The aircraft also had a fuselage mounted synchronized Vickers machine-gun. (Courtesy of Andy Thomas) were all here. We were doing a little serious drinking and Al and Sheila got to cussing at each other. Al was coming back pretty hard and Sheila was determined she was going to have the last word. I didn't like it. I can't bear to hear a man use bad language to a woman.

I told him to shut up. He kept on and I told him again to shut up. He said something to me and we both jumped up and I saw blue for a moment. I took a swing at him and I'd have killed him if Springs hadn't jumped between us and my fist hit his shoulder and he hit Springs in the back. All three of us went down on the floor and got tangled up in the bearskin rug and Cal jumped on me. We got up and shook hands. Damn my temper anyway! It gets away from me in spite of all I can do.

Middleditch[94] and Pudrith[95] have been killed on D.H. Fours. The Lord sure is a good picker!

Stratton got smashed up. He was in a Camel and his machine gun ran away so he crashed to keep from shooting another machine.

April 14th
There's a new order out from Headquarters that no U.S. pilot can come to London without orders. Now isn't that nice? Here we are stationed within the city limits, the tube station is right at the entrance of the field and yet we are forbidden to go down to the center of the town. In other words we are confined to our quarters as if we were under arrest.

The U.S. Army is a great institution. I have been treated like an enlisted man for ten months tho I was never supposed to be one. But I didn't expect the treatment to continue after I became a 1st lieutenant. I suppose if we ever get to be captains, the regulars will all be colonels and captains will be enlisted men still. We all realized that there was a war on and that Washington was too busy to give us our commissions as they promised and we did the best we could in the meanwhile in the best of spirits. We lost our seniority and our pay. A man that was in the same class with me at Ground School and who wasn't good enough to come over with us, went to a flying field and got his commission in six weeks and came over here and was put in charge of some of us. We have all the responsibilities that the British pilots have, we have to do the same work they do, we die the same way they do, we accept orders from the same officers they do when it comes to duty, yet we have none of their privileges. It isn't fair. If Bishop can order me to go up and get killed, which he can, he should be able to give us permission to go into town, which he can't.

I'm glad I had the pleasure of knowing Major MacDill and Colonel Morrow but I can't understand what they are doing in the army. They are gentlemen! There was a major out here yesterday that certainly couldn't qualify. If we had to choose between fighting the Prussian Guard and the West Point Alumni Association, I know where at least two hundred and ten aviators would assemble.

I guess majors are like children around eight and ten. They are just passing thru an ugly age. And these present ones have been hatched so recently that their gold leaves itch.

We are going to the front and get killed off like flies. Two or three get killed in England every week. Yet thee great Moguls are so afraid that we will have a little fun before we do go West that they have forbidden us to come to London to see a show or join our friends and try to forget for a little while what is going to happen to us. It's an outrage. They think we are so much dirt.

We went to the American Officers' club for lunch for a while. They ought to call it the majors' and admirals' free lunch. They think we have leprosy. The club is just around the corner from the house and is very convenient and the food is good but I don't like the company. When Lord Leaconsfield[96] donated his house for the purpose I didn't hear anything said about what officers were to be allowed in it.

Well, we should worry.

I'd rather eat one meal with Bishop than have Admiral Sims[97] and General Biddle[98] pay my board eternally. Thank God the British can recognize a gentleman despite his rank.

These little tin majors give me a pain. They can't find enough aviators in France to cuss at, so they have to run over here every little while and show off their authority by cussing us out before the British. And I must say for the British that they resent it as much as we do.

I'm an American and I'm proud of it but I'm damned if I can take any pride in the boobs that are running the flying corps. For instance how can we fly when our necks are being choked off by these 1865 model collars? The staff must think they are still in Mexico wearing O.D. shirts.

Springs called up and got permission to go down to Headquarters. He came back with three sets of orders for us to go to the dentist until we get our teeth fixed. I guess that will see us thru. Dwyer certainly is a friend in need. He said he's heard about our house unofficially and that we'd better keep it quiet. We will.

Loghran[99] has gone to Turnberry.

We are all broke at the moment and have all cabled home for funds. Cal has a rich grandmother and he and Springs got together and composed a letter to her that was a masterpiece. They told her about the young aviator that had been over here for six months and had been broke and had a rotten time. Then he went out to the front and his father sent him five thousand dollars for a birthday present but he was killed

before he had a chance to get leave and enjoy it. If Springs isn't hung first he'll be a great writer some day. That letter was the work of a master hand.

Wheelock and Berry crashed a Bristol Fighter at Ayr and it caught fire. Wheelock was in the back seat and had a broken arm but managed to get out of the wreckage. Berry was in the front seat and couldn't get out so Wheelock went in after him and pulled him out. Both were badly burned.

April 18th
Gawd, what a life! We get up at noon, breakfast and go to Hounslow on the tube if it's a good day, if not we go down to the Savoy bar and join the gang there. At six we are back at the house unless there's a party at Murray's. Vic Hastings usually comes around before dinner with Col. Hepburn or Cecil Cowan or Nat Ayres and we all go out to dinner after getting well oiled. Vic sent around a couple of cases of Canadian Club from Canadian H.Q. yesterday. That ought to last at least three nights. We went down to see His Lordship's own private wine merchant when we first moved in and he keeps us supplied with some marvelous 1880 port. At least he says it's port. I call it the "answer to a drunkard's prayer".

Then we usually get in our evening dancing at Murray's or the Elysee and then all come back to the house when they close. Anywhere from five to twenty-five of the old detachment usually drop in and we simply can't keep up with our engagements.

We had a full-blooded Sioux Indian in the squadron but he killed himself yesterday by spinning into the ground from a left-hand turn.[100]

Nigger Horn had a crash [see drawing by Clayton Knight]. He was flying an S.E. and had just gotten off the ground when the engine conked. He was headed straight for the town and couldn't turn back. It looked as if he was going to crash into a crowded street but he stuck his nose down and deliberately dove between two little brick buildings on the edge of the field. The buildings tore his wings off clean and he and the fuselage slid along.

Springs has a new girl and my Gawd, what a beautiful thing she is. But she's so stupid it's ludicrous. Nothing but a doll. He says he's suffering from a reaction. The last one had too much brains.

April 20th
It looks like we were going to be delayed. 84 squadron on the same field at Hounslow is ready to go over but the factory is short on Dolphins as they have been using all the new ones to replace Spads at the front. They

have taken our Dolphins and we have to refit with S.E.s.[101] I'm not sorry to get S.E.s but I hate the delay. If we don't get to the front pretty soon there won't be much use in taking us – we'll be too busy fighting off the purple crocodiles.

Mathews, Oliver, Eckert, Newhall, Gile and Hammer[102] are ready to go out to the front to-day. There was a big party last night and we went to a dance at the Elysee Gardens. The whole flying corps was there and all tight as a nun's corset. Hash and Springs held their usual reunion. Springs has something wrong with his left eye and when he drinks too much it closes. I went downstairs in the bar and found Hash holding Springs's eye open with his hand so he could have another drink to Old Nassau. When they meet in hell those two will organize a Princeton reunion.

Cecil gave a dinner party in honor of Peggy and the Doll the same evening. This is a new Peggy – the third. This one came as a present in Murray's the other night. Vic and Barney and Dora were there too. Then we all went to the dance. We decided to go back to the house about one o'clock and the Doll was dancing with some Englishman and Springs and I went out to get her. She didn't want to leave and her partner got the idea that she was objecting to me breaking in. He got very nasty about it and told us to run along and gave me a gentle push. I saw red and took a long swing. Springs saw me swing and jumped in the way. I knocked him flat and then Cal grabbed me. Gosh, it's funny how we three stick together in a crowd. But I wish they'd jump on the other fellow for a change. That's three times they've jumped on me in a fight. We need better team work! Hash has the right idea. He's about six feet four and an old Princeton tackle. He saw the argument and came up and towered over this fellow while Cal was holding me and looked him over and said, "Listen here, young fellow, when he's thru with you, I'll take on what's left".

We abandoned the Doll and all left including Hash and Eckert. We couldn't find but one taxi so all nine piled into it. When we got back to the house we all got out and payed off the driver. Just as he was about to drive off, the door opened again and out stepped Bim. Nobody knew he was with us.

I heard that Stanberry[103] was killed last week on a Camel. He and I were always good friends after our fight at Ground School. There was only one blow struck in that fight and he went out like a candle in the wind. We both apologized and have been good friends ever since.

April 25th
We gave a farewell dinner for 84 at the Criterion[104]. I'll bet the bill for breakage will be more than the one for food. Mac brought back a sign,

"Ladies Room" and hung it over our spare bedroom.

A little girl came around to the house the other night that I've known for some time, named Lily. She's a cute little kid and a good dancer. She's been living with one of the boys for a couple of months. She went up to his squadron and took a house for a while. He's nutty about her and would have married her if she'd tried to make him. She has a sort of past that wouldn't sound well at home but doesn't seem to make much difference over here. At home every woman that isn't a virgin has a past, while over here they've got to shoot somebody, be divorced by somebody who is somebody or get run over by a train.

Well, this particular cadet had just gotten his commission and he celebrated the happy event by diving into the ground from five thousand feet. The poor little girl is all broken up and is scared to death because she thinks she is going to have a baby. She wanted me to tell her what to do. She wanted to know whether to write his people or not. I told her not to. He had done the best he could and it would be a shame to spoil his family's solace in sorrow. They've probably got a dozen artists busy painting wings on all his pictures by this time. I told her if she loved him to say nothing about it and carry on. I gave her what money I had – not much, I'm sorry to say.

Tommy Herbert[105] and Paul Winslow[106] were in the other night full of rumors. They have a scheme for getting switched from Camels, or rather Winslow has. They are ferrying and always take a Bristol Fighter. They are going to pass themselves off as Bristol pilots. Tommy is not so enthusiastic as he crashed a Bristol last week and broke a couple of ribs and sprained his back. I wish he'd sprain his throat so he couldn't sing.

The other evening before going out to dinner we heard a terrific explosion up on the third floor and we dashed up the stairs thinking we were being bombed. Twas only Springs trying to take a bath and the geyser had exploded. The gas in the water heater had blown out and he lit it again after the room was full of gas. Funny things, these geysers. The English stick a tank over the tub and when you turn on the water it turns up the gas to heat it. Springs is short his eyelashes and eyebrows. He didn't have much to start with. Dora says he looks perpetually startled and she's afraid every minute that he's going to run away.

Tom Mooney[107] has been killed. So has Brader.[108]

April 28th
Cal got a cable from his grandmother to-day which called for a hundred pounds. A lot of famous writers' would like to get paid at that rate for their work.

Springs and I went out to a hospital in the suburbs to see Bostick who's back from the front all shot to hell. He flew a Camel into the ground and his face looks like a scrambled egg. His jaw is broken in two places, his arm is broken, and he may lose one eye. On top of that, he's had pneumonia. He couldn't talk much but all that worried him was getting back to the front. He'll never see the front again, poor kid. We took him some strawberries. They are worth their weight in gold over here.

The Royal Flying Corps and the Royal Naval Air Service have been merged into one service known as the Royal Air Force which is to rank equal with the army and navy and be under neither one.[109] From now on it will be the Army, Navy and Air Force. I understand the Navy doesn't like the idea at all. It ought to save a lot of confusion and duplication of work. Some of the non-flyers will lose their jobs which will be a good thing.

May 3rd
Lily, the widow, came around again. It was a false alarm about the baby and she acts as if she might be consoled very easily. However, none of us wanted the job. We wanted to get rid of her but we didn't know how to do it. Then one of these bold, bad, handsome woman stealers came in to call. With a little careful arranging we permitted him to steal our girl right out from under our eyes. Weren't we mad? I hope he gets into trouble as the last time he pulled that little trick he got one that didn't have any label on her addressed to him.

If these boys can fly two-bladers like they can fly fourposters, there'll sure be a shortage of Huns before long.

Springs had a narrow escape. He was about to go up in an S.E. and he just happened to notice in time that his elevator turnbuckle was broken and the controls were held only by a safety wire. He would have gotten off and then it would have broken in the air.

We had a game of follow the leader. Mac was the leader. We had an old two-twenty S.E. and he took it up first. He dove it at the ground wide open and levelled off and ran his wheels along the ground and pulled up in a long zoom and looped. The trick of the stunt is to get over the top of your loop. An S.E. will zoom fifteen hundred feet from the level and that's why they are so good at the front.

Cal was next. The idea was that each man should do the stunt of the preceding man and then set another one for the next man. Cal did Mac's and then half rolled at the top of the loop.

Springs was next and his stunt was a full roll at the top of the loop. Of course he was up above a thousand feet.

I was next and I put my nose down to about two hundred after I did my full roll, and as soon as I started up for my zoom I kicked on full right rudder and pulled the stick back into the right-hand corner. I didn't know what I was doing but I sure did it. I whirled around a couple of times with my nose up and then I whirled around with my nose down and ended up stalled upside down. The motor stopped and I just did get in the field with a dead prop.

It was Thompson's turn next. Mac said what I did was an upward spin followed by an outside spin, whatever that is. I told Thompson how I did it and he went up and started into it with terrific speed. The propeller shaft broke and his prop flew off, just nicking the leading edge of the wing. He got into the field all right. That ended the afternoon performance. Mac and Cal certainly can fly.

About eleven o'clock last night the phone rang and Springs answered. It was a lady and she wanted to speak to His Lordship. Springs got to chewing the rag with her and ascertained the fact that there were two of them and they were alone and would be agreeable to gargling a little champagne. So he and Cal got some pop and went over to call. In about an hour Cal came back without his hat. Springs came in about half an hour later with it and kidded the life out of him. Cal says the lady made an improper proposal to him so when she wasn't looking he departed. Springs says Cal had been making improper proposals himself for half an hour and as soon as the lady began to take them seriously, he lost his nerve. He sure is funny with women.

Give him a piano or a dance floor and a girl and he's like a snake with a toad, – just fascinates them! But as soon as they surrender, he gets stag fever or stage fright or something and takes his foot in his hand.

May 4th

London was too much for us; the house was getting too crowded every night so we decided we'd better leave for a few days and send out the rumor that we had left for good. Everybody in the flying corps knew about the house and came around for a drink after hours and brought their brothers and sisters. The story goes that, we three have been picked by Bishop for his circus*, which is going out to fight Richthofen's[110] Circus, because of our great skill as pilots. Isn't that a joke? Particularly after the stunt I pulled the other day.

*ALL THE PILOTS WERE SPECIALLY SELECTED BY BISHOP.

Bishop had a little Bristol Scout that the general gave him to play around in – pretty little thing, all painted silver and it had a Le Rhone motor.[111] He let me fly it the other day. I took off and the motor cut out cold at about two hundred feet. I tried to land short but I didn't have room enough to even sideslip and I couldn't turn and there was a high fence right in front of me that I couldn't glide over. Then I had a brilliant idea. I pointed the nose at the ground in front of the fence and deliberately bounced. And I bounced over that fence. All would have been well if there hadn't been a football goal-post on the other side of the fence. I hit the cross-bar and the Bristol was reduced to matchwood and I got a bruised knee and a split lip.

Yes, London was getting to be too much for us and so we came down here to Eastbourne to rest up for four days. This is a beautiful place down by the sea, quiet and restful.

We had a funny party the night before we left. Sir Somebody or other and Lord Somebody and their wives came around to the house to call on His Lordship. I explained that His Lordship was in the country and that we were holding down the fort. Then I asked them to come in and crack a bottle with us. They came in and I opened some pop. They were very nice and were much interested in the American Army and asked a lot of questions.

About that time, Cal and Halley and Nigger came in. A nice time was had by all tho no one could figure it out. I believe they thought that Halley lives here too. But they didn't say so, and we couldn't just volunteer the information that she didn't. The titled contingent left and we went down in the kitchen and cooked sausage and mushrooms and made some eggnog.

Vic Hastings came in with two Canadians and two girls. One of them was a raving beauty and the other one wasn't so bad. The beauty and Springs cooked up a mess that was easy on the palate. After a while the Canadians got tired of our kitchen and their dignity got restless and they left. We kept the girls and took them home ourselves. You can't laugh that off!

I wonder what the boys in Texas are doing for amusement. You chase me and I'll chase you! We called the girls Cherubim and Seraphim.

May 6th

We did rest for two days and felt a lot better. Cal, the nice boy, took up with an old gentleman and his charming young daughter. While he was telling them all about the war this morning, Springs and I went out for a stroll. We saw a bottle of ancient pre-war Haig and Haig in a pinch-bottle sitting in a bar window and we went in and tried to buy it.

They wouldn't sell it except by the drink. So we bought it by the drink and sent a messenger after Cal and started on another one. Cal arrived and in order to catch up he poured out half of the other bottle and took it neat. It took effect like dentist's drill and by the time we finished the second bottle, we were ready to fight a buzz saw.

We hired a limousine and told the driver to show us the sights. He took us out to Beachy Head which is a cliff three hundred feet high and showed us Lovers' Leap where all the suicides do their stunt. Cal and Springs began chasing each other around and got over the side of the cliff on a gentle slope. They slipped in the soft dirt and slid right on down the first stage of the cliff to the perpendicular drop above the rocks a hundred feet below. I was scared stiff. They managed to check themselves right on the edge. Cal was all right because he was on his stomach and dug his toes in the soft dirt, but Springs was on his back and the dirt kept crumbling away under his heels, and he slowly slid on down to the very edge.

Cal and I were yelling at the top of our lungs but we couldn't go to his assistance. He held on to a bunch of weeds until he could get his knife out and dig a slot for his heels. I yelled for help and the chauffeur got some officers to come and help us. We made a chain out of our Sam Brownes and some rope and they lowered me and I pulled Cal up easily. But we had an awful time with Springs because he couldn't turn over and didn't dare let go either hand because he was still slipping a little. I don't see why he wasn't killed. We had to lasso him and pull him up backwards.

We decided that since our lives were in jeopardy we ought to have our pictures taken to preserve our likenesses for posterity. The photographer nearly had a fit at our poses.

Then we went down to an indoor swimming pool. There was a flying trapeze over it and Springs insisted on getting up on it as he used to be a trapeze expert at college. He isn't so good now and he missed his jump over shallow water and took all the skin off one side his face, where he cracked the bottom.

Then we went roller skating. That's where I shine. Everybody got off the rink for me and I put on an exhibition for them that was an exhibition. I had on my new pink breeches and when I tried a double reverse, I tripped.

My beautiful pink breeches are ruined! When the place was ready to close the band played "God Save the King". Cal was sitting on the sidelines talking to a girl and he forgot he had skates on and jumped to attention. His feet went out from under him and he lit on the floor on his back. Springs embraced a post for support.

May 10th

The good effects of the Eastbourne trip didn't last long. Kelly came down to town from some ungodly hole and we had a terrible battle. Kelly didn't have a girl so Springs called up and said he was sick and sent Kelly around after his girl. That pair certainly are funny. They aren't satisfied by trying to give each other the shirts off their backs but they want the other to have everything. This time the girl didn't like the idea so well so Kelly came back and they started out together.

We had a fine bomb raid last night.[112] Springs, Cal and I were over at Cherubim's flat. Sherry was there too, and they were playing bridge while I was writing some letters. The Maron, which is the raid warning, went off about ten-thirty. The girls jumped like they had been hit already. They grabbed some camp stools and said they were going down in the tube station. We said we weren't going but they begged us to go with them, so we did. We took along a bottle of whiskey and a plate of cake. The girls were hysterical with fright. Cherry had a sister killed in a raid last year and Sherry had some friend bumped off.

When we got to the station it was already packed. We couldn't get down to the platform so camped on a landing half way down. The air was as foul as the Black Hole of Calcutta and those people certainly were scared. We cheered the girls up and drank the whiskey and felt better. Everyone had brought camp stools and it sure was a funny sight.

I hadn't realized before how successful the raids are. It doesn't matter whether they hit anything or not as long as they put the wind up the civilian population so thoroughly. These people wanted peace and they wanted it quick. Possibly Lord Lansdowne got caught out in a bomb raid.

The air got so bad that we said good-night and left. Outside, the town was absolutely deserted. We waited fifteen minutes for a taxi but there wasn't any so we had to walk home. The city was like a sepulcher except for the terrible racket of the anti-aircraft guns. Not a light anywhere. We didn't hear any bombs explode but Archie kept up a lot of fuss. There wasn't the tiniest crack of light to be seen anywhere. They certainly do enforce the law about lights. They don't have many laws in this country but they certainly enforce what they do have.

There is a battery over in Hyde Park a couple of blocks from the house and it shakes the panes in the windows when it fires. When there's a big raid on, you can sit at our window upstairs and hear the pieces of shrapnel falling in the street like hail. It's just as well to stay indoors. Archie has quit trying to hit anything. They just put up a barrage and hope the Huns fly into it. They have certain areas which they range and certain areas which they leave clear so they won't hit our planes that are up after them. Our night-flying Camels are doing a lot of damage to the raiders and that's the only way they will ever stop them.

Armstrong, the Australian stunt pilot, was over at Hounslow the other day in his specially rigged Camel and gave an exhibition for us. He's certainly a wonderful pilot. He runs his wheels on the ground and then pulls up in a loop and if he sees he hasn't got room enough, he just half rolls at the top. I saw him land from a full roll and he glides and does S turns upside down. I don't think he has long to live, tho, just the same. He says night flying is not so difficult after you once get used to it. And he says it's just as easy to fire at night as in daytime. I don't see how he figures that tho.

After the raid was over an assorted crowd came around to the house. Two of mamma's own little darlings came around with two wild women. I eased them towards the door gently but firmly. One of the boys was highly insulted when I told him that we were glad to have him any time but he'd have to leave his girlfriend at home. He got real nasty and said he didn't know that we were running a nunnery and from what he heard he didn't think we were in a position to object to anything. Then he took a couple of nasty cracks at a few of our friends and regular callers. I told him that after all it was our house and I was sorry that he couldn't see the thing right. We were trying to keep our house respectable. I told him that since we had moved in here, not a woman had spent the night in the house and while I wasn't any inspector of the public morals and hadn't snooped around any, still I'd be willing to guarantee that no one had indulged in any horizontal refreshments here. I wasn't concerned with what they did elsewhere, but this was an amateur gathering and we didn't allow any professional talent or union workers. If he wanted to leave five pounds with his card when he called, it was all right by me, but as for us, alcohol was our weakness. So they left. I should have crowned them. Gosh, it's wonderful the way I control my temper now. I used to like that kid. I remember his mother came out to Mineola to pack up for him and she asked MacDill to please write to her if he didn't behave.

But what I told him was the truth. Some of our guests may be a bit unconventional in their mode of living but they have certainly all been ladies around here. And considering the number that have drifted in and out, I think it's right remarkable. These London women are in a class by themselves. They are good sports, good looking, good dancers, well educated, act like ladies, and they don't sit around and worry about their honor all the time. They aren't a bit conceited about the matter as they all are at home. Virtue over here isn't even its own reward.

Springs and I flew over to London Colney for lunch and heard that Waite[113] killed himself by driving a Spad into the Elstree reservoir. He was firing at the ground target which is in the center of it and his controls must have jammed for he never came out of his dive. London Colney is sure an unlucky place.

Clarence Fry is funnier than ever. He was telling a story on Barksdale[114] about how he went over in a Pup to stunt for his girl. He came out of a spin below the tree tops and couldn't get his motor again and crashed right in her yard. Barksdale is so long he can hardly get in a Pup and flies without his puttees so as not to interfere with his legs. When he crashed he got out of the wreck and confronted his girl with his long underwear sticking out below the breeches. He was so embarrassed his girl thought he was knocked out and wanted to take him to a hospital.

May 11th
The lady that owns the house next door has come back from the country and she wrote a letter to His Lordship complaining about the racket over here. He sent the letter to us and said we had to do something about it. So Springs went over to call on her this afternoon. He was gone a long time and we thought she must have proved to be young and attractive but when he came back he said she had invited him to stay for tea. He said she was awfully nice and her son was killed last year in the

Battle of the Somme. He explained to her how we were just waiting around to go out to the front and expected to go any day now and were just trying to have a little fun before we left. She got to crying and said that was just how her son felt about it before he went out the last time. She ended up by wanting to give us a dinner party and invite some nice girls for us to meet. Springs told her that we knew too many already and that we craved quiet just as much as she did. So we are not going to play the piano after midnight and she is going to withdraw her complaint. You can't beat these English women!

They are having hard luck over at London Colney again. I saw Barksdale in town and he had a long tale of woe. A big two-engined Handley-Page landed on top of an Avro over there the other day. The pilot in the Avro was hurt but not killed and the pilot of the Handley was killed when it nosed on him. The next day the Handley was still standing on its nose and a pilot was taking off in a Spad. The Spad swung 90° taking off and flew right into the tail of the Handley. The Spad turned the Handley over on its back and wrecked the fuselage. The Spad was a write-off, of course. The pilot may live.

Clarence Fry[115] killed himself by stalling a Spad over there. That's too bad. I thought a lot of Clarence. He certainly was a peach.

May 12th

Last night we had another choice assortment of callers. Halley, as usual, was responsible for it. Twas a motley crew. But one of them, oh, la, la, what a knockout! Her name is Billy Carlton[116].

She and I got on like Antony and Cleopatra. How that woman can dance! Well, she ought to be able to, seeing as how she is leading lady in a musical show. She is about twenty-three and has been on the stage since she was eighteen. She sure is witty. She kept us laughing all evening. She had a general in tow that wasn't at all friendly to me. There was a little monologue she gave.

"What, you coward," she would say, "how dare you strike a poor defenceless woman! You contemptible cur, why don't you have courage enough to hit a man? Why don't you hit me? Whow!" And with that she would throw herself on the floor as if she had been knocked down. She had a lot of little stunts like that.

Then she has a cockney song she sings:

> She was poor but she was 'onest,
> Victim of a rich man's crime,
> First 'e wooed 'er and then 'e left 'er,
> Ain't it all a bleedin' shime?

Chorus
It's the sirne the whole world over,
It's the poor wot tikes the blime,
It's the rich wot tikes the pleasure,
Ain't it all a bleedin' shime?

Then the girl went up to London,
For to 'ide 'er bleedin' shime,
There she met another squire,
And 'e dragged 'er down agine.

See 'er in 'er 'orse and kerridge,
Ridin' daily thru the park,
Tho she 'as a dozen rubies,
They don't 'ide 'er bleedin' 'eart.

There she stands upon the corner,
Sellin' flowers to the gent,
She's grown fat about 'er middle,
And 'er golden locks 'as went.

There are a lot more verses and variations to it but these are the only ones I know.

I took her home and the general wasn't very mad! It's getting to be a disgrace the way we welcome our friends and then put them out and keep their girls. Well, they ought to know better!

She has a gorgeous flat and there was a supper waiting for us when we got there and a maid to serve it. She slipped on a negligee and looked like a million dollars.

"I was sitting in jail with my back to the wall,
And a redheaded woman was the cause of it all."

About ten of the boys have given it up and just quit flying. No nerve. They never should have enlisted if they didn't intend to see it thru after they found out it was dangerous. Jeff Dwyer gets them jobs at Headquarters or puts them in charge of mechanics. But yellow is yellow whether you call it nerves or not. I'm just as scared sometimes as any of them.

May 13th
The great McCudden,[117] now Major McCudden V.C, D.S.O., M.C., E.T.C.,

just back from the front to get decorated again, came into Murray's last night for dinner and, oh, boy, what a riot he caused. All the officers went over to his table to congratulate him and the women – well, they fought to get at him just like they do at a bargain counter back home. He's the hottest thing we have now – 54 Huns, [57 by 26 February 1918] five more than Bishop and he's just gotten the V.C. and a bar to his D.S.O. He held a regular levee. I think there are only five airmen living that have the V.C. The first thing you have to do to get it is to get killed.

The girl with him thought she was the Queen of Sheba. She started to pretend she didn't know us. I should have reminded her where we met but I didn't. I saved her life once.

Well, I'm not jealous. I'm going to be hot myself some day.

I'm either coming out of the war a big man or in a wooden kimono. I know I can fight, I know I can fly, and I ought to be able to shoot straight. If I can just learn to do all three things at once, they can't stop me. And Bishop is going to teach me to do that. I've got to make a name for myself, even if they have to prefix "late" to it.

The groundhog captain at London Colney finally got his wish and killed himself in a Pup. He was rolling over the tree tops and his motor cut out and he didn't have enough speed to get around and went into the ground.

I hear that Kissell[118] has been shot down and killed at the front. He was the best Camel pilot we had. He could fly upside down as well as right side up.

Cherubim and Seraphim invited us down to Maidenhead for the week-end at Cherry's house. Vic, Jack May, Barney, Cecil, Dora and the three of us went down Saturday afternoon.

Cherry has a cottage right on the river with a pretty little garden in the back. Jack brought the food down from Murray's and a good time was had by all. Vic found attraction next door and left us for a while. We called on His Lordship and he showed us his country place but I'm not sure he was glad to see us. We were supposed to go to a dance but none of us ever got there, or even came near it.

Everybody went back to town Sunday except Cherry and Sherry and the three of us. We chartered an electric punt and spent the day on the Thames. It's a beautiful spot, a regular fairyland. Little estates come right down to the water's edge and at night it's beyond description. These punts are big flat-bottomed canoes and are run by storage batteries. They have no seats but the bottom is filled with cushions. Anybody can paint the rest of the picture. Somebody gave Springs a bottle of Canadian Club and he got up in the bow and remained there all day like a bowsprit. Cal gave a good imitation of a young man in love. We had lunch on the terrace at Skindle's, which is a big restaurant with a terrace down to the water's edge. We had tea in the punt up at some place above the locks. We went back to Skindle's for dinner and Springs got chummy with a girl over at another table and made a date with her to meet him there later.

We all got back to the cottage after dinner and then Springs got a rowboat and went back to Skindle's after the girl. He couldn't find her and went in the bar. There were a couple of Guards officers in there and they all got to chewing the rag. The Guards officers began taking cracks at the American Army. One of them, a long tall bird, said, "I've been reading in the papers until I'm bloody well sick of it, about the number of American troops that have come over. But what I can't understand is why none of them will fight. Paris is full of them, London is full of them, but they all jolly well stay away from the front. None of them will fight!"

"Well," says Springs, "here is one of them that will". And with that, he hauls off and stretches the long tall bird on the floor. The other one makes a pass at him but he ducks and beats it out and jumps in his boat and shoves off. But in his haste, he forgot his oars. He floated down the river and missed the falls by a miracle. There were no lights showing anywhere and I don't see how he found his way back, but he did. He's got more lives than a cat and needs all of them.

I heard to-day that Hash Gile[119] is missing at the front.

Bob Griffith[120] is dead. The wings of his D.H. Nine came off at ten thousand feet.

May 14th
All aboard for France. Our orders have come thru and we leave next Wednesday.

A ferry pilot brought over my new machine day before yesterday and smashed it all to pieces landing. He got tangled up in the wires coming in. So I decided I'd fetch my own service machine and got Springs to fly me over to Brooklands in an Avro yesterday and I flew it back. It certainly is a beauty. I like these 180 Viper Hispanos made by Wolsey much better than the 220 Peugeots.

Brooklands used to be an automobile race track but is now the depot and test park for the R.F.C. I saw some of the new experimental planes down there. One was the [Sopwith] Snipe, which has the 200 Bentley motor and is going to take the place of the Camel at the front. Another was the [Sopwith] Snark which has the big A.B.C. air-cooled radial. It has a wonderful performance but I understand there's some hitch about it. The Salamander and the Hippo and the Bulldog [all Sopwith types] were all there too. The Hippo is a sort of two-seater Dolphin.

PART ONE: THE UK AND TRAINING

I gave my new plane a work-out in the air to-day. It flies hands off; I put it level just off the ground and it did 130. Then I went up high and did a spinning tail slide. Nothing broke so I have perfect confidence in it. I've been cleaning and oiling the machine guns, tuning up the motor and testing the rigging. The best part of it is that it's mine – no one else has ever flown it and no one else ever will. It's painted green and I have named it the *Julep* and am having one painted on the side of the fuselage. Nigger has the *Gin Palace II* and Springs has the *Eggnog First*.

Larry has had trouble with his motor and is losing sleep over it.

To-morrow, I've got to synchronize my gun gear, set my sights, swing my compass and then I'm ready. Death bring on your sting, oh, grave hoist your gold star!

The bus certainly is plentifully supplied with gadgets. The cockpit looks like the inside of a locomotive cab. In it is a compass, airspeed indicator, radiator thermometer, oil gauge, compensator, two gun trigger controls, synchronized gear reservoir handle, hand pump, gas tank gauge, two switches, pressure control, altimeter, gas pipe shut-off cocks, shutter control, thermometer, two cocking handles for the guns, booster magneto, spare ammunition drums, map case, throttle, joystick and rudder bar. That's enough for any one man to say grace over. It has two guns: one Vickers and one Lewis. The Vickers is mounted on the fuselage in front of your face and fires thru the propeller with a C.C. gear to keep from hitting it. The Lewis is mounted on the top wing and fires over the top of the propeller. It has two sights: a ring sight and an Aldis telescopic sight.

I set both sights and both guns so that they will all converge at a spot two hundred yards in front of the line of flight. When you aim, what you really do is to aim the plane and the guns take care of themselves. The Vickers has a belt of four hundred rounds and the Lewis has a drum of one hundred and we carry three spare drums. To change drums you have to pull the gun down on the track with your hand and then take off the empty drum and put on the full one. It's not hard to do unless you let the wind get against the flat side of the drum, then it will nearly break your wrist. We've practiced changing until we can do it in our sleep. The Vickers is the best gun by far.

Of course, I can't resist the temptation to add a few devices of my own and have also put a cupboard and shelf in for spare goggles, machine gun tools, cigarettes, etc. I am also decorating my cockpit. When you're in the air for two or three hours at a time, you get awfully bored.

We saw "Fair and Warmer"[121] last night. It was opening night and Billy sent us tickets. She's in it. It was quite amusing, especially the audience which always laughed at the wrong time. Their idea of American slang is about as good as our idea of theirs.

Down at Eastbourne we went to a Revue and they sang "Over There" with the chorus dressed in Kilts. You can't beat that!

Yet it is surprising how well Americans are getting along over here – much better than I expected. Every one that has come in contact with the British swear by them. And the British will do more for us than they will do for their own troops. Every club in England that is open to English soldiers is open to Americans. We have every privilege that is offered to their own troops. If the English soldiers are entitled to special prices on anything so are we. We ride on the train at half fare and are entitled to anything we want from their canteens. We even draw what we want from their quartermasters. Yet when the American Commissary was opened up in London, the first rule they made was that no one could buy anything who wasn't in American uniform. To me it hardly seems fair, not to say discourteous. I went down to get some canned stuff the other day but I couldn't get near the counter because the place was so full of the Y.M.C.A. and Red Cross and K. of C. Those boys are going to have the best of everything or know why.

As for me, I'm for the British and I don't care who knows it. Irish papers please copy.

The three of us and Nigger flew up to Maidenhead to call this afternoon. We ground-straffed the place and chased everybody off the terrace at Skindle's. Vic was down there and fell off a haystack watching us. Then we steeplechased all the way back down the river and kept our wheels just out of the water. Nigger dipped his once. Cal missed hitting a bridge by inches and Springs landed with about two hundred feet of telephone wire dragging on his undercarriage.

There was one funny thing. At one long open stretch there was a punt in front of us right in the middle of the river. A man in a bright blazer was standing up in the stern punting and a girl was sitting in the bow with a big pink parasol. As we dove on them, the man fell overboard and the girl lost her parasol. I looked back to see it floating down the river and the man in the blazer floundering about in a regular whirlpool.

We heard that Sanford[122] has been killed out at the front.

When I think of all the good men that have been killed and then see all the bums that are still alive hanging around town, it makes me mad. Justice is blind, all right. And God is not fair about it. Why should he take men like Fry and Stillman and Nathan and all the rest of the good ones and leave bums like me hanging around?

It's not right. I feel sort of ashamed to be here still. I'll bet what the government owes me that I can name those that will be the survivors, if any, of our outfit.

One of our crowd got ambitious and not only got married to two different girls, but tried to give both of them an allotment. That takes nerve!

For a while one of the boys was playing around with a very charming young lady who more or less owed allegiance to a big diplomat who was in Holland on a mission of state. She had a beautiful apartment and he was more or less enjoying himself in the absence of the baron. But the gentleman returned suddenly and he was henceforth out of luck. We were all kidding him about it one night and Springs after listening a while retired and penned a poem on the subject. We all told him how rotten the meter was but he said that was charged up to poetic license. Here's a copy of the revised version:

> A portly Roman Senator was sipping his Rock and Rye,
> When a classic Vestal Virgin caught his educated eye;
> "Ah, ha," he cried, enraptured, "that's just about my style,
> Behold the old come-hither look, that makes the wild men wild!"
>
> The old boy was no novice, for he'd served his time in Gaul,
> And he saw she was a chicken and the flapper pose a stall,
> So he flashed a roll of talents and she flashed him back a smile,
> And she shrugged her architecture in a manner to beguile.
>
> While the young bucks wagered drachmae that his game would never win,
> He was letting her drive the chariot and chucking her under the chin.
> They dined at the smart Lucullus, saw the Coliseum show,
> Supped at the Appian Roadhouse where the party's never slow
> They drank a lot of Roman punch and shook a wicked hip,
> For she taught him the Tiber Grapevine and the Herculeum Dip.
>
> Said he, "If you're a Vestal, it's because you've had no chance, –
> I can see that you're ambitious by the charming way you dance.
> I'm getting rather lonely and I've got a tidy bit,
> Oh, really, you must come over." She answered, "Tempus fugit."
> As he gave his chariot number to the chasseur at the door,
> He heard the garcon whisper. "Sine qua non, caveat emptor,"

He gave her a three-horse chariot, a flat with a cellar of booze,
And introduced her as his niece, who had moved from Syracuse.
He bought her Carthaginian Togas, her sandals came from Thrace,
And her B.V.D.'s were Grecian and were trimmed with Persian lace.
Her hair was bound with fillets of platinum and gold,
And she sprayed her dainty tonsils with a vintage rare and old.

The young bucks were green with envy which but aroused his mirth,
And he boasted, "To hell with all expense, I'm getting my money's worth."
But he had to go to Naples, where some rents were overdue,
While she lingered by the Tiber, complaining of the flu.
And no great time elapsed ere the wise ones slyly winked,
And they whispered, "Habeas corpus," as their golden goblets clinked;
For it was gossiped at the banquets and told o'er games of cards,
That a certain dashing Shavetail of Julius Caesar's Guards,
Was bringing home the bacon, had a latchkey to the flat,
Had soused himself in pre-war stock and was staging a terrible bat.

Now the Senator in Naples was leasing out his piers,
When the gossip from the Tiber was wafted to his ears,
He cursed his Naples real estate and paged his charioteer,
As he scorched along the highway, he pumaced off his spear.
He broke the record back to Rome and arrived with a terrible shout,
But the Shavetail heard him on the stairs and escaped by the gutter spout.
The Senator surveyed his flat, with bottles everywhere,
And picked up some scattered plumage and bits of odd tin-ware.

The lady wept in anguish, but he only mocked her cries,
"I gave you rings for your fingers, now they're beneath your eyes."
The sweet young thing was cagy, she'd expected his return,
And she explained, "Semper fidelis, won't you ever learn!

"Dear Cæsar came to see me, said Pompey's getting hot,
And the Legion's drilling badly and the Navy's gone to pot:
So to stimulate recruiting, I've been flirting with this Wop."
And she slipped her toga's shoulder strap, and displayed a fancy clock.

And the fat and-portly Senator bethought himself of Gaul,
And when garrisoned in Egypt how he used to pay a call,
On a dusky amorous maiden with a houseboat on the Nile,
Whose lingering caresses made Army life worth while;
His thoughts went back to Britain, and he stroked a scarred chin,
Where an angry Celtic husband had expressed his deep chagrin.
And he recalled how his upright figure and the polish his armor bore
Had intrigued the Spanish maidens on that temperamental shore.

And his anger soon abating, he replaced the truant strap,
And she said, "Carpemus diem," as he gave her – cheek a slap;
He patted the tousled curly locks, that on his shoulder lay,
And thought, "She's not hors de combat, 'tis part of an Officer's Pay."

I hear the American Lieut that was at London Colney distinguished himself the other day. His squadron ran into two layers of Huns and leapt on the top layer. He was trying to turn his Camel to the right and he got into a spin and down he went. He got it under control and came out of the spin right in the middle of the lower flight of Huns. They didn't do a thing but shoot him full of holes. He got back a sadder and wiser man. They say he is stout enough and has made a good man. More power to him!

Major and Mrs Bishop at RAF Hounslow with Sopwith Dolphins in the background. (Mark Hillier)

PART ONE: THE UK AND TRAINING

May 17th
We had a bunch of Brass Hats from the War Office down at Hounslow to-day and we put on an exhibition of formation flying and stunting for them that was pretty good.

Nineteen machines in close battle formation are a stirring sight. Everything went off well except Springs's landing. His wheel hit a soft spot and turned him and the other wheel gave way and he turned over on his back and his head was shoved into the mud. He was a great sight when he came walking back to the tarmac where all the generals were standing. He had on slacks and a white shirt and wasn't wearing helmet or goggles and his face and head were all covered with mud. He's got to go over to Brooklands again to-morrow after another plane. I'm going to fly him over in an Avro.

Mrs. Bishop had a lady with her and she invited us to tea with them. We explained that we were all pretty dirty, which we were, but she said to never mind that and come along as we were; so we did. We all went into the squadron office and had tea brought over from the mess. The lady with her proved to be very nice and was very much interested in Americans and America. She was the most patriotic person I've met over here because she was always talking about the King. When I told her how much all the Americans liked serving with the British, she said she was so glad and she knew the King would be delighted to hear it. That sounded a bit far fetched to me.

We got on fine with her and we told her some funny stories and she nearly died laughing. We had a taxi waiting for us and offered to take her back to town with us as soon as we got dressed. She said she'd rather take a bus and get the air and it would take her right by the palace. I didn't get that either. As we went out we saw Cunningham-Reed's mother and she nearly broke a leg curtsying and I noticed Mrs. Bishop do the same thing when we left her and took the lady out to the bus.

I asked Cunningham-Reed why the gymnastics and he told me it was for royalty. I asked him wherefore and he told me the lady was Princess Mary Louise*[123]. All three of us have been trying to remember whether we cracked any jokes about the King or not. Mrs. Bishop must have been laughing merrily. She's a peach. We're all crazy about her. Well, I have pressed the flesh of royalty now. My hand has gotten accustomed

‡ PRESENTED 85 WITH A SILVER FOX ON PLINTH INSCRIBED TO MAJOR BISHOP & OFFICERS. SQUADRON AFTERWARDS CALLED "FLYING FOXES"

to the grasp of nobility and now I know the feel of the real thing. Who said we were Democrats? We're all snobs underneath the cuticle.

When we went into tea an American Lieut. Colonel asked to see Bishop. I think he wanted a plane. Bishop said to tell him to wait and asked us if he should invite him in to tea. We said certainly not; no colonel would ever invite us to anything but a court martial. That colonel got the surprise of his life when he saw these three disreputable looking Americans, with non-reg uniforms and slacks, coming out with Bishop and realized what had kept him waiting. He wasn't very mad. I hope we never see him again.

May 20th
I've been spending most of my time with Billy. She certainly is a wonder and we get on fine together. I wish I had met her sooner.

Earl Hammer[124] has been killed out at the front.

PART II
THE WESTERN FRONT

25 May 1918 and Beyond

War Birds Continued

May 25th
France! Here's where we sober up and get down to real serious work.

Here I am at the front, the victim of many emotions. We had a fine send off and come what may, nothing can ever take away from me the joy that has been mine.

We had a series of farewell dinners and parties. Nigger's father gave us a banquet at the Criterion. He's a fine old fellow, eighty-two years old. He made a pile of money in the wool business in Australia and has five sons in the British Army. Everybody had to make a speech.

Bishop kidded Springs about telling the lady next door that he knew too many nice girls. He wanted to know if he had met any more that turned out to be nice. Then he kidded me about playing football with the Bristol.

The next night Billy came around to the house with some friends. She started to kid me and said I was her cave man. She had a little actress named Babs in too that was sweet and girlish. Springs said that if the cave man stuff would work with one, it ought to work with another. Whereupon he starts to grab Babs.

Babs thought that was fine and she entered into the spirit of the game with great glee. She responded to the cave man treatment by hitting him playfully over the head with an empty port bottle. She was no sylph and it didn't do a thing but knock him cold. It was a terrific crack and he was out for some time and had a big knot on the top of his head. Babs spent the rest of the evening making a fuss over him and I think she meant it. Springs sent her a nice brick all wrapped up in tissue paper the next morning and a couple of hours later a bunch of orchids.

We left Hounslow about eleven and our take-off was a scream.[125] Billy and Babs were there over at one end, Dora and Lillian and Cecil were also present in another group. Nigger's fiancée was there with her family, and the Princess was there with Mrs. Bishop. We nearly broke

Above: Three men of 'C' Flight, 85 Squadron. Standing in front of a Sopwith Dolphin, they are, left to right, Callahan, McGregor and Thomson. The picture was taken at RAF Hounslow in May 1918 prior to 85 Squadron's move to France. (Courtesy, The Springs Close Family Archives, Fort Mill, SC)

Opposite: A portrait of Lieutenant John McGavock Grider. The image was probably taken in April or May 1918. (Courtesy, The Springs Close Family Archives, Fort Mill, SC)

our necks running from one group to another and pretending we didn't know anybody else.

Then the staff arrived from the American Headquarters. We hadn't expected them – Col. Morrow, Col. Mitchell[126], Jeff Dwyer and a couple of others. We tried to get in the ground but couldn't find a hole.

The Princess was very cordial. She said she told the King about us and that he was very pleased to hear that American pilots were so enthusiastic about serving with the R.F.C. and that he hoped some day he would have the opportunity to decorate one of us. Mrs. Bishop made us promise to stick to the major and not let a Hun get on his tail.

That was one morning when I would rather not have been so conspicuous. Our style was badly cramped. Col. Morrow was very nice and spoke of the time I had come to him to enlist and only had one letter

PART TWO: THE WESTERN FRONT

Above: Personnel of 85 Squadron at St. Omer aerodrome, France, on 21 June 1918. From left to right, they are: Cushing, Dymond, Daniel, Canning, McGregor, Callahan, Springs, Horn, Randall, Baker, Cunningham-Reid, Longton, Rosie, Carruthers, Dixon, Brown, Brewster, unidentified, Abbott, and Inglis. (Courtesy, The Springs Close Family Archives, Fort Mill, SC) of recommendation. But that was from the ex-secretary of war so he wrote the other one for me himself.

Dora was much interested in our silk skull caps that we wear under our fur helmets. She wanted to know whose stocking mine was made from.

All nineteen machines were arranged in position for taking off in formation and the engines warmed up. The major's machine was out front in the center and the three flights arranged in a V on each side and in back of him. We'd practiced getting off that way and it was all right as long as no machine got directly behind another and hit the backwash.

Bishop lined us up before the crowd and some general made us a little speech. Then Bishop gave us our final instructions. He told us that Lympe[127] [*sic*] would be our first stop and to be sure and take a good look at the wind sock and to land squarely into the wind. But he didn't call it a sock. He called it by the name we always call it on the field when there are no ladies or gentlemen present. He turned red and the ladies lowered their parasols and he ran and jumped in his machine and we all took off together. I got in Springs's backwash and nearly cracked up getting off.

Cal didn't get far. He disappeared from the formation about fifteen minutes after we took off, and didn't get here until to-day. He had an air bubble in his water line and he had to land in a field south of London to let his motor cool off and get some more water. He got down all right and got out of the field again and decided he'd stop at Croydon[128] and get his radiator drained.

He made a bad landing at Croydon and crashed. So he went back to London for another night and got a new machine from Brooklands the next day.

We stopped at Lympe near Folkstone [*sic*] for lunch and Brown cracked up there. We took off after lunch and Canning cracked up on the beach when his motor conked. We landed at Marquis,[129] near Boulogne, for tea. We had a beautiful trip across the channel. It was as clear as a bell and we crossed at eight thousand feet. My motor was missing a little and I kept picking out destroyers and trawlers below to land beside in case it gave out. MacDonald crashed at Marquis when he landed short in the rough and turned over and Cunningham-Reed washed out his plane by pancaking.

On the way across, Springs motioned for me to come up close to him. I flew up to his wing tip and he took out his flask and drank my health. I didn't have a thing with me but a bottle of champagne and that was in my tool box and I couldn't get to it.

We arrived at our airdrome about six. It's two miles south of Dunkirk and is an old R.N.A.S. station called Petite-Synthe. We are about three miles from the coast and there are two other squadrons on this same airdrome. They are bombers and have D.H. Nines. We had dinner at the 211th Squadron which used to be No.11 R.N.A.S.[130], and they are very nicely fixed in semi-permanent quarters. There is one American over there – Bonnalie[131], who was in Bim's gang. They bomb Zeebrugge and Bruges every day trying to damage the submarine bases there. Just across the canal is another airdrome. There are two squadrons of night-bombers on it with Handley-Pages and Fees and one squadron of Bristol Fighters.

We are in the 65th Wing, which is a part of the 5th Brigade. There is a brigade of the Air Force assigned to every Field Army and consists of four or five wings. A wing consists of five to fifteen squadrons.

211 is a good outfit and we had quite a party. Springs and I got a couple of motorcycles and went out in search of eggs and cream. We found plenty and made a big-tub of eggnog. 88 Squadron[132] came over to see us with a band and we had a regular binge. Capt. Harrison who was our instructor at Thetford is a flight commander over there and he invited us over to spend the night with him. I finally went to sleep laughing over Springs and Dora. After I told Billy good-by rather formally as everybody was watching us, Springs went over to Dora and they put on a burlesque tragic parting that was a scream. Everybody nearly died laughing.

They tell me that our sector of the lines, from Nieuport on the coast to Ypres, is very quiet as there is no possibility of a battle up here. All new squadrons are sent here for a month's final training before going south. 84 has just left this airdrome and gone down to Amiens.

After paying all my bills I had just sixpence left when I took off. Now isn't that perfect! I couldn't have used any more and I couldn't have gotten along on less. That's figuring pretty close. Now I am beyond the reach of money. Eternity has no currency.[133]

May 27th
I'm feeling exceptionally good to-night. I had a nice swim in the moat of Ft. Mardick[134] followed by a glass of eggnog made with real cream, and I can smell a good dinner cooking and I just got some mail, – none from home, just from England. I am at peace with the world. What a strange place to find peace. I can hear the roar of the guns and may be bombed any minute.

There was a letter from Dora to us all. She writes:

PART TWO: THE WESTERN FRONT

My dears:

I hope you have all settled down comfortably to your new careers of rape and robbery. It was really a wonderful sight to see you all go off and then turn and dive on us. If my eyes, ears and nose hadn't been so full of dirt and castor oil, I should have cheered loudly but I defy any one to be festive under those circumstances.

Cal, my dear, I congratulate you most heartily on your somewhat short but extremely concise demonstration of how to crash in safety. You have filled a long needed want and I think it most unselfish of you to take the trouble to come back and take me out to dinner when you had once started over. However, once a gentleman, always a gentleman!

You, you bum: I don't think that in the whole course of my somewhat varied career, I have ever seen such a peculiar figure as you made on Wednesday. In the old days, knights took their lady's glove into the heart of battle with them; but you, moving with times, wear your young woman's stocking as a helmet. It would have been a touching tribute, me-thinks, if you had worn a pair of her knickers as cuffs.

I hope that you will live up to your reputation as a cave man and bite any prisoners you secure. I expect it will soon be quite a familiar sight to see you returning to the landing stage, if you have one, with the scalps of six luckless Germans, who have annoyed you, hanging from your Sam Browne.

Springs, last but not least, my blue-eyed baby – you're a stout fellow. I shall never forget the expression of overwhelming sorrow in your velvety eyes as you kissed me good-by so tenderly under the eyes of the assembled multitude. Thank heaven, whatever happens, I have the thought of your great love to cheer my barren life.

Well, my pinwhiskered and illegitimate trio, all the love of my passionate southern nature. And take care that you all three sit down and write me an epistle at once or it will turn to bitter hatred. We women of Spain are terrible in our rage!

Thine, Dora.

We bought a piano to-day and have a phonograph so the mess is very cheery and excellently equipped with furniture. We are allowed so much cash by the government for furnishing and then have a big private fund. We received several large donations that will come in well. Springs is vice-president of the mess and O.C. drinks. We took a truck and went into Dunkirk to stock up our cellar. We got some Scotch, Benedictine, cognac, champagne, port, white wine, red wine and beer. Dunkirk is not in the "zone des armées" so is under civilian control and we can get what we please. We decided that it was too much trouble to sign chits for drinks, so all drinks are to be free and each man will have to see that he gets his money's worth.

I am certainly glad to be out here at last. I am now going to earn my salt. And there are other reasons I like to be out here. Everybody is in such a good humor and we have a wonderful bunch of fellows. We're about the keenest bunch of fighters that have been gotten together in some time. We're all very congenial and that means a lot. There are three Americans, two New Zealanders, two Australians, one South African, six Canadians, two Scots, one Irishman, and six Englishmen.

Over in England you never could have a cheery mess because everybody was chasing away every evening to see some skirt or other and some of them had wives in the offing that cramped their style. Over here, there are no skirts on our clothesline and there's small chance that we'll see anything eligible for at least three months. That sounds like I am a woman hater, which I am not, but this is the first time in my life that I have ever been entirely removed from feminine influence and for the moment, I like it. I don't expect anybody else would understand this. I want to enjoy my independence a little. I suppose I'll feel different about it before I get my first leave, but just at present, I feel as if I had won the game by default and somebody had arranged a big party in my honor.

Nobody at home seems to be interested in anything but promotions and church attendance.

Our mechanics and baggage have arrived and we are all ready to start work. We did a practice patrol to-day and had a look at the lines.

The major got a Hun two-seater to-day the other side of Ypres. First blood![135]

May 29th
Nigger[136] and Bish[137] each got a Hun to-day. Brown and Capt. Baker each crashed an S.E. on the airdrome. That makes an even break for the day.

Springs and I went into Dunkirk to-day to get some things and I listened to him trying to parlez-vous. He's not so good even if he is educated.

We went into one large store and strolled up to a very pretty little clerk with a big head of blonde hair and opened fire, endeavoring to purchase some toothpaste. She didn't follow him and couldn't interpret his gestures. She thought he was looking for a dentist. She was quite captivating and I commented on how nice she was. She looked as if she knew I was talking about her, so I kept on. I said to him, "She has a pretty face, all right, but fat ankles. Call for a new deal." She gave me a dirty look and Springs tried to brush his teeth with his finger again after his college French failed. I said, "She's sure got the come-hither look in her eyes, but her figure would go better if bustles were back in style. She'd be a knock-out then." She looked mad.

Finally Springs found some new French words that he'd overlooked and she led the way to a counter and he got his Pebeco and paid for it. Then says she, in perfect English, with a glance in my direction, "Do you wish me to wrap it for you or will you take it as it is?" We grabbed the tube and fled. She sure was keen. I'm going back to see her if I ever break my monastic vows. I overlooked the fact that the British have used Dunkirk as a port for nearly four years and wherever there's a Tommy, there is English spoken. It won't be long before all the French women will be speaking with an American accent.[138]

The squadron amusement is diavolo. Somebody found a couple of old sets in Calais and now everybody is concentrated on it. Cal is the champion. He also plays tennis over on 211's court.

The major just blew in raising hell because he picked up the wrong tube and used shaving cream for tooth paste.[139]

June 2nd

One of the supernumerary pilots is looking at the war in my machine, so for the present I am unoccupied and will write a little. I hate for anybody else to fly my machine and this is the first time any one else has touched it. But Nigger wants Inglis[140] to have a look at the lines and get his bearings so when one of us goes West, he will be ready to take his place. I wonder whose place it will be. He's a nice fellow, a New Zealander, and got the D.C.M. at Gallipoli with the infantry.

There are six machines in a flight. Nigger leads and MacGregor and Cal are on his right, behind and a little above. Springs and I are on the left and Thompson is in the center in the space between Cal and me. We fly in the form of a triangle with the back corners high. MacGregor[141] is deputy flight commander and takes command in case anything happens to Nigger. We fly pretty close together and have a set of signals. If Nigger is going to turn sharp, he drops his wing on that side. If he is going to dive steep, he holds up his arm. If he wants us to come up close or wants to call our attention to something he shakes both wings. If it's a Hun, he shakes his wings and points and fires his guns. If he means "yes" he bobs his nose up and down and if he means "no" he shakes his wings.

Captain Edwin Benbow's dog, Ronald, pictured with an Avro 504 in the background. Benbow, one of 85's flight commanders, was the first member of the squadron to be killed in action. He was buried in Duhallow ADS Cemetery near Ypres. (Mark Hillier)

If we see a Hun and he doesn't, we fire our guns and fly up in front and point. We fly at three-quarters throttle so we can always pull up. If he has trouble and wants us to go on, he fires a red light from his Very pistol. If he wants us to follow him out of a fight, he fires a white light. If he wants to signal the other flights, he fires a green light.

MacGregor has been out before. He was out on Pups for six months when they were service machines. He came over with the Australian infantry. Thompson has been out before too. He was out last fall on Camels but crashed too many of them.

We've been doing rather well. We have a score board in the mess and there's a big red 6 staring me in the face now. We don't count any unless they go down in flames or break up in the air or some one sees them crash. The wing commander, Col. Cunningham, is over here all the time and is tickled to death because all this is voluntary for we aren't supposed to get into action the first two weeks. I'm going to get a Hun this week if I pull a wing off in the attempt.

June 3rd
I was censoring some of the men's mail to-day and I ran across this:

> Dear Bill: –
> You remember the big dog back at Hounslow? Well, he ain't got no master no more.

That was Capt. Benbow's dog and we all miss his master. He was buried where he fell, "so what the hell, boys, what the hell!" He died with his boots on and his grave is marked with a cross made from a propeller.[142]

He went out the other day alone and managed to get up in the sun above a flight of Hun scouts. He got on the tail of the rear one and would have gotten him but both guns jammed. Then the others turned back on him and chased him home. He was as mad as a hornet and spent the next day oiling and adjusting his guns. He went back to the same place at the same time and found the same Huns again. No one knows exactly what happened but Archie called up and said they saw him coming out of Hun-land with five Huns on his tail. Just as he got to the lines two of them fired a burst and his plane dived into the ground on our side of the lines and he was killed. He was certainly a fine fellow.[143]

The English have the reputation of being a phlegmatic unemotional race and they certainly try to live up to the part, tho I believe they are very sentimental underneath. It is simply considered bad taste to show it. We all felt pretty bad about Benbow but no emotion was exhibited. I have heard that the *London Times* printed the story of the battle of Waterloo on the inside sheet at the bottom of the page. That's typical. Unless the people at home get an emotional bath every morning they don't think the war is being conducted properly.

It seems funny for me to be censoring these Tommies' mail. The Officer of the Day always has to censor the men's mail. Here I am, Officer of the Day and in one of His Majesty's squadrons and this time last year I hadn't even seen a real live Englishman and sort of regarded them as enemies.

I'm still doing things to my machine. I've taken off the steamlining behind my head so I can see backwards better. I've taken off the windshield steamlining so I don't have to use goggles because the steamline sets up ripples in the air which hurt your eyes and I've put heavier wire on my stabilizer and fin. I've got a new way to fire my guns now that I like much better. I've got a Camel joystick and the triggers are fixed so I can fire both guns with one thumb if I want to.

I got tired of my drab looking cockpit, all full of uninteresting labels and gadgets. And I am now decorating it so I won't be bored upstairs. It's quite like old times playing with my bus. But instead of the spasmodic assistance of a chauffeur, I have three expert Ak Emmas, who do nothing else but look after my bus and do my bidding. They never touch another one and so far, I've managed to keep them pretty busy. Unless I bring down a Hun in a few days I'm afraid they'll get fed up with their jobs. You can tell by their letters that they like to have the machine they work on bring down Huns. You can also tell by their letters what they think of their officers.

They are changing the score now as the major[144] has just come down and has shot down two more Huns – a scout and a two-seater. He's broken the English record and now has more than McCudden. Archie saw one of them go down and another one broke up in the air.*

I pulled a good one. Whenever we come back from a trip over the lines, we're supposed to shoot up all our spare ammunition at a ground target to keep in practice. I asked where the ground target was, and they told me it was a silhouette on the beach north of Ft. Mardick. The first time I came back I went over looking for it. I couldn't find it at first and then I saw a rotten attempt at a silhouette of a plane over in a corner of a field and I dove on it and emptied my guns into it.

I knew my shooting was poor but I didn't think it was that bad and it took me a hundred rounds to get on the target. When I got back to Petit Snythe, there was a big straff on.

A Belgian major had telephoned over that a plane with my letter on it was over shooting at their landing 'Tee' and they were all in the dugout and to please send over and stop it before their mess was all shot to pieces. That's what I call good camouflage when they can hide a whole squadron. Either that or I am blind as a bat.

There's only one objection to this locality. Dunkirk is only twenty miles from the lines and it has a big harbor with three canals running into it and it is just as easy to find it in the moonlight as in the daylight. And this field is right between two canals and there's a railroad siding back of the mess so they always know where we are. The Huns bomb Dunkirk every clear night and it's gotten tiresome already. And every day about noon, they shell Dunkirk with a long range gun from Ostend. The civilian population live in cellars and spend most of the day down there too. I don't see why they don't all move.

The first couple of raids didn't bother us at all. We stood out in front and watched and thought it was good fun. But one night it suddenly began raining nose fuses around us and some friendly Hun dropped a bomb in the middle of the field. Since then we have swallowed our pride and taken shelter in the dugout. It's carefully sandbagged and has a telephone in it and a special compartment for the officers which is fairly comfortable. But I don't like it. You read too much about bombs falling on dugouts and if they get a direct hit, it will kill every one in it.

* BISHOP COULD, AND DID, SAW THROUGH A PLANE MAINSPAR WITH ONE BURST OF FIRE.

We are doing regular patrols now, one in the morning and one in the afternoon. We stay over the lines two hours each trip and our beat is from the coast to Courtrai, which is about fifteen miles east of Ypres, commonly known as Wipers. It's a comparatively quiet sector in daytime but a lot of dirty work goes on at night. The French and Belgian Armies hold the trenches so look after their own artillery and reconnaissance. Whenever we are looking for Huns we go down south of Wipers in the Salient where they are as plentiful as niggers in a watermelon patch on a moonlight night.

June 4th
Everybody in the squadron has some sort of a dog. Cunningham-Reed had a forced landing and came back with a Belgian fox terrier that can do everything but talk. I have a chow that was born in the hangars at Hounslow, – a real dog of war.[145]

Springs got all full of enthusiasm and went out by himself the other day to do battle with the Hun in spite of what Nigger told him. His ambition was rewarded and he managed to find six Hun scouts south of Courtrai. They chased him all over the sky and he had a time getting away from them. He finally just put his tail plane forward and dove wide open. Not orthodox but if your plane stays together, it's all right. Nothing can hit you while you're doing two hundred and fifty unless they are right on your tail and I guess it would be impossible to get there at that speed. And even more difficult to get out alive after you get there. He tore all the fabric loose on his top wing coming out.

He was still so excited when he landed that he ran into the major's plane and locked wings with it on the ground.[146]

The major was all set to bawl him out but Springs walked up to him and ran his finger across his row of ribbons and said, "You see these medals?" Bish nodded. "Well," says Springs, "I just want to tell you that you are welcome to them!" With that he walked on into the bar. Bish laughed tho he wasn't pleased about having his machine smashed.

They say Archie is the most useless thing in the war, but that machine gun fire from the ground is greatly to be feared. That's what got Richthofen. I think so too, for I came back to-day and found a couple of bullet holes in my rudder. I think I know where the fellow lives that did it and I am going back to-morrow and fill his dugout with lead. Machine guns only carry up to about twenty-five hundred feet but Archie can go higher than we can.

It's surprising how personal the war in the air gets. Whenever there's anything going on, you know that each little lead bullet or Archie shell is meant for you personally. And when you fire, you don't just fire towards Berlin and then wait until some one telephones you whether or not a Hun stopped it. No, you wait until you are in the correct position on a Hun's tail and then you open fire and see your tracer bullets going past him or into him and if you get him you see him go spinning down, maybe in flames.

Meanwhile Mr. Hun has been practicing target shooting and is ready to do a half roll as soon as you start your dive. Or he may have it all fixed up with Archie to range a certain area and then lure you into it. And Mr. Hun is on the job too. Just do a bad turn or a sloppy half roll and you'll hear him play your swan song on his Spandaus.

Archie has a funny sound. A burst near you sounds like a loud cough and as soon as you hear it you start zig-zagging. When you hear it you know that burst won't hurt you – it's the one you never hear that does the dirty work and tears the bag – but it does mean that the battery has your range and the next one is sure to come closer unless you fool him and sideslip, zoom, turn or throttle down. Then he fires where you should have been but weren't. He's easy to fool but you must do something. The best thing to do is to change your course twenty degrees every twelve seconds. That gives you time to get out of the way of the one that's coming up at you that moment and doesn't give the gunners time to get your deflection for the next shot.

I've been out baiting Archie several times and it's great sport. You can make him waste five thousand dollars' worth of ammunition on you in no time. And then think how mad the old Hun gunner must get! I'll never be happy until I get a chance to open up on one of them with my machine guns.

The Huns use shrapnel which bursts black and the Allies use high explosive which bursts white. There is an Austrian naval battery at Middlekerke [Middelkerke] that bursts pink. Scared me to death the first time I saw it.

There's one Hun gunner over at Dickybush [Dickebusch] that is so good he never fires but one salvo of four shots at you. If he doesn't hit you the first time, he doesn't waste any more ammunition on you unless there's a big formation where he's got a chance to get a trailer. But he knows it's useless to fire at a plane that is trying to dodge him. He nearly got one of us – a shell burst between Cal and myself. Cal got a piece of it in his arm and we tried to make him put up a wound stripe but he wouldn't do it. It was the first salvo and I was asleep and didn't even know we had crossed the lines. The best thing that Archie does is to signal. You can see an Archie burst twice as far as you can see a plane and our Archie is very good about warning us of the approach of Huns up in the sun when we can't see them. I was out the other day alone and our Archie put a burst up close to me to call my attention to a scout formation in Hunland.

I went up to test out my new engine and landed up north of Dunkirk where I heard there was an American squadron. They didn't seem particularly glad to see me tho the C.O. invited me to lunch. These boys certainly are down in the mouth. They think the Hun has won the war and are worrying about their baggage and girls in Paris. Why didn't I just write baggage? Hobey Baker is a flight commander up there. He used to be a great athlete at Princeton. A fine fellow he is. I've heard Hash and Springs talking about him. Poor Hash is a prisoner now.

I asked some of them to come over and have dinner with us. They said they couldn't as they had no way to get over there. They haven't much transport and they have to account for every drop of petrol. I offered to send over our car for them and they said they'd like to but didn't show much enthusiasm. They aren't enjoying the war much. They didn't have a bar and their mess wasn't much to boast of. I gather that Uncle Sam is pretty stingy with his nephews on this side, particularly those in the air. Me for the R.F.C.

There's one thing about the British that I like – they realize the importance of morale. The British try to build it up, the Americans try to tear it down. You can't expect men to have any pep after they've been cheated out of their seniority and pay, lost faith in their government after broken promises and been treated like enemy prisoners by the higher officers. Only the enormous patriotism and determination of our young men have prevented serious trouble. Our army seems to think that all they have to do for morale is to send along a couple of Y.M.C.A. secretaries and a few professional song leaders. Wait and see what happens to them.[147]

June 5th
Springs went back after the six Huns that chased him home. Nigger and MacGregor wanted to go hunting so they all went together. My engine was giving trouble so I couldn't go. Just after they crossed the lines Bish joined them and led them down on the same six Huns at the same place where Springs found them before and at the same hour. They must have been the same ones that got Benbow. Methodical, these Huns are.

They were in two layers of three each. Bish and Mac took the lower ones and Springs and Nigger took the top ones. Bish and Mac each got one and Springs got one down out of control but no one saw it crash so he doesn't score. It must have been a good fight while it lasted. They were Pfaltz [sic] scouts and are easy meat for S.E.s.[148]

The wind shifted and they had to land the short way when they came back. There was a train on the siding when Springs came in and he just glided over the box cars and tried to make a slow landing. His undercarriage crumpled up and stuck in the ground and he slid along in the fuselage like it was a canoe but didn't go over on his nose. Bish told him to fight on our side for a change and to quit bringing down S.E.s. Brown washed out his third to-day trying to land cross wind. It can't be done in an S.E. Not with the undercarriage where it is. I don't see why they don't move it forward.

Springs says he feels like a little boy that got licked in a fight and went home and got his big brother and came back.

June 6th
The new flight commander for A flight arrived. His name is Randall[149] and he is known as Randy. He was badly wounded at Gallipoli and got trench fever when he was with the infantry. Then he was transferred to the flying corps and was out on D.H. Twos. He was shot down by Richthofen. He says that Richthofen may have the reputation of being a good sport but that he showed him no mercy – shot his engine up and then followed him down while he was trying to land and shot him three times. He got one bullet in his rear and they had to cut off a slice. He sits down and leans like the tower of Pisa.

Cal said he'd be fine for sitting on stairs. He went up to have a look at the lines and crashed landing and turned over on his back. That's the trouble with these S.E.s; they don't like the ground.

I went up and had a private battle of my own. I saw a Hun two-seater away the hell and gone over Roulers. I chased him a bit but I couldn't catch him. Then about three Archie batteries opened up on me! The whole sky turned black. A barrage grew up in front of me like a bed of mushrooms and I swung around just in time to avoid it. Scared? Of course, I was scared. There were heavy clouds below me and I didn't know where the lines were. My compass was spinning around so fast that I couldn't tell anything from it. Then I forgot whether the sun set in the east or the west and had to stop and figure it out.

Every time Archie would get close to me, my heart would skip a beat. It has an awful sound when it's close, like a giant clapping his hands and it has a sort of metallic click. So I put my nose down and ran for it. First Archie would be 'way behind me and then he'd get 'way in front and I'd zoom and he'd be a mile away. I crossed the lines down below Wipers where I didn't know the country and for a few minutes I was lost. I got out my maps and found a town on the map that I located on the ground and then I came on back by Bergues.

Springs is all right until he gets mail from home, then he gets into a terrible rage and wants to fight the wide, wide world. He and his father

seem to carry on a feud at long range. He's got so now he doesn't open any letters until after he's had a few drinks and some of them he doesn't open at all. His father writes him full details and instructions in triplicate about how to do everything and finds fault with everything he does. He showed me a couple of them and they certainly were nasty. Springs is no saint but he isn't nearly that bad. I don't see why he cares what's going on at home. He worries about everything his father says and takes all his criticism to heart, tho why he should worry over it when he's three thousand miles away is beyond me. He's three thousand miles closer to hell.

He must be awfully fond of his father to care what he thinks about things he doesn't know anything about. And the idea of losing sleep because some one three thousand miles away hasn't got sense enough to understand English when you write it to them, is absurd!

There was a bomb raid on last night and the dugout was stuffy so he and I went out and crawled under a boxcar on the siding. It's about as good shelter as you can get. A direct hit will kill you anyway in the dugout and the boxcars will protect you from the nose fuses and fragments. We got to talking about home. He said that he had to get killed because he couldn't go home. He said if he got killed, his father would have a hero for a son and he could spend all his time and money building monuments to him and make himself very happy and proud. But if he lives thru it and goes home, he says his father will fight with him for the rest of his life. No matter what he does, his father will say it's wrong and worry over it.

I told him he was crazy but he was quite serious about it. He says it's a family trait. He says he wants to last long enough to make a name for himself so his father will have something to build a monument to, and then get bumped off with a lot of fireworks the last week of the war. He says if he lives thru it, his father is determined to make him go down in a cotton mill and work five years as a day laborer and live in the mill village. Some sort of foolishness about starting in at the bottom and working up. And the slightest mistake he makes will break his father's heart. He says he owns one mill himself but that won't make any difference to his father who won't want him to have it.

I asked him what he wanted to do. He said he wanted to write but his father is determined to make a horny-handed hardboiled superintendent out of him. He's all the time scribbling now. He's always stopping something important to jot down a plot, as he calls it, for future reference. He's got a brief case full of them already – plays, short stories, poems, sketches or what have you. He's tried to read me some of them several times.

Above: Personnel of 85 Squadron in France. Fulford's original caption states that they are, from left to right, 'a visitor, Tiny Dixon, Diamond [Dymond], Horn, Bishop, Callahan, Fulford'. Fulford points out that Longton is present, but was standing behind Callahan. (Mark Hillier)

Below: Another image of officers from 85 Squadron. Left to right can be seen Fulford, MacDonald, Inglis and Bishop. Fulford noted beneath the image that 'Bishop objects to the photographer'. (Mark Hillier)

PART TWO: THE WESTERN FRONT

His grandfather left him a big plantation in South Carolina, about three thousand acres, and he wants to go there to live. There's a big brick house on it that was built by his great-grandfather and he wants to fix it up like it was originally. We talked it all over. He wants me to come and live with him and run the farm in case we both get thru. He says he's got plenty for both Cal and me. If he doesn't live thru it he's left a will which leaves enough to Cal and me to get us started after the war. He damn near had me crying. I can't leave him and Cal anything but I told them that if anything happened to me to help themselves to my stuff.

The farm idea sounds good to me. He wants to build a tennis court and a swimming pool and a landing field for a plane. He's going to build the pool so he can jump right out of the bedroom windows into it.

Cal is in the banking business, or rather was, and Springs says he thinks he owns a lot of stock in some bank and Cal can run it.

All that sounds fine but I don't guess there's much chance of all three of us getting thru. And judging by the letters I've seen, I can imagine what his old man would say if we came down to live with him while he's doing his five years' penance in overalls. Besides that, I've got business to attend to myself after this scrap is over.

We were just about ready to jump out of the window into the pool when the Huns arrived in force and proceeded to drop thirty-two bombs just across the canal on the Handley-Page airdrome. That's the worst raid I've seen.

They dropped a parachute flare first that lit up the ground like an arc light. Then they dropped a phosphorus bomb on a hangar and set fire to it. They dropped a big bomb on a dugout and killed forty officers and men. Fortunately most of the Handleys were out on another raid themselves. The field was so full of holes that they couldn't land on it and either had to stay up all night or go over and land on the beach. Some splinters from one bomb hit one of the wheels and it rained nose fuses.

I heard in Boulogne that Dick Mortimer[150] has been killed.

Springs and I were sitting in the mess alone yesterday afternoon doing a little light drinking when in walked a man in naval officer's uniform. "Cheerio," says he. "Chin-chin," say we, "have a drink". "Thanks," says he, joining us and reclining on the back of his neck with us. He didn't seem like the naval officers we had met before and we gathered that he was just paying the flying corps a social visit and came over here after a Bronx, for which 85 is famous. He and Springs got into a heated literary argument. I held my fire until they got on my subject.

Later on Capt. Baker told us who the bird was. It was Arnold Bennett[151], the writer, who is out here getting some local color for a book.

June 8th
This morning I arose at three-thirty – two-thirty real time – and by six I was back for breakfast and the Huns had wasted a thousand pounds' worth of Archie shells on us. Our hands might have been a bit steadier as we raised a coffee cup, but a little exposure to the hate of the Hun does give you a wonderful appetite. This Archie gunner at Middlekerke is no amateur – his first burst almost made me loop! After that dodging was easy.

Before breakfast I went over to a farmhouse in a sidecar and got some cream for our cereal. Springs has taught the cook to make Eggs Benedict and we breakfast well.

As a matter of fact we live well. We went down to Boulogne and got an ice cream freezer and we are the only outfit at the front that has ice cream for dinner every night. "In the midst of life we are in death" And in the midst of death we manage to have a hell of a lot of fun. Bronx cocktails, chicken livers en brochette, champagne, strawberry ice cream, and Napoleon brandy. That's the way we live. I don't think Bish is sorry he brought us along.

We had a lot of trouble getting that ice cream freezer. We went down to Boulogne to a department store and Springs opened fire with his drugstore French. They brought him an egg beater. He tried again and they insisted that what he really wanted was an ice pick. They brought him a dictionary but it wasn't in it.

So he called for, "machinery to make cream hard". They brought him a churn and then a cream whipper. We gave it up and walked out. Then we saw one in the window and went back and got it.

Again at eleven I went out to do battle. We got into a dogfight over Ostend and had a merry little fracas.

I was up above the main formation to see that nothing dropped down out of the sun and a Pfaltz dove on me. He came right out of the sun but I've learned to put my thumb up and close one eye and unless they are at a dead angle, I can see them. I saw this one in time and just as he opened fire, I turned quickly and threw his sights off. His tracer was going a hundred feet behind my tail. The Hun went on by and half rolled onto my tail. I kept turning to keep his sights off me and he followed. We turned around and around – each maneuvering to get into position to fire a burst at close range. But I had learned my lesson well at Ayr and I could do perfect vertical banks and I began gaining on him.

I was getting in position to open up when he half rolled to break away. I half rolled after him and was on his tail like a hawk after a chicken. I let him have both guns at close range. My sights were dead on his cockpit and I must have got in about a hundred and fifty rounds. My Lewis jammed after fifty rounds but my Vickers kept going. The Hun started to turn, then he flopped over on his back and went straight down. He was last seen headed towards his future home and breaking all records – hell bent for hades!

I couldn't see him crash so I only got an "out of control". But I know I got him. At the speed he was diving he never could have pulled out. And I know now that I can fight as well as fly. It was quite evident that one of us had to die but I was cool as a cucumber and when we were turning around each other I could almost hear Nigger thru the earphones from the front seat of an Avro telling me: "Little top rudder now. Easy. Keep your nose level. Pull your stick back. Take off a little aileron. Now cross your controls."

Our pink-cheeked little boy, commonly known as Lady Mary, decided it was high time he shot down a Hun so went up in search of one. The result has caused much merriment. He found plenty of Huns all right, enough to last him the rest of his life if taken singly. He ran into a school of them and didn't see them until they were right on top of him. As near as we can figure out the Huns must have gotten in each other's way getting to him or been laughing so hard they couldn't shoot straight. Anyway, he's back and is now a member of the "sadder-and-wiser-club" of which Springs is president. Maybe the Huns' wings pulled off when they tried to dive after him.*

Trapp also qualified for membership in that august body. He met a couple of two-seaters and chased them twenty miles into Hunland. They saw their own airdrome and took courage and turned around and chased him all the way back.

Springs got in a fight and shot his own propeller to pieces and Cal had his tire punctured by an energetic Hun.**

Late every afternoon there is the most unearthly racket [at the] back of the mess on the tracks.

Several thousand Chinese or rather Annamite coolies come back from where they work during the day. Their camp is about a mile below here on the canal. I hear that there are two hundred and fifty thousand of them in France. They were brought over to fill sand bags and dig reserve trenches behind the lines. There are trenches all the way back to the

* FIRST 85 MAN TO GET AN OBSERVATION BALLOON, NEVERTHELESS.

** THEY WOULD FIRE IN A DIVE WITH ENGINE FULL ON! A BULLET FIRING 1,000TH OF A SECOND LATE MEANT A DIFFERENCE OF NEARLY 8° IN POSITION OF PROP BLADE

PART TWO: THE WESTERN FRONT

One of 85 Squadron's pilots, Captain Malcolm McGregor D.F.C., pictured at Hounslow in front of a Sopwith Dolphin. McGregor died as the result of injuries sustained during a crash whilst landing a Miles Falcon at Rongotai Aerodrome, Wellington, New Zealand, on 19 February 1936. Fulford's original caption states: 'A magnificent pilot. Sat up one afternoon at 16,000ft waiting for stray Huns, and read Richthofen's book to pass the time.' (Mark Hillier) coast now. We can retreat twenty miles and still have prepared positions. But just think of bringing these Chinese all the way around the world. That just shows how scarce man-power really is in Europe ... I talked to one of the officers in charge of the Chinese. He told me they were organized into military companies and regiments. Each one has an identification tag welded around his neck and they can speak a little pigeon English. He said they were fine workmen and give little trouble. They are scared to death when there's a bomb raid on and that's the only time he has any trouble with them. They have their own camp well sandbagged, I noticed.

This Dunkirk district certainly gets well straffed. Every clear night it gets bombed. The Huns pass over here on their way to London, Calais and Boulogne and use the harbor to set their sights on. If they don't reach their objective they let Dunkirk have their bombs on the way back, or if they have any left over they save them for us. I think they must send over all their new men to practice on Dunkirk. We don't get much sleep because they are over here all night. The only defence is Archie and these cable balloons. Both are worse than useless. They send up about a dozen balloons as soon as the last one of our machines is down and they are held by strong cables. The idea is that some Hun might run into one of them.

And every morning the long range gun at Ostend sends over four big shells addressed to the major of Dunkirk. This has been going on for four years and the civilian population seems to have gotten used to it. A shell hit a shoe store the other day and knocked the front of it down. We were in town that afternoon and business was going on as usual with the damaged boots out in front being sold at a discount.

The Germans certainly are methodical. They send over the same number of shells at exactly the same hour. Everybody knows when to take shelter and Mournful Mary, the siren, goes off automatically ten minutes before.

We have a fine place to swim tho the water is pretty cold. There's a big moat around Ft. Mardick about twenty feet wide that has a canal running down to the ocean. Sometimes we go in the surf.

The French towns with their walls and moats are awfully pretty. There's a little town just below here named Gravelines that has walls shaped exactly like a star and the sun, sparkling on the moat, makes it look like a jewel. It's about a mile inland and has a canal running out to the ocean.

June 10th
Nigger let Thompson[152] lead a patrol. We weren't too keen about it tho he has been out to the front before. Cal, Springs, Inglis and I went along.

We were supposed to patrol the coast between Ostend and Bruges to see that no high two-seaters came over to take photographs of the bomb hits last night. There were heavy clouds at ten thousand feet and we had trouble getting thru them as Thompson flew a jerky pace. I didn't pay much attention to where we were but I thought it was funny that we weren't getting Archied. Boulogne, Calais, Dunkirk, Nieuport, Ostend and Bruges are all along the coast about twenty miles apart and they all look alike from fifteen thousand feet. Thompson got Dunkirk and Boulogne mixed up and proceeded to do a very daring patrol over Fernes on our side of the lines, thinking he was up near Bruges. We figured out that he was doing about as much good there as anywhere and wandered off on our own.

I went over and had a good look at Wipers. It made me sick. There's not a wall standing running north and south. And there's a stretch of country forty miles square that's as flat as a piece of paper – no trees, no houses, nothing! I could see the flashes of the guns and see the smoke and dust where the shells burst. We hear firing twenty-four hours out of the day. And down on the ground it looks as if some one had drawn a lot of pencil marks in a row. That's the barbed wire! We were up over Holland the other day but we were too high to see the electric cable.

What a nightmare this war is! I'm beginning to understand the term "Anti-Christ".

Both the Allies and the Germans pray to the same God for strength in their slaughter! What a joke it must seem to Him to see us puny insignificant mortals proclaiming that we are fighting for Him and that He is helping us. Think of praying to the God of Peace for help in War! The heavens must shake with divine mirth.

I can't kick. It's the best war I know anything about. It's been worth a lot to me so far. Sooner or later I'll join the company of the elect but I want to get a Hun first. I want to get one sure one – a flamer or a loose-winged flop. I know how hard it is, but unless I get one, the government will simply be out all it cost to train me. If I get one, it'll be an even break. If I get two, I'll be a credit instead of a debit on the books.

Nigger is going to play the dive and zoom game. An S.E. will outzoom anything built and if we get above the Huns we can dive and fire and then zoom away. I understand a Fokker can outmanoeuvre an S.E. and if you dogfight with them they can outturn and outclimb you. A Fokker triplane can lick anything that has ever been built but they have a bad habit of falling to pieces in the air so the Huns are washing them out. I wonder how long it will be before we will have the Snipe and the Snark that we saw tested at Brooklands.[153]

June 11th
We had a proper binge last night. We invited the C.O. and the flight commanders of 211* over for dinner to return their hospitality and a colonel from the A.S.C. who was a friend of MacDonald's in Saloniki [Salonika]. Every one calls the C.O. Bobby. He is a great drinker and has the reputation of being able to drink the rest of the world under the table.

MAJOR ROBERT LORAINE

We certainly gave him a good opportunity to exhibit his jewels. Springs and I were detailed as pacemakers and we mixed up a big bowl of punch and we all had a bottoms-up contest that was a classic. We had speeches from every one after dinner and the colonel tried to get on the table to make his but it wasn't strong enough to hold him. Then we had a football game in front of the mess. Cal and Bish collided head on in the dark at full speed and were both knocked cold. Bobby lived up to his reputation and won the contest easily. We had to carry the colonel out and put him in his car feet first. He came back to-day and wanted to know what was in that punch. When we told him what was in that innocent drink he nearly fainted. These Britishers will learn some day to respect our concoctions. They don't think a drink is strong unless it tastes bad.

Mac sure is funny when he dips into the flowing bowl. He's very much in love with a girl at home, or thinks he is, which is just as bad. She was only sixteen when he left and he hasn't seen her in four years. He still thinks she is young and innocent and sixteen. And every time he gets plastered he gets to worrying over the fact that she's such a sweet little thing and he's so tough. He says he isn't good enough for her and he's going to write and tell her so. He actually sheds tears over it. Then we get to kidding him and tell him that she probably has grown into the wildest thing in town and he'll be too tame for her when he gets home. That makes him cry out in agony and then he wants to fight. He bores every one to death talking about her all the time.

Then he gets one more drink and tells us about the little widow at Malta that he used to give a little dual to when he was stationed there. Springs pretends to get the two mixed up and Mac spends the rest of the evening trying to straighten it out. Mac admits in all seriousness that the widow's morals were not what they might be, but claims that the climate of Malta is responsible and then he admits that he was a bit insistent.

Living here together the way we do, it doesn't take long to exhaust all the topics of conversation and unless we are talking shop we all know what everybody else is going to say. When we have a binge everybody makes exactly the same speech that they made before, but as long as our guests laugh, so do we.

Cal ... can wear anybody's clothes and does. He never worries about anything and hasn't a nerve in his body.

He'd be happy in a shell hole on iron rations. All he wants is to be left alone. He's got no ideas or ambitions beyond the next meal. He plays the piano as if he'd never heard of a score and he never knows himself what he's going to play next. *(Bought piano in Dunkirk)* But he can rag a piano like no one else on earth. He can play classical stuff but doesn't very often. It's too much trouble.

The gunnery officer[154] plays according to Hoyle, and Cal sits down beside him and jazzes the treble. He's the best natural pilot we have. Takes his flying just like his bridge. Nigger says he has the smoothest hand on the stick he ever saw. He's all right until he starts to figure. He and Springs argue for two hours after every patrol. We are all getting so we can see pretty well in the air now but at first we had to use our imaginations to keep up with Nigger and Mac.

Mac had all his teeth knocked out in a Pup crash last year[155] and the other morning before the dawn patrol he lost his false teeth. Gosh, he was funny. He couldn't talk at all and he couldn't go on the patrol because he was afraid he'd get shot down without them.

Springs is just the opposite of Cal. He worries more over things at home than if he was there. He was almost in tears the other day because he found out his father had shown one of his letters about. He said he hated not to write to his father – he felt it was his duty – but his father would show the letters about and make a fool of him no matter what he wrote.

I told him he was the fool to worry over it. He might as well be worrying over his great-grandfather or great-grandchildren.

June 13th
We have a steady job now escorting the Nines over to Zeebrugge and Bruges every morning while they bomb the submarine bases. Bish[156] leads the whole squadron and we are just spoiling for a good fight.[157] The Nines take a half hour start and we meet them at twelve thousand feet out at sea. Then we climb together up to fifteen and come in over the Dutch border and shoot back across Belgium wide open. We stay up above them and they drop their bombs and one machine stays behind to take pictures of the hits.

We get all the Archie that was intended for them. There were some Fokkers up yesterday but we were too strong for them and they wouldn't fight. We can see the ships that the British sunk in the harbors at Zeebrugge and Ostend. It doesn't look to me as if they are completely blocked. It was certainly a stout effort. We hear that they are going to do it again. They have dismantled some of the submarines and are taking them out overland from Bruges.

There is an American Naval squadron at Dunkirk flying French machines. We ran into a couple of the pilots and had lunch with them at the Chapeau Rouge.

We seem to be the only Americans in Europe that are really enjoying this war. All the others I have met seem to be having to work or sleep without sheets or eat out of mess kits or do something unpleasant to spoil their holiday.[158]

PART TWO: THE WESTERN FRONT

June 14th
You can't appreciate the R.F.C. until you see a squadron on the move. We came back from a dose of Archie without suffering from his hate about seven o'clock and after a good breakfast I got tired of baseball and decided I'd take a nap.

About ten my batman shook me and said, "Orders has come, sir that we are to move at twelve o'clock". At twelve o'clock our baggage, transport, equipment and dogs left and at four we flew down to our new airdrome at St. Omer.[159] We thought we might as well pick up a Hun on the way so had a squadron show. Bish led and we crossed the lines at Wipers and worked on down south to the Forest of Nieppe but we didn't see anything.

It was the wrong time of day. Early in the morning or late in the evening is best. That's our new beat, from Wipers [Ypres] to Nieppe.

At one place near Hazebrouck, the ground for about three square miles is dull yellow in color. That's where there has been a gas attack.

Above: Two pilots pictured at Hounslow in front of a Sopwith Dolphin. Fulford has captioned this image as being of 'Kelly and Warner, original members of 85, both killed'. (Mark Hillier)

PART TWO: THE WESTERN FRONT

Above: 'The Move'. Some of 85 Squadron's transport pictured during its move from Petit Synthe near Dunkirk to St Omer in June 1918. (Mark Hillier)

Below: Members of 85 Squadron on 'moving day'. The individual second from the left appears to be Lieutenant Peter Rosie, the Engineering Officer. (Mark Hillier)

Above: Some of 85 Squadron's personnel resting outside huts at St. Omer. From left to right are: McGregor, unidentified, Billy Bishop, and unidentified. (Mark Hillier)

Below: Another snapshot of 85 Squadron's personnel outside huts at St. Omer. McGregor is in the centre facing the camera, whilst Bishop is on the right just behind the goat. The latter appears in a number of the squadron's photographs. (Mark Hillier)

Our airdrome is an old French one on a plateau about three miles from St. Omer.[160] They are expecting a big battle down here.

Our new quarters are very comfortable. We are up on a beautiful wooded hill overlooking the field and there's a pretty sylvan glade on the other side where we can lie in peace and snooze in the breeze. Not bad at all but there's no place to swim.

After our transport left, we decided we'd go for a last swim and borrowed a tender from 211 to take us over to the beach by Ft. Mardick. Randy came along and when he undressed he was certainly a sight. There's hardly a spot on his body that isn't cut or shot. He ought to be in a museum. His back and chest look like he was tattooed by one of those futurist artists.

We were out in the surf when we heard a terrible explosion and saw the smoke the other side of the fort. Before we could get out of the water, there were about four more. Randy yelled that the long range gun was shelling the fort and to get out of the water on account of the concussion.

We didn't know what to do. I never felt so naked in my life, standing there with shells bursting two hundred yards away and the debris flying up a hundred feet. We grabbed our clothes and ran for the tender which was nearly a mile away. We beat all existing records getting there and jumped into the tender and told the driver to drive like hell away from the fort. Then he told us what the trouble was. The French were exploding a lot of German mines that the mine sweepers had brought in. The joke was on us.[161]

June 16th
My new motor is a dud. It chewed up a valve but I got back to the drome all right.

We're worried about Mac.[162] When he was seen last we were going down on nine Huns about fifteen miles the other side of the lines.[163] He got away from them all right, I think, but it's three hours since we got back and there's no word of him yet. I guess he had engine trouble for there wasn't much of a scrap. If he only gets back across the lines! We are all rather nervous.[164]

My dog has fleas.

June 17th
Mac was all right. He shot his own prop off but he got back across the lines and landed about twenty miles from here all O.K. He came back on the truck that went after his plane and brought a cow[165] back with him, so we have our own dairy now. Rosie has been trying to milk his goat without success.

PART TWO: THE WESTERN FRONT

Above: Fulford captioned this picture as being of 'Bishop's brother-in-law (in light tunic)', on the left, and himself. Bishop's brother-in-law was Captain Henry John 'Hank' Burden, a Canadian flying with 56 Squadron when this photograph was taken. Fulford's caption goes on to state that Burden 'got three Huns the following day', which would date the image to 11 August 1918. (Mark Hillier)

Opposite: Lieutenant Peter Rosie, 85 Squadron's Engineering Officer, pictured with his goat and Captain Horn's dog Lobo. (Mark Hillier)

I got a paper from home and read a column by "Biddy Bye". She gives a "Loyalty Menu" for loyal housewives to serve poor starved patriots. It read like an a la carte menu at the Ritz before the war. I'd like to find the lady and shove her menu down her throat. Hope our "Loyal Ones" aren't getting thin and wasting away. This is in a military zone and food and licker are scarce. We have to send to Dunkirk for extra supplies.

Springs had a letter from Kelly and he's ready to come out and Bish is going to arrange for him to come to us.

We have another one of the Oxford Cadets with us, Rorison[166], who is assigned to B flight. He's from Wilmington, N.C. He's a serious youth and can figure out anything on paper with a slide rule.

We have another patrol to do and then Bish and Nigger and the three of us are going over to their old squadron to dinner. As it is one of the best squadrons at the front, it ought to be a cheery evening. Bish and Nigger were both flight commanders there last year.

I had no idea there was so much to learn about this game. When you get to the front, you are just starting. There's something new to learn about your game every flight and then there're the idiosyncrasies of the Hun to be studied with your ear to the ground as well as the geographical and meteorological conditions.

For instance, there's a Hun balloon that's rather close to the lines. They always pull down the others when they see us coming but they leave this one up. It looked like easy pickings and Springs and I asked Nigger if we couldn't drop down and get it some time when the wind was with us strong. Nigger said he'd investigate and that we'd better leave balloons alone until we were sent after them because they were very dangerous toys.

He got word from the brigade that this balloon is a dummy and is there as a decoy. About four Archie batteries have it ranged and instead of having a passenger basket, it's loaded up with amanol [an explosive] and as soon as some sucker dives on it, the Huns will explode it and that will be the last heard of him. And you have to come thru the Archie barrage to get to it. Archie has no bite at all – all bark – but it's hard on the nervous system. This is certainly a nice friendly little war. The Canadians originated that balloon trick.[167]

June 18th
It was a good party. I think we won as when we left their C.O. was doing a Highland Fling with a couple of table knives for swords.

Coming back, we just got inside the gates of St. Omer when the Huns began to bomb it. And they were after the town too, no mistaking it. You should have seen us getting out of it. Not a light showing anywhere and crooked narrow streets. Our chauffeur didn't know the town very well and we all five were yelling at him at the same time. A bomb burst about a block from us and we climbed the curb twice in our haste.

We were in bad shape for the early patrol. It was pretty dud looking when we got up at four-thirty. Nigger said he didn't think the fog would lift and there wasn't much use going out. He went back to bed and told Springs to take the two of us up and do a safety first patrol if it cleared up enough for us to get off. It cleared up about six and we took off and worked up towards Wipers.

Springs led us about five miles over between Wipers and the Forest of Nieppe, but we didn't see anything as there was still a pretty heavy fog.

We got a lot of Archie but that was all. We had about given it up as a washout when we spotted a two-seater on the other side of Estaires. Springs waggled his wings and pointed and we waggled back that we thought it was a Hun too and then we went down with our motors wide open.

I warmed up my guns on the way down and was all ready. When Springs was about four hundred yards away and a thousand feet above him, the Hun turned and the observer opened fire on him as he came in close. Springs got underneath him and Cal came down and cut him off from the other side and made him turn back. I came straight down from above and he was right in position for me and I put in a good burst from both guns right into his cockpit.

We were all firing and I could see my tracer going right into his fuselage. I almost ran him down and just as I leveled off and pulled up, the Hun burst into flames and went down in a dive. The pilot must have fallen on his stick and I saw him go down like a comet. As he hit the ground a pillar of flames and smoke shot up.

We were so low by that time that the machine guns and pom-poms on the ground opened fire on us and I had the pleasure of watching a few tracers go thru my wings. We were too low for Archie.

Nigger said he'd sent us out to do a safe and sane patrol and not to win the war before breakfast. He bawled Springs out and said that by the law of average we should all have been killed. We didn't pay any attention to him because our heads were all swelled up over getting a flamer.

There was no use all three of us claiming the Hun and we were going to just one of us take him. Cal and Springs were going to let me have him but Canning who saw the fight from a distance put in a claim too, because he said he was firing at him, so we all took one fourth each. If Canning had kept out one of us would have got credit for one whole Hun. Fractions don't mean anything. But as long as Canning was coming in any way we might as well all stay in. But I know I got that Hun.[168] Springs and Cal were firing at him too but I could see my tracer going right into his fuselage.[169]

Bish[170] got one about noon and Lady Mary [Cunningham-Reid] went out and bumped off another one.

MacDonald has been missing since yesterday.

June 19th

We have got to get up every morning at three from now on and go down to the hangars and stand by and be ready to leave the ground at five minutes' notice. That means we have to keep our motors running to keep them warmed up. The Hun is supposed to be going to start a push any moment and everything is ready for the counter attack.

We have bomb racks fitted to our fuselage and we carry four twenty-pound copper bombs to use ground straffing. They think the Hun is going to push in front of Hazebrouck and try to pinch off the Salient. We aren't going to give an inch of ground but are going to start a counter attack and push back.

We had a squadron show and Thompson, Trapp, Lady Mary and myself had to go down and reconnoiter the road from Bailleul to Armentières at a couple of hundred feet looking for signs of troop movements. To protect us, were Nigger, Cal, Springs and Mac at one thousand feet and the rest of the squadron were at five thousand.

We flew down the road the whole way and back again but didn't see much except a lot of tracer bullets coming up at us. And I saw some flaming onions up close. They are nice little things – a lot of phosphorus balls that come up in front of you like a swarm of bees, and if you run into them, it's good-night!

I saw Thompson get hit.[171] He landed and turned over. I think he's alive as the machine certainly was under control. Trapp is missing but I didn't see him at all.[172]

Lady Mary[173] found a balloon and shot it up and set fire to it on the ground. I got a few holes scattered about the plane but nothing serious.

If the Huns are going to attack there, they are mighty quiet about it. I dropped my four little bombs on a truck train.

The top flight got into a dogfight and Bish dropped a Fokker.[174] A flight lost a man.[175]

June 20th

MacDonald is back. He got lost coming back from a patrol in the fog and landed a hundred miles from here. He made sure he wasn't in Germany all right. He was out of gas when he ceased to flee and it took two days to get a truck down there to him. A Frenchman entertained him royally at his château and Mac fell in love with his beautiful niece and kept the truck waiting an extra day. Moral: Always pick a good place to get lost. He brought a mangy looking cur back with him. Our menagerie is growing.

Heard that Joe Trees and Dick Reed have been killed.[176] The colonel came over and congratulated us on our reconnaissance. He's a brother to one of the flight commanders at London Colney, Capt. Cairns the fellow with one leg. He's with 74 now.

June 21st

Bish has been recalled to England to help organize the Canadian Flying Corps. Before he left he went up to have a final look at the war. He ran

Above: Three of 85 Squadron's pilots. On the left is Captain S.B. Horn M.C., in the centre Lieutenant J. Dymond, and on the right Captain W.H. Longton D.F.C.. Horn was Mannock's senior flight commander on the squadron. (Courtesy of Andy Thomas)

into five Hun scouts.[177] He picked off the last one and the two in front collided when they did a climbing turn to get back of him. Then he got another one and on the way back he ran into a two-seater and got it.* Pretty good morning. His score is now seventy-two!

That's something for the boys to shoot at. Next to him is McCudden and then Mannock. We all went down to Boulogne to see him off and had a big champagne lunch.[178]

An American Division was landing at Boulogne and these boys certainly have got funny ideas. They think they are crusaders and talk like headlines. They are full of catch-phrases and ideals. We talked to a bunch of them in the bar. They think they are on the way to a Sunday school picnic.

The Japanese think if they get killed in battle they will go to heaven. They've got nothing on these boys. They think they are going to get a golden harp just for enlisting.

One of the boys asked me where the Red Light district was. I told him that if God would paint the moon red, then Europe would be properly labeled.

‡ *The only time in 85 he damaged his guns, due to too-prolonged bursts of fire. They were speeded up to 900/1000 rounds per minute.*

WAR BIRDS

PART TWO: THE WESTERN FRONT

Above: A further picture of the men and machines of 85 Squadron at St Omer Aerodrome, 21 June 1918. Similar to the image on page 98, this time the serial numbers have not been obscured. Again, from front to back, they are C1904, D6851, C1931, B7870, C1928, and C6486. From left to right, the men in this group image are: Canning, McGregor (holding a pet), Callahan, Springs, Horn (with his dog, Lobo, in front of him), Randall (also holding a dog), Baker, Cunningham-Reid, Longton, Rosie, Carruthers, Dixon, Brown, Brewster, unidentified, Abbott, and Inglis. (Courtesy of Andy Thomas)

Opposite: Royal Aircraft Factory S.E.5a aircraft of 85 Squadron at St Omer Aerodrome, 21 June 1918. The serial numbers, which have been blanked out by the censor, are known to be, from front to back, C1904, D6851, C1931, B7870, C1928, and C6486. The dog that can just be seen standing by the cockpit of the first aircraft is Lobo, which belonged to Captain Horn. Whilst C1904 had been flown by Billy Bishop, on his posting away from 85 Squadron it was taken over by Horn who flew it for the remainder of his time with the unit. (Courtesy of Andy Thomas)

There were two officers at the next table to us at lunch. One of them saw my R.F.C. wings and wanted to know why I was wearing a crown above my wings. I told him because I was a qualified R.F.C. pilot.

"Well," says he, "you can wear a crown if you want to. But as for me, – I can't get enough eagles on. I just want eagles all over me."

They had on funny belts. I said, "Where'd you get the funny Sam Browne belts?"

"Sam Browne belts?" said one of them. "These ain't Sam Browne belts. These is Liberty belts!!!"

Above: Men of 'C' Flight, 85 Squadron, pictured in front of a dispersal hut at St. Omer. In the front row, left to right, are: Horn, Thomson, Callahan, Grider. The pair in the back row are McGregor (on the left) and Springs. The dog beside MacGrider is Horn's Alsatian, Lobo. (Courtesy, The Springs Close Family Archives, Fort Mill, SC)

That gave the squadron a laugh. They've been kidding us about it ever since. They call us the Liberty Boys and want to see our eagles.

We came back and had a patrol to do at five. Nigger took off down wind and we all followed him. Springs and Cal got to bouncing before they had flying speed and smashed their undercarriages but they didn't go over on their backs. Springs nearly landed on top of Cal and just did bounce over him. Mac broke a bracing wire but came on with us.

June 22nd
I got up this morning feeling like a week-end in the city tho I had no reason to. I drank too much coffee before going up and I'm as nervous as a kitten now. Must be getting the Woofits.

I had rather a surprise yesterday. I was some distance back of the patrol and saw a Hun two-seater about three miles across the lines so went for him. I expected about thirty seconds at close quarters under his tail and then to watch him go down in flames. It looked like cold meat. I started my final dive about one thousand feet above him and opened fire at one hundred yards.

Then I got a surprise. I picked the wrong Hun. Just as I opened fire, he turned sharply to the left and I was doing about two hundred so couldn't turn but had to overshoot and half roll back. As I half rolled on top of him, he half rolled too and when I did an Immelman [sic], he turned to the right and forced me on the outside arc and gave his observer a good shot at me as I turned back the other way to cut him off from the other side.

I fired a burst from my turn but my shots went wild so pulled up and half rolled on top of him again and opened fire from immediately above and behind. He stalled before I could get a burst in and sideslipped away from me but gave me a no-deflection shot at him when he straightened out. I didn't have to make any allowance for his speed or direction and his observer was shooting at me. The observer dropped down in his cockpit so I suppose I killed him. But I couldn't get the pilot. He put the plane in a tight spiral and I couldn't seem to get in position properly. Cal and Tiny Dixon came in about that time and everybody was shooting at him from all angles. I know he didn't have any motor because he came down very slowly and didn't attempt to maneuver. We were firing from every conceivable angle but we couldn't seem to hit the tank or the pilot and every now and then he'd take a crack at me with his front gun when I'd try him head on.

He was a stout fellow, a good fighter and I hope he is still alive. If his observer had been any good I wouldn't be writing this now. He hit one of my front spars and that was all. I left him at one hundred feet as my engine was overheating and was sputtering and I've had enough machine gun fire from the ground to last me for a while and I don't like field guns from directly in the rear. Accidents will happen. So I started back and joined the patrol. Archie simply went mad.

The infantry reported the fight and said that the Hun was under control when he went down the other side of Kemmel Hill.

Then we all came down low over the trenches later and had a sham battle among ourselves. Nigger and I dove furiously on each other just back of No Man's Land and Springs and Cal and Mac rolled and looped desperately trying to get on one another's tails. The boys in the trenches must have enjoyed it. None of the Huns fired at us at all and even Archie the Avenger left us alone tho we were within range. Then we spied some field sports four or five miles back of our lines and we started for

Above: The 85 Squadron S.E.5a, D6933 'N', flown by Lieutenant J.C. Rorison – an American who joined the squadron in June 1918. (Courtesy of Andy Thomas) them. They were very appreciative as they stopped the game to watch and wave at us. Must have been a Canadian Division for they had a baseball diamond. Mac ran his wheels on it.

We've gotten quite good at stunting in close formation. We fly very close together and can loop and roll in formation. Nigger signals and loops straight over. Mac and Cal loop with right rudder on and Springs and I loop with left rudder. That spreads us out and then we come back in close as we come out of the dive. Nigger puts his motor at half throttle so we can pick up our places. When we roll, Nigger and Cal and Mac roll to the right and Springs and I roll to the left.

A photographer with a movie camera came over last week and got some movies of us doing it. We fly up close enough to get our wings between the front man's wings and tail.

June 23rd

We were out on patrol this morning and just across the lines we saw a two-seater. Nigger was leading and signaled to us to follow and dove after him. It was a pretty silver L.V.G. and he turned and Nigger missed his first dive. The Hun circled and I overshot and half rolled to make sure of him. Springs missed too and Cal, who had turned higher up, came right down on his tail as Mac went under. Cal got him and the Hun turned over on his back and went down and crashed into the ruins of Sailly. Archie was right put out about it but was nowhere near us. The gunners are rotten down here.

We climbed up high and about a half an hour later saw about thirty machines in the sky at different levels. Six machines of ours were in the middle layer and we saw them dive on the lower ones. Then I saw one of the Huns from above dive vertically for three thousand feet and flatten out and open fire right on the tail of one of our machines. Most wonderful sight I ever saw. I wouldn't have believed it possible. That lad was good. But one of our machines jumped on his tail and while he was firing too long at the front machine, our plane got him and he went down in loose spin.

About that time we reached the fight on a long dive and went in. There were plenty of Huns to go around and there were Huns diving and firing all about us. Worst dog fight I can imagine. Everybody was firing short bursts at everybody else. We had the advantage coming in on top and were having a fine time. Suddenly everybody pulled out and Archie opened up. A new bunch of ten Huns came up and we went back in again but there was too much confusion.[179]

Nigger and Springs went down on a black Pfalz and got him.[180] He went into a spin and crashed into a wood. The other S.E.s were from 74 and they got two Huns and lost one man.

The General came over and had tea with us and asked us who we wanted for C.O. He wanted to send us McCudden*[181] but we don't want him. He gets Huns himself but he doesn't give anybody else a chance at them. The rest of the squadron objected because he was once a Tommy and his father was a sergeant major in the old army. I couldn't see that that was anything against him but these English have great ideas of caste.

McCudden did come for about 7 days.

PART TWO: THE WESTERN FRONT

Above: Captain Horn's dog Lobo at St Omer. (Mark Hillier)

We asked for Micky Mannock who is a flight commander in 74. He's got around sixty Huns and was at London Colney when we were in January. He wanted to take the three of us out with him in February but we weren't thru at Turnberry. They say that he's the best patrol leader at the front – plans his squadron shows a day in advance and rehearses them on the ground. He plans every maneuver like a chess player and has every man at a certain place at a certain time to do a certain thing, and raises merry hell if any one falls down on his job.

74 is a stout outfit. We knew them all at London Colney where they mobilized. The other day, Grid Caldwell[182], the C.O., and Capt. Cairns collided in a fight. Cairns got down under control but the whole squadron saw Grid go spinning down.

That night they had a wake and all got drunk and turned it into a celebration. About midnight Grid walked in. They thought they were seeing a ghost as he was all bloody and his clothes were torn to pieces. He had set his tail stabilizer and gotten out of his seat and crawled out on the wing and gotten the plane out of the spin. His aileron control was jammed and part of his wing tip was gone but he balanced it down and landed it this side of the trenches by reaching in and pulling the

Fulford's handwritten note on this picture clearly explains who features in it. Another caption he had added to the page also states that Mannock had 'one eye quite sightless' and that the 'small "dug-out" is for dogs and Rosie's goat'. (Mark Hillier) stick back before he hit. The plane turned over and threw him into a clump of bushes. It had taken him ever since to get back as he crashed about thirty miles away. So he resumed command and took charge of the drinking and when the squadron went out for the dawn patrol, he led it. Then he went to the hospital.

Mannock trained Taffy Jones[183] who was a pupil with us at London Colney. Taffy has eight Huns [eighteen by this date] now and Mick says he's the best shot in the squadron. Mick has marvellous eyesight tho he only has one eye. He's to get two weeks' leave and then come to us. In the meantime Baker[184] is in command.

June 24th
We found nine Hun scouts yesterday and dove on them but they wouldn't fight and ran for home. We chased them but couldn't catch them.

Something funny about that. It must be a new type of plane and they were just practicing. They were fast whatever they were. My motor got to acting funny and the water began to boil. It cut out a few times and I just did get back and landed between Kemmel and Popheringhe [Poperinghe] in a big field that was mostly shell holes. There were some American troops up there of the 30th Division and they helped me to get some water and get going when it cooled off. It got me home but didn't run any too well.

They have retimed it but unless it turns up better I am going to ask for a new one. These Hispano Vipers are fine when they are all right but the slightest trouble bawls them all up. Springs was messing around over by Messines and flushed a two-seater out of the clouds and got him. Tiny Dixon was firing at him too, so they halved him. Randall knocked down a high two-seater and Hall is missing.[185]

We have a new pilot to take Thompson's place, Capt. Webster, a quiet, reserved fellow.[186] He's not a captain in the flying corps but in his infantry regiment. When any one transfers from their regiment to the flying corps they come in as second lieutenants but keep their honorary rank in their regiment and draw the pay of that rank. Then after they transfer, if they prove they're good and get a flight, then they become temporary captains and rank as captains in the flying corps and draw a captain's pay but keep their old regimental rank.

We have seven captains now but only three of them rank as such and those are all lieutenants in their regiments. There's one man who is known in the gazette as, "Lieutenant, temporary brigadier general". He must be good! That's the right system. In our army, if a major transfers to the aviation corps he comes in as a major and bosses men who have

Major Edward Mannock pictured in the cockpit of a S.E.5a whilst the OC of 85 Squadron. (Courtesy of Andy Thomas)

PART TWO: THE WESTERN FRONT

Captain A.C. 'Snowy' Randall, 85 Squadron, photographed during 1918. Having been 'B' Flight's commander, he also served as 85 Squadron's CO. (Courtesy of Andy Thomas) been flying for years and know more about it than he will ever know. I don't know who's going to do our fighting but I know who's going to get all the rank and all the medals.

June 25th
Springs and I flew up to Dunkirk to get some champagne yesterday. We landed at Petit Snythe and found an American squadron was being organized there, the 17th. Sam Eckert[187] is C.O. and Tipton[188] and Hamilton[189] and Newhall[190] are the flight commanders. They've got Le Rhone Camels and may the Lord make His face to smile upon them because they are going to need more than mortal guidance.

There was a brand new American major up there in a new Cadillac named Fowler. We turned our nose up at him but he insisted on being nice. His brother, who was killed at Issoudon, went to Princeton with Springs so they got to chewing the rag. He was so new the tags were still on his gold leaves and he didn't know how to salute – saluted like an Englishman.

When he heard why we'd come up he insisted on driving us into Dunkirk in his Cadillac. We got the champagne and he insisted on taking us into the Chapeau Rouge for a drink. We shot down a couple of bottles of champagne and he was all right, we thought, even for a new Kiwi.

He kept on asking such simple questions. He wanted to know all about how our patrols were led and if we led any ourselves and how we got along with the British. He acted awfully simple, just like an ordinary U.S. major, and we did the best we could to enlighten him as to the proper method of picking cold meat and bringing most of our men back. His ideas were all wrong and we concluded that he must have been reading some of the books by the boys at home. We got a snoutful and he brought us back to the field and we invited him down to dinner at 85 and then he left. We asked Sam what Fowler had done to get a gold leaf and he told us that Fowler had been out with the British since 1914 and had the Military Cross and had done about five hundred hours flying over the lines. The joke is certainly on us.

But he ought to know better than to fill a pilot full of champagne and then ask him how good he is. To tell the truth I think we were very modest. And why doesn't he wear wings or his decorations? If I had the M.C. all the rules that Pershing can make couldn't keep it off my chest.

I heard up there that about fifteen of our boys have been killed. Hooper[191] and Douglas[192] are among them.

We went down to have dinner with Nigger's brother at the 2nd A.D. They received us with open bottles. Those boys must have been in training for the event. That's the third of Nigger's brothers that has tried to uphold the family honor.

I heard a funny story down there. The Germans took Lille and the Allies held Armentières. For a long time they continued to run the factories in Armentières on electricity that came from Lille. A Frenchman was kept to run the power plant by the Germans and he didn't cut Armentières off. It was several months before he was caught.[193]

June 27th
Springs is missing.[194] He and MacGregor and Inglis were out this morning on the dawn patrol. Mac was leading and spotted a two-seater over Armentières. They went after him and had to chase him a bit further. Mac got to him first and missed his dive. Springs got under him and stayed there. The Hun stalled up and the observer was shooting down at Springs when Mac got back in position and got him. That was the last seen of Springs. Inglis says he saw some smoke coming out of his fuselage when the observer was shooting at him. It's afternoon now and no word has come from him so I guess he's cooked. Requiescat in pace, as he would say! I've got to go on a balloon straff now.[195]

June 29th
Springs is back. He brought back a school of pink porpoises and a couple of funny stories. His guns jammed when he went under the two-seater and he was trying to clear the stoppages when the observer hit his oil pipe. His motor didn't stop at once but brought him back a little way before the bearings melted. He glided back just across the lines and crashed down wind in a machine gun emplacement.

His face is a mess where the butt of his Vickers* gun knocked a hole in his chin and he got a crack on the top of his head and a pair of black eyes. One of the longerons tore his flying suit right up the back and just grazed his skin and removed his helmet. Some Tommies fished him out and sorted the ruins. He says the first thing he thought of when he came to was his teeth on account of Mac. He ran his tongue around his mouth and couldn't find any front teeth. He let out a yell.

"What's the matter, sir?" a Tommy asked him. "My teeth," sobs Springs, "they're all gone!" "Oh, no they ain't, sir," says the obliging Tommy, "here they are, sir!" and with that he reaches down and pulls his lips off his teeth. His teeth were all right, they were just on the outside of his face.

LEWIS - VICKERS WAS OUTSIDE COCKPIT

There wasn't any anaesthetic up there but somebody brought a bottle of cognac. Every time he'd try to take a drink of it, it would all run out of the hole in his chin. So he spent the morning with his head tilted back and his mouth open while an Irish padre poured the cognac down his throat for him. He said after a little while the pain let up but they brought him another bottle so he kept up the treatment.

He got back into the Forest of Nieppe and telephoned back to the wing that afternoon for a tender to come and get him. Then some doc up there gave him a shot of anti-tetanus serum. The tender came up after him and they started back, stopping at every estaminet on the way. He didn't have on a uniform, just his pajamas under his flying suit but had two or three hundred francs in his suit so they would stop and he'd buy champagne for the mechanics to pour down his throat.

They got back here about dark, all of them tight as sausage skins. We had a celebration[196] and made some strawberry julep to pour down his throat and we all managed to light up. Then someone noticed that his face needed a bit of hemstitching so we took him down to the Duchess of Sutherland's hospital in the woods below here. The doctor down there seemed to think the crack on his head was serious.

We were in a hot room and none of us felt too good. The doc told him to stand up and close his eyes and then open them. Of course he couldn't focus his eyes. I could have told the doc that. Then he told him to close them again and keep them closed. He swayed a couple of times and then keeled over on the floor and passed out of the picture. "Ah, ha," says the doc, "I thought so! Concussion of the brain! We'll have to keep him in bed for a while." So they sewed up his face and he didn't know a thing about it next day. The doc says we can't see him for a few days as he must be kept absolutely quiet. I'd like to see them do it.

June 30th
We got into a dogfight this morning with the new brand of Fokkers and they certainly were good. They had big red stripes on the fuselage diagonally so they must be Richthofen's old circus. There were five of us and we ran into five Fokkers at fifteen thousand feet. We both started climbing, of course. And they outclimbed us. We climbed up to twenty thousand five hundred and couldn't get any higher.

We were practically stalled and these Fokkers went right over our heads and got between us and the lines. They didn't want to dogfight but tried to pick off our rear men. Inglis and Cal were getting a pretty good thrill when we turned back and caught one Hun napping. He half rolled slowly and we got on his tail.

Gosh, it's unpleasant fighting at that altitude. The slightest movement exhausts you, your engine has no pep and splutters; it's hard to keep a decent formation, and you lose five hundred feet on a turn. The other Huns came in from above and it didn't take us long to fight down to twelve thousand.

We put up the best fight of our lives but these Huns were just too good for us. Cal got a shot in his radiator and went down and Webster had his tail plane shot to bits and his elevator control shot away. He managed to land with his stabilizer wheel but cracked up. I don't know what would have happened if some Dolphins from 84 hadn't come up and the Huns beat it. I think we got one that went down in a spin while Cal was shooting at it but we couldn't see it crash.

I got to circling with one Hun, just he and I, and it didn't take me long to find out that I wasn't going to climb above this one. He began to gain on me and then he did something I've never heard of before. He'd be circling with me and he'd pull around and point his nose at me and open fire and just hang there on his prop and follow me around with his tracer. All I could do was to keep on turning the best I could. If I'd straightened out he'd have had me cold as he already had his sights on me. If I had tried to hang on my prop that way, I'd have gone right into a spin. But this fellow just hung right there and sprayed me with lead like he had a hose. They have speeded up guns too. All I could do was to watch his tracer and kick my rudder from one side to the other to throw his aim off. This war isn't what it used to be. Nigger has noted the improvement in the Huns and is awful thoughtful.[197]

We went to see Springs this afternoon and he seems to be doing all right. He's … a mouthful of thread and a couple of black eyes. We took him a couple of bottles of champagne but he didn't need it as they serve it to him there. Things have been sort of quiet at the front lately in this sector and there were only three of them in there. One is a brigadier general who had been wounded seven times before this last shot in his leg. He and Springs were full of champagne and have a bar rigged up in a tent outside. The third is a Chinaman from a labor battalion who has been parted from his appendix forcibly.

There are about eighteen nurses there and it is the custom for all the nurses from the Duchess down to walk by and ask each patient how he feels each morning. The general says if they just had short skirts on and would whistle he'd applaud and join the chorus. Springs's face is going to be all right because they sewed it up from the inside.

Mac made a date to call on a pretty little nurse. That boy is a fast worker. I'll bet he gets sick in a few days.

July 1st
I hear that Mathews[198] is now a member of the sadder-but-wiser club. He dove straight down on a two-seater and the observer didn't do a thing but shoot the front end of his plane full of holes. He got back to the lines but cracked up and lit on his neck. These boys will learn some day that one two-seater can lick one scout any time unless the scout can stick under his blind spot

But these Hun two-seaters haven't got any blind spot. The long ones have a hole in the bottom of the fuselage and they can shoot down at you and these new ones have a double tail and are so short that the observer can stand up and fire right down at you while the pilot simply pulls up in a stall. And you can't take them from a front angle because the observer can traverse his guns over the top of the upper wing. Of course, if there're two of you, that is another story, but it takes two scouts to lick a good two-seater. These Bristol pilots say they can lick two scouts. They fight them like scouts and the observer simply guards the tail. If you want to go to heaven, the easiest way I know is to dive on a two-seater. We all do it and take a chance but the percentage of gentlemen who get cured of it is mounting.

July 2nd
Springs came back last night. He walked back in red silk pajamas and a pair of fur flying boots. The doctor decided he was nutty and wanted to send him back to England. They took his clothes away from him so he lit out like he was. The reason the doc was so sure he was crazy was that he overheard a telephone conversation.

Major Fowler's adjutant called up to tell him that he'd been made a flight commander in the new American squadron up at Dunkirk. Springs said he didn't want to be a flight commander and he didn't want to go to any American squadron. He told the adjutant to give the job to some one else quick. The doc overheard him refusing promotion and was sure he was cuckoo. The doc came over after him but we persuaded him that Springs wasn't nutty and after we filled him full of julep he finally said he could stay but that he mustn't fly for a week.

We got hold of Col. Cairns and he said he'd arrange for him to stay here and report him unfit for duty. But G.H.Q. called up later and said that he had to go anyway so he's to go up to Dunkirk tomorrow. It's either that or back to the hospital and the doc will sure send him home. But he isn't in any shape to take charge of anything.[199]

July 5th
Cal [Callahan] and I flew up to Petit Snythe yesterday for a baseball game between the mechanics of the 17th and the 148th U.S. squadrons. We couldn't stay long as we had to get back for a patrol.

Mort Newhall is C.O. of the 148th and Bim Oliver[200] and Henry Clay[201] are the other flight commanders besides Springs. Springs made some horrible punch that knocked out everybody that got a smell of it. He wants Cal and me to join his flight and Fowler[202] said he'd arrange it but we said nothing doing. I don't want to fly Camels and certainly not Clerget Camels. I told him I'd crown him eternally if he got me put on those little popping firecrackers. My neck isn't worth much but I want an even break.

Bobby was there and kept in the limelight by getting hit by a foul ball. They say that his latest stunt was a bear. His squadron had been working pretty hard and the colonel gave them a holiday to rest up. Instead of letting his squadron rest, he decided that they ought to practice moving.

So he made them pack up everything on the place and load it on the lorries and move it down the road ten miles. Then he drove up magnificently in the squadron car and inspected them and gave orders to them to move back again and unpack. They were so mad they wanted to kill him. Imagine a practice move!

He was a colonel once but he got demoted for one of his celebrated stunts! When the Hun broke thru on the Somme in March, the infantry retreated so fast that the mechanics on the airdrome didn't have time to get away and joined the infantry and fought with them. At one place they weren't able to save the planes because of a fog.

Bobby was in command of a wing, and he decided that he ought to prepare for such an emergency and ought to train his mechanics as infantrymen. So he got rifles for them and had regular drill. That part was all right and met with the approval of the brigadier. But he decided that he ought to have a sham battle as well. He had two squadrons entrenched along the canal at the far side of the airdrome, and then he had two other squadrons representing Huns to attack them. He was to be the hero of the occasion. About that time some inspecting general happened by and saw Bobby, with sword waving, tight as a tick, dashing madly across the airdrome at the head of the charge. He won the battle but lost his job. At least that's the story I heard. I'll say this for him. If likker was ammunition he'd be a field marshal.

There's quite a few of the old Oxford gang up there. Clay, Oliver, Curtis[203], Fulford[204], Forster[205], Whiting[206], Ziztell[207], Kindley[208], Clements[209], Knox[210], Hamilton, Campbell[211], Dixon, Goodnow, Dorsey[212], Avery and Desson. Stew Welch is over at 211 with Bonnalie.

July 7th
The new Fokkers are giving us hell. A flight lost two men yesterday and Webster got all shot up again. He doesn't consider the day well spent unless his mechanics have a few holes to patch.[213]

Capt. Baker, who is acting C.O. until Mannock gets here,[214] put Springs in for a decoration, the D.F.C. which is the Royal Air Force's Military Cross. The colonel sent the citation back. He said he was a good fellow but he'd only gotten four Huns and that wasn't worth a decoration. But just think what would have happened if he'd been down on the French front with an American squadron! He'd have gotten a D.S.C. and a *Croix de Guerre* for each Hun.

I flew up to see him yesterday and he sure was a funny sight. He's all swollen up like a poisoned pup and is red as a beet and broken out all over – inside as well. The anti-tetanus serum was sour and it has poisoned him.

John Goad is dead.[215] He was shot down in flames flying a Bristol Fighter. When the flames got too hot he turned the machine upside down and jumped.

July 10th

Springs and Oliver came down for dinner the other night. Gosh, they were funny telling about their Camels. They had a Crossley car with a general's veil on it to keep the wind off the back seat and were certainly hot. The squadron has both British and American transport so Mort has a Cadillac and the flight commanders have the Crossley and all the rest have sidecars.

Springs is a wreck. He's blind in one eye and the other one isn't much good. He's got haemorrhage of the retina, whatever that is, but the doc says it will clear up in a little while. He's also got cirrhosis of the liver from that serum. He'll be a fine flight commander. Between all that and the stiff neck he ought to be one of their best assets. Bim says they are the tin woodman and the scarecrow from the land of Oz and they are looking for Dorothy to put them together again. They kept us laughing all evening and everybody got plastered.

Mannock[216] has arrived to take charge all rigged out as a major with some new barnacles on his ribbons, and he certainly is keen. He got us all together in the office and outlined his plans and told each one what he expected of them. He's going to lead one flight and act as a decoy. Nigger and Randy [Arthur Clunie Randall] are going to lead the other two. We ought to be able to pay back these Fokkers a little we owe them.

I hear that Deetjen[217] is gone. They're going so fast now that I can't keep track of who's dead and who's alive. I guess I'll find out before long tho. I heard in Boulogne that Alan Winslow is missing.[218]

July 11th

One of our dashing young airmen, who, according to his own story had done innumerable deeds of valor but had never been caught in that act, changed his tune yesterday. He landed after he'd been out alone and his plane had about fifty holes in it. His altimeter and Aldis sight were both hit. He was as limp as a rag and had to be assisted to his quarters. There he remained as sick as a dog for two days.

When questioned about what happened to him he would get hysterical and sick at his stomach again. The wing doctor came over to see him and sent him to hospital tho there's nothing wrong with him except he's badly frightened. That's the last of his illustrious career. He'll go home and write a book on the war now. I always did think he was yellow.

What I believe happened to him is this. He's been telling so many lies about what he's been doing that he believed some of them himself and decided he'd go out and really have a look at a Hun. The first ones he saw shot him up and his constitution couldn't stand the fright. One thing about this game out here: those that are good are awfully good, and those that are bad are awfully sour. Thank God the Huns have the same trouble. Six real good determined pilots could shoot down twenty of this kind that have business to attend to after the war.[219]

July 18th

Mannock led a show yesterday and gave us all heart failure. He was leading the bottom flight with three men and found ten Fokkers and

PART TWO: THE WESTERN FRONT

played them for fifteen minutes.[220] At any moment it looked as if we were all going to get shot down but Mannock knew what he was about and kept the top flight up in the sun. He sucked the Huns into where he wanted them and went right under them. They knew there was a flight above up in the sun so only five of them came down.

Then Randy and three men came down on them just as they got to Mannock, and instead of their top five getting the cold meat as they expected, Nigger, Mac, Cal, Inglis and myself leapt on them so that our eight below had a picnic with the bottom five Huns*. They got two of the bottom ones and Mac got one of the top ones that tried to get down to join the fight below.

*SQUADRON GOT 8 HUNS IN 2 PATROLS AND RECEIVED CONGRATULATORY WIRE FROM AIR BOARD, LONDON.

MacDonald got his wish and got hit in the arm and is now in the Duchess's hospital with the world in his lap. Lucky dog. I'm willing to compromise with the Lord on an arm or leg any time. I'll spot Him one and shoot Him for the other.

We are certainly getting away with some good patrols. Mick is master. He has taken Cal with him and is going to train him as deputy leader. If the Huns would just figure with Cal instead of fighting with him he'd argue himself to Berlin. He takes his fighting just like he takes his bridge. By the time he and Mick are ready to go into a fight they know what the Huns had for breakfast.

Tiny Dixon and Canning have both been promoted and sent to other squadrons as flight commanders. Dixon ought to make a good one*.[221]   BOTH DID.

July 20th
Mannock is dead, the greatest pilot of the war [note that here the diary is again incorrect as Mannock was actually killed on 26 July]. But his death was worthy of him. Inglis had been doing a lot of fighting but had never gotten a Hun. But he tried hard and Mannock told him that he would take him out alone and get him a Hun. So just the two of them went out late in the afternoon*.

VERY MISTY. HAD TO FLY LOW.

* THIS IS A MISTAKE; IT WAS EARLY MORNING. A.A. GUNNER CAME TO CONFIRM INGLIS'S REPORT

Mannock picked up a two-seater over Estaires and went down after him.[222] Mannock has a special method of attacking a two-seater. He takes them from the front at an angle and then goes under them if he misses his first burst. It is very hard to do but is unquestionably the best method. Instead of going under and getting him for himself, he held his fire and turned the Hun and held him for Inglis.

Inglis got him and they started back but they were down low. Mannock got hit by machine gun fire from the ground just like Richthofen and dove right on into the ground. Inglis went back and flew right down to the ground and saw the wreck and is sure he's dead.

Mannock is the only man I've known who really hates the Hun and he certainly does. He wants to kill every man that was born in Germany. He was a Member of Parliament from Ireland before the war and quite a politician. He seems to hold the Germans responsible for the yellow cowardly contemptible part that Ireland has played in the war. He certainly did cuss the Germans and their Irish sympathizers. He told us if we ever let a German get away alive that we could have killed, he'd shoot us himself. He was also the most accomplished after dinner speaker I ever heard.[223]

We've had the two finest C.O.s that the flying corps had and the general came over and asked us who we wanted next. We are glad to know that we are going to get Billy Crowe, he ought to fit in with this outfit.

Tubby Ralston had a dud bus and they wouldn't give him a new one so he decided he'd crash it deliberately. He picked out a good place to do it and went down and pancaked. He crashed it all right and nearly killed himself doing it.

Loghran has been killed. He was at Hounslow when we first went there.[224]

July 23rd

I have learned many things, especially that discretion is the better part of valor. And in this game, not only the better part, but about ninety-nine per cent of it. When there are more than two Huns above you and your immediate vicinity is full of lead, well, my boy, it is high time to go home. Never mind trying to shoot down any of them. Go home and try again to-morrow. How do you go home? You are far in Hunland and you are lonesome. If you put your nose down and run for home you will never live to tell it. All the Huns will take turn about shooting at you until you look like a sieve. These new Fokkers can dive as fast as we can.

First you must turn, bank ninety degrees and keep turning. They can't keep their sights on you. Watch the sun for direction. Now there's one on your right – shoot at him. Don't try to hit him – just spray him – for if you try to hold your sight on him you'll have to fly straight and give the others a crack at you. But you put the wind up him anyway and he turns. Quick, turn in the opposite direction. He's out of it for a moment. Now there's another one near you. Try it on him – it works! Turn again, you are between them and the lines. Now go for it, engine full on, nose down!

Two of them are still after you – tracer getting near again. Pull up, zoom and sideslip and if necessary, turn and spray them again. Now make another dive for home and repeat when necessary. If your wings don't fall off and you are gaining on them, pull up a little.

Ah, there's Archie, that means they are behind you – woof – that one was close – you now have another gray hair – they've been watching you – better zigzag a bit. You can laugh at Archie, he's a joke compared to machine guns. You dodge him carefully and roll in derision as you cross the lines and hasten home for tea – that is if you know where it is. That is discretion – many a man has gotten one out of a fight only to lose to the others who have nothing to do but shoot him down at leisure.[225]

[*July 26th*[226]]

July 28th
McCudden the great has been killed.[227] He was taking off in an S.E. and he hit a tree. He'd just gotten back from England and had been flying with a light load over there. He forgot that he had four bombs on now and a full load of ammunition and he pulled up too steep. I guess he deserves a lot of credit. His brother was shot and is a prisoner.

I can't write much these days. I'm too nervous. I can hardly hold a pen. I'm all right in the air, as calm as a cucumber, but on the ground I'm a wreck and I get panicky. Nobody in the squadron can get a glass to his mouth with one hand after one of these decoy patrols except Cal and he's got no nerve – he's made of cheese.

But some nights we both have nightmares at the same time and Mac has to get up and find his teeth and quiet us. We don't sleep much at night. But we get tired and sleep all afternoon when there's nothing to do.

I got shot up by a damn two-seater yesterday[228] and then got dived on by a couple of ambitious Fokkers. My tail plane looked like a Swiss cheese.

This war gets more dangerous every day. And now this colonel has gotten bloodthirsty and wants some balloons. He's welcome to them. It

means in addition to other things that we will carry flat-nosed Buckingham to set the balloons on fire and if we get shot down in Hunland they will shoot us at once on the ground if they find any of it in our guns. It's dirty stuff and the phosphorus in it burns you so that the wound will never heal. But the Huns use it all the time so I don't see why we shouldn't too.

Cal picked one of them out of his spar the other day and there's no question as to what it was because it kept burning and you could smell the phosphorus and see by the hole it made that it was flat-nosed. It's not soft-nosed – that's dum-dum and is barred by the Hague treaty. I don't think either side has ever used any of that. I understand that the British have an enormous quantity of it and are ready to use it if the Huns ever start. I carry a belt arranged with one round of tracer and one round of Buckingham and one round plain when I am expecting to go down on a balloon. Then I am ready for anything. Since I set fire to that two-seater with plain tracer I am perfectly content with it but I guess Buckingham is surer.

July 31st

We saved Springs's bacon to-day. He and four little Camels were over by Roulers at nine thousand feet. Some Fokkers chased away his top patrol – they can't get above fifteen thousand with these Clergets; and then took their time to finish him off.

The five Fokkers were above just ready to attack, and in spite of that he went down on a balloon. The Fokkers went down on the Camels and we came up just at that point and leapt on them. We had a merry little dogfight. Imagine these poor benighted Camels wandering about Hunland and going down on a balloon with no top protection! Can you beat that! Why you can't even tie it! It turned out to be another dummy and they got a regular bath in Archie and pom-poms.

17 and 148 may be awfully good, I guess they are, but they can't get away with that sort of stuff. Springs called up later to thank us and confirmed a Hun for Nigger.[229] He said it was his twenty-second birthday to-day but his next would be his thirty-third as he had aged ten years to-day. I talked to him and asked him what sort of a bloody fool had he turned out to be. He said he wasn't leading that patrol. His deputy flight commander was leading it and was trying to show him a good time. I told him he'd better lead himself even if he was blind in both eyes. At least he's got a head.

Poor old 74 took an awful beating yesterday. Cairns was killed and two others. He had a wing shot off.

We don't get a chance to scrap on this side of the lines often or even within ten miles of the lines but one of these new Fokkers came over after a balloon and A flight nailed him after he got two and was trying to get back.

We went up to see it. They have the new motor in them – the B.M.W., I think it's called. It's a lot better than the old Mercedes. I know that without seeing one on the ground. It's a beautiful plane – has a fuselage made of welded steel tubing and has an extra lifting surface on the undercarriage.[230]

August 8th
Springs flew down this afternoon for tea. He's still all shot to pieces but has been leading patrols right along and got a Fokker the other day over Ostend.[231] He said it was pure self-defense. The doc thinks he's got ulcer of the stomach and he's on a licker allowance. He claims he can drink all right but he can't eat. That's a new disease.

They must have a great outfit in 148. They are all First Lieutenants and every one bawls everybody else out to suit themselves. And they have about six different bosses and get orders from all over the world. And they all hate Camels except Clay who wants to do like Tipton and win the war before breakfast. Springs got a couple of cases of port from His Lordship's wine merchant and he brought down a couple of bottles to us*.

Longton took his Camel up and did things with it that I didn't know any machine would do. Longton has been decorated with the A.F.C. for developing a two-seater Camel last year. What I can't see is why he didn't come out on Camels if he's so good on them. His prize pupil didn't last long.[232]

Jerry Pentland[233] was over the other night for dinner. He's a flight commander in 84. He was on crutches as a two-seater hit him in the foot. We called him Achilles and kidded the life out of him about going thru Gallipoli and then coming to France and getting hit by a two-seater. Jerry swears that he was at twenty-two thousand. No wonder we can't get up to these high Rumplers. But a Dolphin will go higher than that if you don't freeze first.

24 squadron got caught out by a bunch of these new Fokkers and got shot up badly. They had to have some men with experience so we sent over Capt. Caruthers and Rorison.[234]

※ WAS THE FINEST CAMEL PILOT OF ALL. COLLIDED WITH ANOTHER PLANE AT AN AVIATION MEETING AFTER THE WAR, & WAS KILLED.

August 11th

Again I've got that feeling, gee, it's great to be alive! The last three days have been particularly strenuous and eventful. Ordinarily I wouldn't be able to sleep at all, but I'm so tired that I slept like a baby last night. And I'm getting so bored at being shot at that I don't bother to dodge any more. I sat up in the middle of Archie bursts yesterday for five minutes, yawned and refused to turn until they knocked me about a hundred feet. I used to be scared to death of Archie and gunfire from the ground. Now it almost fails to excite even my curiosity.

Day before yesterday we had four dogfights. In the morning we attacked five Huns. I paired off with a Fokker on my level and we maneuvered for a couple of minutes trying to get on each other's tail. I finally got inside of him, put one hundred rounds into him and he went down out of control. Another one was after me by that time and we had quite a scrap but he made the fatal blunder of reversing his bank and I got on his tail and pumped about two hundred rounds into him.

I couldn't see what happened to him as another one was coming down on me from above. This one should have gotten me but he didn't. He had every advantage and one of my guns jammed. I was down on the carpet by that time and had to come back low for five miles with this Hun picking at me while I was trying to clear the stoppage and do a little serious dodging.[235]

Yesterday we did ground straffing down south. That's my idea of a rotten way to pass the time. Orders came thru after dinner and all night

I felt just like I did that night before the operation. I shivered and sweated all night. I took off with four little twenty-pound bombs strung under my fuselage; then we flew over about four miles across the lines at three thousand feet.

Nigger gave the signal when he saw what we were after which was Hun transport and we split up and went down on the carpet. All the machine guns on the ground opened up and sprayed us with tracer and a few field guns took a crack at us but we got thru somehow and dropped our messages with pretty good effect and shot up everything we could see on the ground. I saw what looked like a battery and emptied my guns into it and then chased home zigzagging furiously.

As soon as we got back, they told us to get ready to go out and do it again. So over we went and this time I saw a road packed with gun limbers. I dropped my bombs on them and then started raking the road with my guns. My bombs hit right on the side of the road and everything scattered. Two planes were shot up pretty badly and A flight lost a man.[236] Don't know what happened to him.

Then we did a high patrol with A flight. They got after a two-seater and there were some Fokkers up above them that didn't see us on account of the clouds. We went down after them and three of them pulled up to fight us. Inglis and I took them on and the rest went on down. I got into a regular duel with one of them and we fought down from eight thousand to about fifteen hundred. He did a half roll and I did a stall turn above him and dropped right onto his tail. I'd have gotten him if the other one hadn't come on down after me. Then it was my turn to half roll and I was careful to do a good one and not lose any altitude. He half rolled with me a couple of times but the dogfight was working down and he decided to postpone the engagement and dove for home. Zellers[237] and Dietz[238] and Paskill[239] have been killed.

August 14th
We have moved south for the battle of Amiens and have an airdrome at Bertangles four miles from Amiens.[240] 17 and 148 are down in this region somewhere.

I heard that Walter Chalaire got shot in the leg on a D.H. Four.[241]

August 17th
I'm not feeling very well to-day. I fought Huns all night in my sleep and after two hours of real fighting to-day, I feel all washed out.

Yesterday produced the worst scrap that I have yet had the honor to indulge in. It lasted about twenty minutes and the participants were nine little Fokkers and myself. I say participants because each Hun fired at me at least once and I fired at each one of them several times, collectively and individually. We went down on a two-seater and I stuck with him and fought him on down after the others pulled up. It was one of these new Hannoveranners and he licked me properly. They just haven't got any blind spot at all and the pilot was using his front gun on me most of the time.

On my way back I spotted a flock of Fokkers about three thousand feet above me. I didn't know what was going on, but it looked to me as if the thing to do was to suck those Fokkers down on me and then there would be plenty of our machines up above to come down on them and get some easy picking. I knew I was a good way over but I thought sure there would be a squadron of Dolphins about in addition to the S.E.s, so I climbed for all I was worth and waited for the Huns to see me and come down. Archie put up a burst as a signal and I didn't have long to wait.

I turned towards the lines and two of them came down. I put my nose down and waited for them to catch up. As soon as one of them opened fire I pulled up in a long zoom and turned. One Hun overshot and I found myself level with the other one. He half rolled and I did a skid turn and opened up on him. He wasn't much of a pilot because I got about a hundred and fifty rounds into him. He went into a dive. But that first lad was all that could be expected. He got a burst in my right wing on his first crack and now he was stalling up under me and the first thing I knew about it was when I saw his tracer going by. I half rolled and sprayed a few rounds at him and went on down out of it too. I was getting worried about where the rest of the boys were and couldn't see any signs of an S.E. Three Huns came down on me from above and played their new game. They try to fight in threes. They have some prearranged method of attack by which one sits on your tail while the other two take time about shooting from angles. They were all three firing and all I could do was to stay in a tight bank and pray. I thought I was gone.

One of them pulled up and then came straight down to finish me off. I turned towards him and forced him to pull up to keep from overshooting. As soon as I saw his nose go by, I put mine down for I saw it was time to think more about rescuing the decoy than holding any bag for the rest of them. One Hun was on my tail in a flash and we were both doing about two hundred and fifty. I turned around to see what he was doing and as soon as his tracer showed up close, I pulled straight up. He tried to pull up but overshot and went on by, about fifty feet from me. I was close enough to see his goggles and note all the details of his plane, which was black and white checked with a white nose. I waved to him and I think he waved back, tho I'm not sure.

I tried to turn my guns on him but he went up like an elevator and tried to turn back to get on my tail. I put my nose down again and we more or less repeated. The rest of his crew didn't seem to be in a fighting mood and only picked at me from a distance so I got away. I had to come back on the carpet and I shot up some infantry on the ground but it was too hot for me and I zigzagged on home. I felt fine then but before I got back I was shivering so I could hardly land. And I haven't been feeling right since. My heart seems to be trying to stunt all the time.

These present quarters aren't much and the food down here is terrible. Bully beef, boiled potatoes and Brussels sprouts. I've never been able to understand those people who go out into the woods with a tent and a frying pan and have such a wonderful time. And now that I am actually in possession of a tent and a frying pan, I understand that form of exercise much less. Bring back, oh, bring back, my shower and breakfast in bed! True I can't really call this roughing it, with a valet to bring me hot water when there is any water, and a good chef to cook for me when there is anything to cook, and a bartender to shake up a drink when there is anything to shake; but this is closer to nature than my table of organization calls for. Don't bother about my liberty, give me a suite!

A general came over to see us the other day. I was down at the hangars and he walked up unannounced and we started conversing. I didn't know who he was as his insignia wasn't showing on his flying suit and he spoke so familiarly of various matters that I thought he was a captain and we had quite a little argument about these new Hun planes.

It turned out that he was the general in London who fixed it up for us to come out with Bish. These British great moguls are the finest in the world. They make Lord Chesterfield appear like a truck driver for polish. He invited me over to his château for dinner next week.

I hear Cheston[242] has gone West. He was shot down in flames on D.H. Nines.

I was over at a Nine squadron the other day and saw Clayton Knight.[243] He showed me some sketches he had made of planes and fights. They were very good. That boy will be an artist some day if he lives thru it.

August 19th
We got permission from the colonel to put on a joint decoy stunt with Springs's flight. Cal and Springs worked out the details. The point of the story was that the Hun was supposed to be surprised.

Nigger led and the five of us flew over to 148's drome and rendezvoused at five thousand feet at five yesterday afternoon. We both climbed on the way to the lines and they crossed at about thirteen thousand. We stayed back and climbed up to seventeen thousand and had four planes from A flight up above us. We stayed between Springs and the sun and kept about five miles from him so that Huns wouldn't see us. He worked on over about twelve miles getting some Archie.

Then six Fokkers came up to see what was going on and the Archie ceased. It looked like cold meat to the Huns but they wanted to make sure of it and took their time. They came down to about a thousand feet above Springs and he dove back towards us to get them in proper position for a thorough slaughtering. Everything was working beautifully and we were waiting for the Huns to start their dive. The trap was all ready to be sprung when the Hun Archie opened up. They didn't fire at us or at Springs but at the Huns. The Huns got the signal and must have seen us as we started down for they put their noses down and beat it back for all they were worth. We didn't get within two miles of them.

But we'll pull our little stunt again and when we do, the slaughter will be terrific.

I don't know which will get me first, a bullet or the nervous strain. This decoy game is about the most dangerous thing in the world. I know I'll never be able to shoot at a bird again. I know too well how they must feel. I also sympathize with [those] who dodges baseballs with his head thru a hole.

Cal is prostrated. His family passed one of his letters around and it got in the papers. Needless to say he is going to write nothing more about the war. I saw a letter from his father. It was a peach. He was trying to cheer Cal up instead of making him gloomy with a lot of bum advice. I should like to meet him some day. He certainly has a sense of humor. I don't think he will take me off to one side and ask me if Cal took anything to drink during the war. I imagine he will get on well with any of Cal's friends.

We are going to form a new society – "The Society for the Extermination of Amateur Aerial Authors", the purpose of which will be to protect the public from a flood of bunk. "Sergeant Pilot Wright" is to be our first Honorary Member. With each fresh paper from home we get a list of new victims. One writer who signs himself the "Terror of the Huns" writes in his article that he opened fire "violently". Wonder he didn't break the trigger! He's proud because he got his Hun right over his own airdrome. Lord, I wish I could catch one within five miles of the lines much less across it. We have to go over to their airdromes after them.

Which reminds me that this volume is getting to be quite a book. I've written three whole books full of it. I am a bit worried about what to do with it. I guess some one will take care of it if anything happens to me. Springs asked me to leave it to him, but he's on Camels and it wouldn't be safe with him. Cal will look after it as long as he is here. It will never do to let the people at home find out the truth about this war. They've been fed on bunk until they'd never believe anything that didn't sound like a monk's story of the Crusades.

Every time I get a paper from home I either break into a loud laugh or get mad. I'm as bad as Springs. I see where all the patriotic women are studying public speaking and bird life. I can't see the why of either.

The Women's Committee of the Council of National Defense is certainly taking a step in the right direction. They have issued special rules about Service Stars regulating how people may proclaim to the world at large that a member of their family is a hero. A man is killed in action – certainly somebody ought to be able to swank about and get his glory! But I don't think they go far enough. Why not benefit the living as well as swank for the dead? Why not help out those that live thru it? Let the bona fide wives of dead heroes wear a gold star with an edging of mourning. Let the war brides of lucky cannon fodder wear two gold stars and mourning. Let the would-be wives of eager and successful belligerents wear a single plain gold star and black stockings. Let the anxious and unsuccessful ones wear a gold star and colored stockings. Thus every woman could swank, mourn, and advertise all at the same time, and the itinerant doughboy would be saved much curiosity and vain labor.

Yes, the Women's Committee is certainly on the job when it comes to winning the war. The American attitude towards soldiers is without parallel or equal and beyond the imaginative concept of even Jules Verne. Every day I hear something new which makes me glad I am in France.

If it were the lower classes who indulged in the rotten, cheap, maudlin sentimentality that even the French peasants scorn, I could understand it. But no, in America our best people have proved the contention of democracy that all are equal by showing how poor democracy's best are, and stooping to a level that aristocracy's servant's scorn.

Of course, American people are proud that their men are fighting for what they think is right, but at the same time they must go about proclaiming it to the world, taking credit for it, boasting of it, advertising it and endeavoring to transfer the pride in the soldier to selfish egotism. Will American families wear the decorations, wound stripes and service chevrons of their beloved ones also? Why not?

One thing I will say: America's attitude has turned out a fine army of fighters. When they go into battle they fight to the finish because the people at home have shown them just how valuable life is. A British staff colonel told me in Boulogne that the division of U.S. troops that have been with them was the finest body of fighting men that he'd ever seen. He was very flattering but he didn't think much of their higher officers. He said they'd all be killed if they were turned loose with American staff work.

The French are willing to let us have their share of the war cheap. They admit cheerfully that we saved Paris and they are perfectly confident that we are going to win the war without any further argument. We get great news from the South. I hope it's all true. But everybody thought the Cambrai show last Fall was the beginning of the end. Then the Huns turned around and chased us back the whole way and absolutely wiped out the cavalry.

My eyes are so sore that it's getting hard to write. You can't wear goggles when you are out hunting and the wind blows your eyelids when you sideslip or skid. And our ears are ruined forever. The sudden changes of altitude play hell with them. Going up in an elevator a few hundred feet used to affect mine. Now I dive five thousand at a crack and they ache all night.

August 20th
We're doing ground straffing and go out in pairs or alone and make three or four trips a day.[244]

I was out yesterday afternoon and had a busy hour. And I got a chance to see a battle from a grandstand seat. There were heavy clouds at two thousand so I crossed over under them, and looked for a target. As I crossed the lines I saw about forty white puffs of smoke in a line, about twenty feet apart. That was a barrage and as the puffs would die away, more would take their places.

Nothing could be seen on the ground at all. Further over was a village and high explosive shells were rapidly obliterating it. I would see several buildings rise about twenty feet in a mass, then disintegrate, muck fly about, and then as it settled, I would hear a dull thud and my machine would wabble from the concussion.

Two miles farther I saw some Hun artillery on a road and went down on the carpet. I dropped my bombs and then saw some troops just off the road and put about five hundred rounds into them. Machine gun fire from the ground was pretty hot and then I heard a crack, crack, crack, pitched in a higher key. I looked around and coming down out of the clouds were five Fokkers. Two of them were firing and I could see their tracer coming towards me. I twisted and turned and tried to work back. I was right on the carpet and over a little ruined village. I kept zigzagging and eventually reached a point that I knew was occupied by our troops. Then I drew the first breath in three minutes.

Shells were bursting everywhere – shrapnel in the open spaces with its white puffs and high explosive with its cloud of dust and debris on the trench parapets. Here and there were tanks, some belching lead and some a mass of flames or a misshapen wreck, hit by field guns. I was down right on the ground but saw very few dead bodies but any number of dead horses. The ground was all pockmarked and what little vegetation remained was a light straw in color from the gas.

Further down I saw the Huns using gas, a thin layer of brownish green stuff was drifting slowly along the ground from a trench about three hundred yards long. But no men were to be seen anywhere. Only dead horses and tanks.

The Fokkers were hovering about in the clouds waiting on me to come back or for some other cold meat. I looked my plane over carefully and couldn't see any holes so started back. I was right over our reserve lines and our artillery was banging away and the concussion was making me bob about so I was nearly seasick.

I got an idea. The Huns were up in the clouds. Why not beat them at their own game? So I climbed up into the clouds and headed towards where I thought they would be. The clouds were intermittent so I had to climb up to nine thousand before I got high enough to see any distance. I saw my Huns, seven of them now, and worked into position between them and the sun. They went into a cloud and I lost them. Then I got myself lost. I found out where I was and found my Huns again, four of them this time. But before I could get into position I lost them in the clouds.

I went down thru a gap and deposited the rest of my ammunition in the Hun trenches and along the roads and went on a personally conducted tour of the battlefield. I saw everything – advanced trenches, reserve trenches, tanks, reserve tanks, armored cars, artillery in action, support going up, demolished towns, cuts that once were railroad beds, thousands of yards of barbed wire – in fact the whole rotten business.

The British seem to be going after the control of the air. So far neither side has ever had the control of the air. First one side and then the other has had the supremacy of the air depending on superiority of planes and pilots but neither side has ever been able to do its air work unmolested or keep the other side from doing theirs. Both sides have accomplished certain things and had to fight constantly to do it. But the British seem to be planning to drive the Huns out of the air by carrying the aerial warfare back to their airdromes.

I understand that the Huns have a decided supremacy over the French and Americans. I'd like to get down on the American Front with a British squadron and get some cold meat. I'm tired of having to go so far over. Makes the odds too high against you.

If I was running the war the first thing I would do would be to get control of the air no matter what it cost. That's what's saved England all these centuries – control of the seas. And her fleet is big enough to keep control without fighting. The Air Force would do the same thing.

August 21st
More rumors of more battles. We were in the Folkestone in Boulogne and Henry told us that there is going to be a big push shortly. Push? What's a push to us? That's for the Poor Bloody Infantry to worry over. We push twice a day, seven days in the week. We go over the top between each meal. Oh, yes, the flying corps is the safe place for little Willy – that is as long as he doesn't have to go near the front!

Nigger and I flew up for tea with Springs. He was not too good. He and Bim have had tombstones made for themselves. They are hollow and if they go down on the Hun side, they are to be filled with high explosive and dropped over, if they are killed on this side, they are to be filled with cognac so it will leak on them.

Mac is back with a new version of the widow of Malta.

Hilary Rex has been killed. He was in a fight with a Fokker and his machine was disabled and he had to land. He landed all right and got out of his plane. The Hun dove on him and shot him as he was standing by his plane.

Armstrong is in the hospital with an explosive bullet in his back.

[*August 22nd*[245]]

August 23rd
The colonel has decided that we are to pull a daylight raid on a Hun airdrome. That's a good idea! The 5th group pulled one off up at Varssenaere but there are not so many Fokkers up there. We'd never get away with it down here. That was a fine show up North tho. One of the American Camel squadrons, the 17th, did the dirty work and went down on the carpet. Here's the official report I got out of "Comic Cuts":

"A raid was carried out by No. 17 American Squadron on Varssenaere Aerodrome, in conjunction with Squadrons of the 5th. Group. After the first two Squadrons had dropped their bombs from a low height, machines of No. 17 American Squadron dived to within 200 feet of the ground and released their bombs, then proceeded to shoot at hangars and huts on the aerodrome, and a château on the N.E. corner of the aerodrome was also attacked with machine gun fire. The following damage was observed to be caused by this combined operation: a dump of petrol and oil was set on fire, which appeared to set fire to an ammunition dump; six Fokker biplanes were set on fire on the ground, and two destroyed by direct hits from bombs; one large Gotha hangar was set on fire and another half demolished; a living hut was set on fire and several hangars were seen to be smouldering as the result of phosphorus bombs having fallen on them. In spite of most of the machines taking part being hit at one time or another, all returned safely, favorable ground targets being attacked on the way home."[246]

[*August 24th*[247]]

August 25th
Cal was missing all day and gave me an awful sinking spell. It just made me sick at my stomach to think of him gone.

He came back late in the afternoon with a beautiful package. He had a spar in his bottom wing shot thru in a dogfight and it broke in two and he sideslipped back and landed in the support trenches. He wiped off the undercarriage but didn't hurt himself. He spent the day with an Archie battery. It was a Naval outfit and so had plenty of issue rum. The British Navy seems to do everything but get wet.

Cal spent the day swilling rum with the C.O. They let him fire the guns occasionally and he saw a couple of fights thru the glasses and brought back a couple of shells to be made into cocktail shakers. He says that the Archie gunners don't expect to hit anything, they just fire for the moral effect.

August 27th
Many things have happened. I hear that Bobby got shot down up at Dunkirk and is no more. Tommy Herbert has been shot in the rear with a phosphorus bullet. Leach has been shot thru the shoulder and isn't expected to pull thru. Explosive bullet. Read[248] is dead and so is Molly Shaw.[249]

Alex Mathews[250] is dead. He was walking across the airdrome after a movie show over at 48 and a Hun bomber saw the light when the door was opened and dropped a two hundred and twelve pound bomb on him. They dropped about thirty bombs on the airdrome and killed about forty of 48's men and set fire to the hangars.

They broke all the bottles in our bar. Cal and Nigger and I were further ahead and threw ourselves into a ditch. Nothing hit us but we sure were uncomfortable. The night flying Camels brought down one of the Huns, it had five engines and a crew of six men. It came down in flames and lit up the whole place.

Barksdale got shot down in an S.E. and landed in German territory but set fire to his plane and got in a shell hole and covered himself up with dirt. The next morning the British attacked and took that sector. Barksdale said the Scotsman who pulled him out couldn't speak English any better than the Germans and he thought he was a prisoner at first.

One of our noblest he-men, a regular fire-eater to hear him tell it, has turned yellow at the front. He was quite an athlete and always admitted he was very hot stuff. He was ordered up on a bomb raid and refused to go.

The British sent him back to American Headquarters with the recommendation that he be court-martialed for cowardice. He would have been too, if his brother hadn't have been high up on the A.E.F. staff. He pulled some bluff about the machines being unsafe and they finally sent him home as an instructor and promoted him. He may strut around back home but I'll bet he never can look a real man in the eye again.

Springs had a wheel shot off in the air last week. Ralston came back and took up a wheel to show him and everybody ran about the airdrome firing Very pistols and holding up wheels for him to see. He understood and sideslipped down all right without killing himself. He said he saw a Dolphin pilot kill himself several weeks ago landing with a wheel gone. The Dolphin pilot didn't know it was off and the plane turned over on him.

Bonnalie was never considered much of a pilot. He was an aeroplane designer before he enlisted and knew a lot of theory but he took a long time to learn to fly and no one thought he would ever be much good. He put on one of the best shows on record and has been decorated with the D.S.O.[251] His citation appeared in *The Gazette*. Here it is:

"On the 13th of August, this officer led two other machines on a long photographic reconnaissance. Bonnalie, in spite of the presence of numerous enemy aircraft, succeeded in taking all the required photographs and was returning to our lines; they were intercepted by six Fokker biplanes which dived to the attack. In the ensuing combat Lt. Bonnalie perceived one of our planes making its way to the lines with an Enemy Aircraft on its tail.

"This officer at once broke off combat with the remaining E.A. and dived to the assistance of the machine in trouble. He drove off the E.A. regardless of the bullets which were ripping up his own machine from attacking E.A. Eventually, half of Lt. Bonnalie's tail plane was shot away and the elevator wire shot thru and the machine began to fall out of control in stalling sideslips. Lt. Bonnalie managed to keep the machine facing towards our lines by means of the rudder control while the observer and the third machine drove off the E.A. which were attacking.

"Eventually with the aid of his observer who, as the machine was tail heavy, left his cockpit and lay along the cowling in front of the pilot, Lt. Bonnalie recrossed the trenches at a low altitude and managed to right the machine sufficiently to avoid a fatal crash. The machine crashed within four miles of the lines. Lt. Bonnalie's machine was riddled with bullets."

Now that's what I call a good show. Who would have thought it?

There's an R.F.C. officer over at 20 Squadron on Bristols, from New York, named Paul Iaccaci, who has the D.F.C. and is quite a pilot.[252]

17 and 148 have been having a hard time. 17 has lost Campbell, Hamilton, Glenn, Spidle, Gracie, Case, Shearman, Shoemaker, Roberts, Bittinger, Jackson, Todd, Wise, Thomas, Frost, Wicks, Tillinghast and a couple of others. Hamilton and Tipton were the two best Camel pilots we had. And they have about six others in the hospital, too. Wicks and Shoemaker collided in a fight.

148 has lost Curtis, Forster, Siebald, Frobisher, Mandell, Kenyon and Jenkinson; and Dorsey and Wiley and Zistell are in the hospital. Jenkinson, Forster and Siebald went down in flames. Frobisher was shot thru the stomach and died later.

Of course that's not a bad showing when you consider that they have shot down a lot of Huns and done a lot of ground straffing and have been flying Camels which were all the British could spare them. The British have washed out the Camels and are refitting their own squadrons with Snipes. A Camel can't fight a Fokker and the British know it.

But we've lost a lot of good men. It's only a question of time until we all get it. I'm all shot to pieces. I only hope I can stick it. I don't want to quit. My nerves are all gone and I can't stop. I've lived beyond my time already.

It's not the fear of death that's done it. I'm still not afraid to die. It's this eternal flinching from it that's doing it and has made a coward out of me. Few men live to know what real fear is. It's something that grows on you, day by day, that eats into your constitution and undermines your sanity. I have never been serious about anything in my life and now I know that I'll never be otherwise again. But my seriousness will be a burlesque for no one will recognize it.

Here I am, twenty-four years old, I look forty and I feel ninety. I've lost all interest in life beyond the next patrol. No one Hun will ever get me and I'll never fall into a trap, but sooner or later I'll be forced to fight

PART TWO: THE WESTERN FRONT

Above: Elliott White Springs photographed in front of an upended Sopwith Camel of the US 148th Aero Squadron at Remaisnil Aerodrome, France, on 16 September 1918. During a combat with a number of Fokkers, Springs' Camel, that seen here, lost its left wheel. Spings attempted to make a landing on the aerodrome, at which point the undercarriage leg dug in, tipping the aircraft on to its nose. Springs recalls that 'the funny thing was there was a movie man on the drome to take some pictures and he had his camera all set and had taken a movie of the whole thing'. At the time of the crash, Springs was serving with the 148th, having been posted out from 85 Squadron. (Courtesy, The Springs Close Family Archives, Fort Mill, SC)

---

against odds that are too long or perhaps a stray shot from the ground will be lucky and I will have gone in vain. Or my motor will cut out when we are trench straffing or a wing will pull off in a dive. Oh, for a parachute! The Huns are using them now.

I haven't a chance, I know, and it's this eternal waiting around that's killing me. I've even lost my taste for licker. It doesn't seem to do me any good now. I guess I'm stale. Last week I actually got frightened in the air and lost my head. Then I found ten Huns and took them all on and

175

I got one of them down out of control. I got my nerve back by that time and came back home and slept like a baby for the first time in two months. What a blessing sleep is! I know now why men go out and take such long chances and pull off such wild stunts. No discipline in the world could make them do what they do of their own accord. I know now what a brave man is. I know now how men laugh at death and welcome it. I know now why Ball went over and sat above a Hun airdrome and dared them to come up and fight with him. It takes a brave man to even experience real fear. A coward couldn't last long enough at the job to get to that stage. What price salvation now?

No date
War is a horrible thing, a grotesque comedy. And it is so useless. This war won't prove anything. All we'll do when we win is to substitute one sort of Dictator for another. In the meantime we have destroyed our best resources.

Human life, the most precious thing in the world, has become the cheapest. After we've won this war by drowning the Hun in our own blood, in five years; time the sentimental fools at home will be taking up a collection for these same Huns that are killing us now and our fool politicians will be cooking up another good war. Why shouldn't they? They have to keep the public stirred up to keep their jobs and they don't have to fight and they can get soft berths for their sons and their friends' sons. To me the most contemptible cur in the world is the man who lets political influence be used to keep him away from the front. For he lets another man die in his place.

The worst thing about this war is that it takes the best. If it lasts long enough the world will be populated by cowards and weaklings and their children. And the whole thing is so useless, so unnecessary, so terrible! Even those that live thru it will never be fit for anything else. Look at what the Civil War did for the South. It wasn't the defeat that wrecked us. It was the loss of half our manhood and the demoralization of the other half. After the war the survivors scattered to the four corners of the earth; they roamed the West; they fought the battles of foreign nations; they became freebooters, politicians, prospectors, gamblers, and those who got over it, good citizens.

Opposite: Signatures gathered by Fulford during an event hosted by 85 Squadron – note the Flying Fox emblem – on 21 November 1918. The names include members of other squadrons, such as 41 Squadron and 2 Squadron AFC, all of which shared the same airfield at the time. (Mark Hillier)

PART TWO: THE WESTERN FRONT

85
SQUADRON
21st Nov 1918.

5 LEFT OF ORIGINAL SQUADRON

Signatures gathered during a celebration meal on 11 November 1918. (Mark Hillier)

PART TWO: THE WESTERN FRONT

My great-uncle was a captain in the Confederate Army and served thruout the war. He became a banker, a merchant, a farmer and a good citizen, but he was always a little different from other men and now I know where the difference lay. At the age of seventy he hadn't gotten over those four years of misery and spiritual damnation. My father used to explain to me that he wasn't himself. But he was himself, that was just the trouble with him. The rest were just out of step.

My father used to always warn me about licker by telling me that uncle learned to drink in the army and it finally killed him. I always used to think myself that as long as it took forty years to do it, he shouldn't speak disrespectfully of uncle's little weakness. And as the old gentleman picked up stomach trouble from bad food in the campaign of '62, I always had a hunch that perhaps the licker had an unfair advantage of him.

The devastation of the country is too horrible to describe. It looks from the air as if the gods had made a gigantic steam roller, forty miles wide and run it from the coast to Switzerland, leaving its spike holes behind as it went.

I'm sick. At night when the colonel calls up to give us our orders, my ears are afire until I hear what we are to do the next morning. Then I can't sleep for thinking about it all night. And while I'm waiting around all day for the afternoon patrol, I think I am going crazy.

I keep watching the clock and figuring how long I have to live. Then I go out to test out my engine and guns and walk around and have a drink and try to write a little and try not to think. And I move my arms and legs around and think that perhaps to-morrow I won't be able to.

Sometimes I think I am getting the same disease that Springs has when I get sick at my stomach. He always flies with a bottle of milk of magnesia in one pocket and a flask of gin in the other. If one doesn't help him he tries the other.

It gives me a dizzy feeling every time I hear of the men that are gone. And they have gone so fast I can't keep track of them; every time two pilots meet it is only to swap news of who's killed. When a person takes sick, lingers in bed a few days, dies and is buried on the third day, it all seems regular and they pass on into the great beyond in an orderly manner and you accept their departure as an accomplished fact. But when you lunch with a man, talk to him, see him go out and get in his plane in the prime of his youth and the next day some one tells you that he is dead – it just doesn't sink in and you can't believe it. And the oftener it happens the harder it is to believe.

I've lost over a hundred friends, so they tell me – I've seen only seven or eight killed – but to me they aren't dead yet. They are just around

WAR BIRDS

Above and opposite: 85 Squadron's card for Christmas 1918. The original drawing was, Fulford points out, done by Squadron Mechanic Arnold. (Mark Hillier)

PART TWO: THE WESTERN FRONT

(ON REVERSE SIDE OF CARD)

CHRISTMAS 1918

THE OFFICERS N C O's AND MEN

OF THE

UMPTEENTH SQUADRON R.A.F.

IN THE FIELD

SEND

GREETINGS

TO THEIR

FRIENDS, WIVES & SWEETHEARTS.

(ORIGINAL DRAWN BY A SQUADRON MECHNIC. ARNOLD)

the corner, I think, and I'm still expecting to run into them any time. I dream about them at night when I do sleep a little and sometimes I dream that some one is killed who really isn't. Then I don't know who is and who isn't.

I saw a man in Boulogne the other day that I had dreamed I saw killed and I thought I was seeing a ghost. I can't realize that any of them are gone. Surely human life is not a candle to be snuffed out. The English have all turned spiritualistic since the war. I used to think that was sort of far fetched but now it's hard for me to believe that a man ever becomes even a ghost. I have sort of a feeling that he stays just as he is and simply jumps behind a cloud or steps thru a mirror. Springs keeps talking about Purgatory and Hades and the Elysian Fields. Well, we sure are close to something.

When I go out to get in my plane my feet are like lead – I am just barely able to drag them after me. But as soon as I take off I am all right again. That is, I feel all right, tho I know I am too reckless. Last week I actually tried to ram a Hun. I was in a tight place and it was the only thing I could do. He didn't have the nerve to stand the gaff and turned and I got him. I poured both guns into him with fiendish glee and stuck to him tho three of them were on my tail. I laughed at them.

I ran into an old Harry Tate over the lines the other day where he had no business to be. He waved to me and I waved back to him and we went after a balloon. Imagine it! An R.E. Eight out balloon straffing! I was glad to find some one else as crazy as I was. And yet if I had received orders to do it the night before, I wouldn't have slept a wink and would have chewed up a good pair of boots or gotten drunk. We didn't get the balloon – they pulled it down before we got to it, but it was a lot of fun. That lad deserves the V.C. And he got all the Archie in the world on the way back. So did I, for I stayed with him. He had a high speed of about eighty and was a sitting shot for a good gunner but I don't think he got hit. I didn't.

I only hope I can stick it out and not turn yellow. I've heard of men landing in Germany when they didn't have to. They'd be better off dead because they've got to live with themselves the rest of their lives. I wouldn't mind being shot down; I've got no taste for glory and I'm no more good, but I've got to keep on until I can quit honorably. All I'm fighting for now is my own self-respect.

17 and 148 seem to get a lot of Huns these days. That's one thing about a Camel; you've got to shoot down all the Huns to get home yourself. There's not a chance to run for it. Clay[253], Springs[254] and Vaughn[255] are all piling up big scores. But their scores won't be anything

to those piled up on the American and French fronts. Down there if six of them jump on one Hun and get him, all six of them get credit for one Hun apiece. On the British front each one of them would get credit for one sixth of a Hun. Of course, what happens up here is that the man who was nearest him and did most of the shooting gets credit for one Hun and the others withdraw their claims. Either that or the C.O. decides who should get credit for it and tears up the other combat reports.

Cal has five or six now and I've got four to my credit.

Springs and Clay have been decorated by the King with the D.F.C. Hamilton and Campbell[256] got it posthumously and Kindley and Vaughn have been put in for it.

Cal is going to get it too. Springs tells me that Clay is the finest patrol leader at the front. He's certainly gotten away with some good work from all reports. And on Clerget Camels too! These boys are lucky if they just get back.

I heard unofficially that Clay and Springs are going to get squadrons of their own and that Cal and I are to take their flights. Not if we can help it! Tubby Ralston is down there in Springs's flight now and he reports hell on roller skates.

I hear that Tipton[257] and Curtis[258] and Tillinghast are prisoners. I'm glad they aren't done in for good.

Clay and Springs got separated from their men after a dogfight the other day and decided they'd have a look at Hunland by themselves. They found a formation of ten Hannoveranners and jumped on them.

These Hannoveranners have been licking us all so regularly that they wanted to make sure of getting one so they both leapt on the rear plane to make sure of it and one took him from above and the other from below. The rest of them mixed in and they had trouble getting out of it. They kidded each other all day about what rotten shots they were and that afternoon Rainor of 56 flew over to tell them that he was down below and saw their Hannoveranner crash. They thought he was kidding them at first but he gave them the pinpoints and they flew over there again and sure enough there was the crash.

Our infantry pushed the next day and they went up in a tender and got up to the crash. They were stripping it when the Hun artillery opened up on them and all they brought back was the black crosses off the fuselage and the machine guns. The pilot's seat looked like a sieve where Clay had got a burst in from below and the cowling was full of holes from above where Springs was decorating the observer. That's some shooting. They said the way the plane hit it looked like one of them must have still been alive as it wasn't smashed up badly. It had one of the new Opal [sic] motors in it. That's the hardest plane to fight on the front.

Everybody in 17 and 148 are still 1st lieutenants. Yet all the regulars and politicians' sons stay at home and get their promotions automatically.

I heard that Ed Cronin was killed on D.H. Fours down South. He was sent out late in the afternoon and had to land in the dark when he came back and cracked up. Jake Stanley was shot down on Bristols and is in a German hospital. Anderson, Roberts, Fred Shoemaker[259], Wells, Leyson and Bill Mooney are all missing.

Touchstone[260] is a prisoner of war and wounded and so is Clayton Knight with a bullet in his leg. Knight got into a fight with a bunch of Fokkers and they shot his machine all to pieces. He was flying a D.H. Nine and his observer was wounded early in the fight so all he had was his front gun. They thought he went down in flames but got a postcard from him later that he was alive. Frank Sidler has been killed and so has Ritter[261] and Perkins and Suiter and Tommy Evans[262] and Earl Adams.[263]

I saw Springs the other day in Boulogne. He said his girl at home sent him a pair of these Ninette and Rintintin luck charms. Since then he's lost five men, been shot down twice himself, lost all his money at blackjack and only gotten one Hun. He says he judges from that that she is unfaithful to him. So he has discarded them and says he is looking for a new charm and that the best one is a garter taken from the left leg of a virgin in the dark of the moon.

I know they are lucky but I'd be afraid to risk one.[264] Something might happen to her and then you'd be killed sure. A stocking to tie over my nose and a Columbian half dollar and that last sixpence and a piece of my first crash seem to take care of me all right, tho I am not superstitious.

Here the diary ends due to the death of its author in aerial combat. He was shot down by a German aircraft twenty miles behind the German lines. He was given a decent burial by the Germans and his grave was later found by the Red Cross.

PART TWO: THE WESTERN FRONT

Appendices

I	Major W.A. Bishop's Combat Report, 30 May 1918
II	Major W.A. Bishop's Combat Report, 31 May 1918
III	Major W.A. Bishop's Combat Report, 31 May 1918
IV	Lieutenant M.C. McGregor's Combat Report, 1 June 1918
V	Major W.A. Bishop's Combat Report, 1 June 1918
VI	Major W.A. Bishop's Combat Report, 4 June 1918
VII	Major W.A. Bishop's Combat Report, 15 June 1918
VIII	Account of McGregor's Combat, 16 June 1918
IX	Major W.A. Bishop's Combat Report, 16 June 1918
X	Lieutenant L.K. Callahan's Combat Report, 16 June 1918
XI	Lieutenant A. Cunningham-Reid's Combat Report, 16 June 1918
XII	Major W.A. Bishop's Combat Report, 17 June 1918
XIII	Major W.A. Bishop's Combat Report, 18 June 1918
XIV	Major W.A. Bishop's Combat Report, 19 June 1918
XV	Lieutenant A. Cunningham-Reid's Combat Report, 25 June 1918
XVI	Lieutenant M.C. McGregor's Combat Report, 27 June 1918
XVII	Lieutenant A. Cunningham-Reid's Combat Report, 29 June 1918
XVIII	Lieutenant J. Dymond's Combat Report, 30 June 1918
XIX	Lieutenant A. Cunningham-Reid's Combat Report, 3 July 1918
XX`	Captain S.B. Horn's Combat Report, 7 July 1918
XXI	Major E. Mannock's Combat Report, 7 July 1918
XXII	Lieutenant W.H. Longton's Combat Report, 10 July 1918
XXIII	Major E. Mannock's Combat Report, 14 July 1918
XXIV	Captain A.C. Randall's Combat Report, 14 July 1918
XXV	Lieutenant J.C. Rorison's Combat Report, 14 July 1918
XXVI	Lieutenant W.H. Longton's Combat Report, 14 July 1918

XXVII	Major E. Mannock's Combat Report, 19 July 1918
XXVIII	Major E. Mannock's Combat Report, 20 July 1918
XXIX	Major E. Mannock's Combat Report, 22 July 1918
XXX	Captain M.C. McGregor's Combat Report, 24 July 1918
XXXI	Lieutenant W.H. Longton's Combat Report, 24 July 1918
XXXII	Captain A.C. Randall's Combat Report, 24 July 1918
XXXIII	Lieutenant O.A. Ralston's Combat Report, 24 July 1918
XXXIV	Lieutenant D.C. Inglis's Combat Report, 24 July 1918
XXXV	Captain A.C. Randall's Combat Report, 31 July 1918
XXXVI	Captain M.C. McGregor's Combat Report, 3 August 1918
XXXVII	Lieutenant W.H. Longton's Combat Report, 9 August 1918
XXXVIII	Captain A.C. Randall's Combat Report, 9 August 1918
XXXIX	No.85 Squadron Combat Report, 22 August 1918
XL	Lieutenant J.W. Warner's Combat Report, 15 September 1918
XLI	Second Lieutenant R.A.H. Lloyd's Combat Report, 16 September 1918
XLII	Captain S.B. Horn's Combat Report, 17 September 1918
XLIII	Lieutenant J.W. Warner's Combat Report, 25 September 1918
XLIV	Captain M.C. McGregor's and Lieutenant P.D. d'Albenas' Combat Report, 8 October 1918
XLV	Lieutenant D.C. Inglis's Combat Report, 9 October 1918
XLVI	Captain C.B.R. MacDonald's Combat Report, 23 October 1918

Appendix I

Major W.A. Bishop's Combat Report, 30 May 1918

Squadron:	No.85
Type and No. of Aeroplane:	S.E.5a C/6490
Armament:	1 Vickers. 1 Lewis
Pilot:	Major W.A. Bishop, V.C., D.S.O., M.C.
Observer:	
Date:	30th May, 1918
Time:	7-53 p.m.
Locality:	Armentières
Duty:	In search of E.A.
Height:	15,400 feet
Result	{Destroyed 1 {Driven down out of control {Driven down

Remarks on Hostile Aircraft: 2 Albatrosses DV.

NARRATIVE

I attacked the top one of 2 Albatross, after slight manoeuvring I opened fire while on a turn, firing 20 rounds E.A. fell and crashed ½ mile N.W. of Armentières, I then fired on 2nd E.A., and fired 30 rounds from 200 yards range at him, E.A. went into a spin which I think was controlled.

Appendix II

Major W.A. Bishop's Combat Report, 31 May 1918

Squadron:	No.85
Type and No. of Aeroplane:	S.E.5A. C/6490
Armament:	1 Vickers. 1 Lewis
Pilot:	Major W.A. Bishop, V.C., D.S.O., M.C.
Observer:	
Date:	31st May, 1918.
Time:	3-5 & 3-15 p.m.
Locality:	Quesnoy & Lille.
Duty:	In search for E.A.
Height:	
Result	{Destroyed {Driven down out of control 1 {Driven down 1

Remarks on Hostile Aircraft: Out of control

NARRATIVE

At 3-05 p.m. 14,000 feet over Quesnoy 5 miles N.E. of Armentières. I attacked one of 3 Phalz scouts sitting 2,000 feet above a formation of about 14 E.A. I fired 20 rounds at 20 yards range from behind. E.A. immediately fell completely out of control. I was unable to watch it owing to presence of the remainder of the E.A. formation.

At 3-15 p.m. 6 miles S.W. of Lille at 11,000 feet. I attacked a two-seater E.A. who was evidently an Artillery Observation machine, I fired a long burst from rear at 100 yards range, E.A. turned to left, then dived fast and landed in a field.

APPENDICES

Appendix III

Major W.A. Bishop's Combat Report, 31 May 1918

Squadron:	No. 85
Type and No. of Aeroplane:	S.E.5A C/6490
Armament:	1 Vickers & 1 Lewis
Pilot:	Major W.A. Bishop, V.C., D.S.O., M.C.
Observer:	
Date:	31st May, 1918
Time:	8-15 p.m.
Locality:	2 miles N. of Estaires
Duty:	In search of E.A.
Height:	11,000 feet

Result {Destroyed   1
        {Driven down out of control
        {Driven down

Remarks on Hostile Aircraft: Phalz [sic] Scout, painted black.

NARRATIVE

Seeing white Archies 2 miles East of Hazebrook I flew in that direction, and saw one E.A. Scout underneath me near the A.A. burst. I dived at him but suddenly saw another E.A. higher just recrossing the enemy lines, followed him and fired 20 rounds from each gun at 50 yards range. E.A. fell to bits, and fell 2 miles North of Estaires.
This E.A. must have been seen by A.A. Batteries of the 2nd Army as visibility was very good.

Appendix IV

Lieutenant M.C. McGregor's Combat Report, 1 June 1918

Squadron:	No. 85
Type and No. of Aeroplane:	S.E.5A C/6472
Armament:	1 Vickers & 1 Lewis.
Pilot:	Lieut. M.C. McGregor
Observer:	
Date:	1st June, 1918
Time:	8-10 p.m.
Locality:	La Gorgue
Duty:	In search of E.A.
Height:	11,000 feet
Result	{Destroyed {Driven down out of control 2 {Driven down

Remarks on Hostile Aircraft: Pfalz. Black, white tails.

NARRATIVE

While on practice patrol I followed Major Bishop down on six E.A. I fired a long burst into one E.A. who turned over on his back, and went down completely out of control a long way. Major Bishop saw this machine and confirms it.
I fired a burst at another E.A. who went down completely out of control.

APPENDICES

Appendix V

Major W.A. Bishop's Combat Report, 1 June 1918

Squadron:	No.85
Type and No. of Aeroplane:	S.E.5A C/6490
Armament:	1 Vickers & 1 Lewis
Pilot:	Major W.A. Bishop, V.C., D.S.O., M.C.
Observer:	
Date:	1st June, 1918
Time:	8-10 p.m.
Locality:	La Gorgue
Duty:	In search of E.A.
Height:	11,000 feet
Result	{Destroyed 1 {Driven down out of control {Driven down

Remarks on Hostile Aircraft: 6 Pfalz.

NARRATIVE

While on practice patrol, I led patrol consisting of Captain Horn, Lieut. McGregor, Lieut. Springs, diving on 6 E.A. I fired 4 bursts at one E.A., zoomed and dived again on to leader's tail fired 30 rounds from 50 yards, E.A. went down in a straight dive, then spun and crashed near La Gorgue. During fight I saw Lieut. McGregor shoot down E.A., which fell completely out of control a long way and another E.A. fell completely out of control from above me. This must have been shot down by Lieut. Springs, I saw it still out of control quite low down. Lieut. McGregor also shot down another E.A. out of control. Lieut. Springs confirms the E.A. I shot down.

Appendix VI

Major W.A. Bishop's Combat Report, 4 June 1918

Squadron:	No. 85
Type and No. of Aeroplane:	S.E.5a C/6490
Armament:	1 Vickers & 1 Lewis
Pilot:	Major W.A. Bishop, V.C., D.S.O., M.C.
Observer:	
Date:	4th June, 1918
Time:	
Locality:	
Duty:	In search of E.A.
Height:	

	{Destroyed	1
Result	{Driven down out of control	1
	{Driven down	

Remarks on Hostile Aircraft: Albartoss [*sic*] Scouts.

NARRATIVE

Time: 11-28 a.m.
Locality: Half-way between Nieuport & 3 miles out to sea.
Height: 14,000 feet.

Seeing a formation of 8 E.A. out to sea, I flew towards them from the East & diving, attacked a straggler, after 10 rounds from each gun, he burst into flames and fell burning brightly. I zoomed away and escaped.

Time: 11-37 a.m.
Locality: Leffinghe.
Height: 15,000 feet.

I attacked another straggler of the same formation. Diving from the East on them and zooming away, fired 30 rounds from each gun at 75 yards range. E.A. which was a silver Albatross, fell completely out of control and passed through clouds 8,000 feet below still out of control.

Appendix VII

Major W.A. Bishop's Combat Report, 15 June 1918

Squadron:	No.85
Type and No. of Aeroplane:	S.E.5A C/1904
Armament:	1 Vickers & 1 Lewis
Pilot:	Major W.A. Bishop, V.C., D.S.O., M.C.
Observer:	
Date:	15th June, 1918
Time:	6-55 p.m.
Locality:	3 miles East of Estaires
Duty:	In search of E.A.
Height:	17,500 feet

Result {Destroyed 1
{Driven down out of control
{Driven down

Remarks on Hostile Aircraft: E.A. consisted of Pfalz and Albatross. Pfalz had red fuselage and black wings.

NARRATIVE

I attacked one of four E.A. which were sitting above large formation of E.A. In course of combat I fired at 3 of the 4, finally shooting one Pfalz down in flames from 50 yards range and behind.

Appendix VIII

Account of McGregor's Combat, 16 June 1918

"Two days after the squadron had taken up its new quarters, Mac had an exciting experience and nearly ended his days as a prisoner of war.

"After his flight had completed the afternoon patrol, he remained behind with a view to seeking Germans flying over the lines. Observing a burst of our 'Archie' in its vicinity, he spotted an enemy machine a few thousand feet above him. He tried to climb to the same level, but the enemy pilot saw him and hurried for home.

"Mac followed, some distance below, trying to sink him by stalling up and firing short burst at intervals. Unsuccessful in this Mac turned back and a little later saw four other enemy aeroplanes some distance below him. He dived on one, when all four evidently decided to call it a day and dived steeply away. Mac followed and, traveling at over 180 miles an hour, was firing a good burst into the machine he had selected, when he shot away one blade of his propeller. The terrific vibration which ensued, caused by the uneven swing of the propeller and peaking of the engine (the revolutions jumping from 2,000 to nearly 5,000) nearly destroyed the machine. Screws fell out of the fascia board, flying wires slackened, and everything that was not split pinned came adrift. Fortunately, his previous experience at Hounslow had shown him how to stop the vibration. He therefore switched off the engine, and stalled up until the propeller ceased to revolve.

"Gliding slowly back to our lines, he was amused to see three of the Germans flying parallel; with him, just out of range (the fourth whom he had engaged, was by this time nearing Berlin). They made no attempt to attack, although it would have been a simple matter to have shot Mac down, as he was unable to travel at more than 70 miles an hour. Had he exceeded this speed, the propeller would have spun and recommenced the vibration.

"The Germans doubtless suspected that he was playing some trick to entice them within easy range. Mac managed to get over the lines, some 20 miles from his aerodrome, being 'archied' vigorously the while, and – 'plonked the old machine down without any damage to myself but plenty to the bus'. From an infantry battalion headquarters he telephoned the aerodrome." (Taken from *Mac's Memoirs: The Flying Life of Squadron Leader McGregor*).

APPENDICES

Appendix IX

Major W.A. Bishop's Combat Report, 16 June 1918

Squadron:	85 Squadron
Type and No. of Aeroplane:	S.E.5A C1904
Armament:	1 Vickers & 1 Lewis
Pilot:	Major W.A. Bishop, VC, DSO, MC.
Observer:	
Date:	16th June, 1918
Time:	
Locality:	
Duty:	In search of E.A.
Height:	

Result {Destroyed   2
        {Driven down out of control
        {Driven down

Remarks on Hostile Aircraft: Crash

NARRATIVE

At 8-20 p.m., 1,800 feet, 5 miles East of Armentières.
I chased a two-seater from our side of the lines climbing up to him finally getting to 100 yards range fired 20 rounds from each gun. E.A. smoked then burst into flames and fell.

At 8-28 p.m., 8,000 feet, over Armentières.
4 Albatross scouts attacked me from the sun and head on continued their dive to 4,000 feet below me. I watched for a few minutes and dived onto rear one, opened fire at 75 yards from behind and in the sun. E.A. went down vertically and crashed on western edge of Armentières. E.A. dived to below me I think owing to presence of one of our formations 3 or 4 thousand feet above.

APPENDICES

Appendix X

Lieutenant L.K. Callahan's Combat Report, 16 June 1918

Squadron:	No.85
Type and No. of Aeroplane:	S.E.5A D/6871
Armament:	1 Vickers & 1 Lewis
Pilot:	Lieut. L.K. Callahan
Observer:	
Date:	16th June, 1918
Time:	7-20 a.m.
Locality:	Estaires
Duty:	Offensive patrol
Height:	2,000 feet
Result	{Destroyed 1 {Driven down out of control {Driven down

Remarks on Hostile Aircraft:

NARRATIVE

I followed Capt. Horn upon 10 Pfalz, and saw the E.A. which he fired at go down completely out of control. Later I followed Capt. Horn in a dive upon a two-seater and fired 200 rounds. The two-seater went into a vertical dive and was seen to crash near Estaires by Capt. Horn and was followed till near the ground by Lieut. Springs.

Confirmation

I saw a two-seater close to the line near Estaires. I dived with the patrol and fired 50 rounds at it. Lieut. Callahan followed on and fired a long burst into the E.A., which I saw dive vertical and crash in some ruins close to Estaires.

APPENDICES

Appendix XI

Lieutenant A. Cunningham-Reid's Combat Report, 16 June 1918

Squadron:	No.85
Type and No. of Aeroplane:	S.E.5A D/6859
Armament:	1 Vickers & 1 Lewis
Pilot:	Lieut. A. Cunningham-Reid
Observer:	
Date:	16th June, 1918
Time:	12-30 p.m.
Locality:	South of Ypres Menin Road near Kruiseik
Duty:	Patrol
Height:	500-100 feet
Result	{Destroyed One Balloon {Driven down out of control {Driven down

Remarks on Hostile Aircraft: One Balloon on ground.

NARRATIVE

After zooming away from firing at a long line (about a company) of infantry concealed in a ditch along the Ypres Menin Rd. I saw a balloon on the ground near Kruiseik. I dived within 100 yards of it firing continuously and zoomed away directly I saw it go up in a cloud of smoke. I was making for another balloon camouflaged on the ground and beyond the first one, when both my guns jambed. Ammunition used one S.P.G. tracer to 2 R.F.C. Special (both guns).

Appendix XII

Major W.A. Bishop's Combat Report, 17 June 1918

Squadron: No. 85
Type and No. of Aeroplane: S.E.5A C1904
Armament: 1 Vickers & 1 Lewis
Pilot: Major W.A. Bishop, VC, DSO, MC.
Observer:
Date: 17th June, 1918
Time:
Locality:
Duty: In search of E.A.
Height:

Result   {Destroyed   3
                                   {Driven down out of control
                                   {Driven down

Remarks on Hostile Aircraft: 3 crashed

NARRATIVE

10-25 a.m. Staden & Hooglede. 18,000 feet.
i) Between Staden & Hooglede, 18,000 feet at 10-15 a.m. I turned back a two-seater who was approaching our lines, finally closing to 75 yards. After 20 rounds he burst into flames.

10-50 a.m. Sailly-sur-le-Lys. 4,000 feet.
ii) over Sailly-sur-le-Lys 4,000 feet at 10-50 a.m., seeing 1 Albatross I zoomed into the edge of a cloud. Albatross passed cloud & I secured position on tail. After 15 rounds he fell and crashed just South of village.

10-55 a.m. Laventie (near). 2,000 feet.
iii) After attacking (ii) I saw a two-seater E.A. quite low, I dived at him from East but he turned and got East of me. After 2nd burst of 20 rounds he fell in a turning dive, then crashed near Laventie and main road.

APPENDICES

Appendix XIII

Major W.A. Bishop's Combat Report, 18 June 1918

Squadron:	No.85
Type and No. of Aeroplane:	S.E.5A C1904
Armament:	1 Lewis & 1 Vickers
Pilot:	Major W.A. Bishop, VC, DSO, MC.
Observer:	
Date:	18th June, 1918
Time:	10-45 a.m.
Locality:	6 miles N.E. of Ypres
Duty:	Search of E.A.
Height:	9,000 feet

Result {Destroyed 2
{Driven down out of control
{Driven down

Remarks on Hostile Aircraft: Albatross Scouts, natural wood fuselage.

NARRATIVE

While looking for one of the Squadron Patrols I saw E.A. scouts in a gap in the clouds circling around each other. I dived into the cloud and came out in the gap just above them, secured position on tail of one. After very short burst, he seemed to explode and went down in flames. At same moment one of the other 3 spun away, of the remaining two, one attacked me the other firing wildly from 300 yards on one side. I fired a long burst in a deflection shot at E.A. fighting me, and he smoked then burst into flames. 4th E.A. then spun away and I fired 20 rounds at him with no result.

Appendix XIV

Major W.A. Bishop's Combat Report, 19 June 1918

Squadron: No.85
Type and No. of Aeroplane: S.E.5A C1904
Armament: 1 Vickers & 1 Lewis
Pilot: Major W.A. Bishop, VC, DSO, MC.
Observer:
Date: 19th June, 1918
Time:
Locality:
Duty: In search of E.A.
Height:

Result   {Destroyed   5
                      {Driven down out of control
                      {Driven down

Remarks on Hostile Aircraft: 5 Crash

NARRATIVE

1,100 feet. 1mile E. of Ploegsteert. 9-58 a.m.
After crossing the lines in the clouds I came out over Ploegsteert Wood, saw 3 Pfalz Scouts which I attacked. 2 other Pfalz then approached from East I fired short burst into one of original 3 E.A. He went down in vertical dive. 2nd & 3rd E.A. then while circling about me collided and fell together. 1st E.A. crashed and burst into flames 1½ miles E. of Ploegsteert. Remaining 2 E.A. turned and flew E. I gave chase and opened fire on one at 200 yards range. E.A. spun into ground. Last E.A. zoomed into clouds and escaped.

900 feet. Between Neuve Eglise & Ploegsteert at 10-10 a.m.
I met a two-seater and attacked from behind and underneath. E.A. burst into flames. I then fired on a small body of troops on the ground scattering them. Climbed into clouds and flew West.

APPENDICES

Appendix XV

Lieutenant A. Cunningham-Reid's Combat Report, 25 June 1918

Squadron:	No.85
Type and No. of Aeroplane:	S.E.5A D/6859
Armament:	1 Lewis & 1 Vickers
Pilot:	Lieut. A. Cunningham-Reid
Observer:	
Date:	25th June, 1918
Time:	(i) 6-45 p.m. (ii) 7-30 p.m.
Locality:	(i) Nieppe (ii) E. of Ypres
Duty:	In search of E.A.
Height:	

	{Destroyed	1
Result	{Driven down out of control	1
	{Driven down	

Remarks on Hostile Aircraft:

NARRATIVE

I climbed East though clouds at 10,000 feet over Nieppe Forest; at 6-45 p.m. on emerging below clouds again I saw a formation of five single seater E.A. below me, who had apparently not seen me. I dived under the tail of one of the rear machines, and fired a burst from both guns at close range. The E.A. went down completely out of control.

At about 7-15 p.m. I saw 2 two-seaters E. of Ypres, making for our line. Each time I attempted to approach them they turned East, which manoeuvre was repeated several times. So climbing away West I entered the clouds, turned East again, and was then enabled to make a surprise attack on one of these machines, which was then making for our lines again. I came up under its tail and fired a short burst at very close range; E.A. immediately went down out of control at 5,000 feet, and on looking back I saw he had burst into flames. The locality was about half-way between Voormezeele & Gheluvelt. This second machine was later confirmed by "R" A.A. Battery as having been brought down in flames.

1 Decisive   1 Indecisive pending confirmation.

Appendix XVI

Lieutenant M.C. McGregor's Combat Report, 27 June 1918

Squadron:	No.85
Type and No. of Aeroplane:	S.E.5A C1931
Armament:	1 Lewis & 1 Vickers
Pilot:	Lieut. M.C. McGregor
Observer:	
Date:	27th June, 1918
Time:	9-15 a.m.
Locality:	Erquingham
Duty:	Offensive Patrol
Height:	8,000 feet

Result	{Destroyed	1
	{Driven down out of control	
	{Driven down	1

Remarks on Hostile Aircraft: Two-seater

NARRATIVE

While leading the patrol I saw a two-seater at 8,000 feet East of Estaires on which we all dived. I fired a good burst into him. He went into a steep dive afterwards going into a slow spin, continuing on until he crashed into the ground near Erquingham.
This machine was seen to crash by Lt. Inglis.
On the way home at 1,500 feet we attacked another two-seater East of Bailleu at close range. After a few bursts the observer ceased fire and the machine was driven east.

While following Lt. McGregor on an Offensive Patrol after dropping our bombs we saw an E.A. two-seater 2,000 feet below us East of Estaires on which we dived. Lt. McGregor got in a good burst after which the machine went into a steep dive which turned into a slow spin from which he didn't recover and crashed into the ground.

Decisive 1
Indecisive 1

Appendix XVII

Lieutenant A. Cunningham-Reid's Combat Report, 29 June 1918

Squadron: No.85
Type and No. of Aeroplane: S.E.5A C/1922
Armament: 1 Lewis & 1 Vickers
Pilot: Lieut. Cunningham-Reid
Observer:
Date: 29th June, 1918
Time: 8-17 p.m.
Locality: Kemmel
Duty: Offensive Patrol
Height: 1,5500 [sic] feet

Result   {Destroyed   1
                             {Driven down out of control
                             {Driven down

Remarks on Hostile Aircraft: Pfalz.

NARRATIVE

Whilst on patrol an E.A. dived on me & then on Lieut. Dixon, I did a climbing turn and went down after it, I got several good bursts into it from close range & following it down to 7,000 feet. I then watched it down till I saw it crash.

APPENDICES

Appendix XVIII

Lieutenant J. Dymond's Combat Report, 30 June 1918

Squadron:	No.85
Type and No. of Aeroplane:	S.E.5A C.6486
Armament:	1 Lewis & 1 Vickers
Pilot:	Lieut. J. Dymond
Observer:	
Date:	30th June, 1918
Time:	1-5 p.m.
Locality:	Berthen
Duty:	Line patrol
Height:	18,500 feet
Result	{Destroyed 1 {Driven down out of control {Driven down

Remarks on Hostile Aircraft: D.F.W. two-seater.

NARRATIVE

At 12-55 p.m. I was flying at 18,500 feet and saw E.A. two-seater flying West at about 17,000 feet. I overtook E.A. unobserved in the sun and dived from the front, getting a good burst with bot guns at close range. E.A. went down in a straight and very steep dive Northwards not attempting to turn East. At 7,000 feet flames began to burst from the Fuselage. This is confirmed by "H" Battery A.A.

APPENDICES

Appendix XIX

Lieutenant A. Cunningham-Reid's Combat Report, 3 July 1918

Squadron:	No.85
Type and No. of Aeroplane:	S.E.5A C/1922
Armament:	1 Vickers & 1 Lewis
Pilot:	Lt. A. Cunningham-Reid
Observer:	
Date:	3rd July, 1918
Time:	12-15 p.m.
Locality:	Bruges – Thielt
Duty:	Search of E.A.
Height:	1,000-2,000 feet

Result
{Destroyed   1
{Driven down out of control
{Driven down   1

Remarks on Hostile Aircraft: Pfalz. Red & Black.

NARRATIVE

Descending through clouds I found myself at 3,000 ft., East of Nieuport and observed two E.A. proceeding towards Thourqut. I was able to catch them up without being seen by keeping in and out of the clouds and got in a burst at very close range into one causing it to go into flames. Immediately afterwards I was attacked by about 4 other E.A. that I had not previously seen, these prevented me from returning into the clouds. I engaged them until my Lewis ran out and my Vickers jambed and then changing my drum I got a good burst into one which immediately went down, this enabled me to regain the clouds.

1 Decisive
1 Indecisive

APPENDICES

Appendix XX

Captain S.B. Horn's Combat Report, 7 July 1918

Squadron:	No.85
Type and No. of Aeroplane:	S.E.5A C.1904
Armament:	1 Vickers & 1 Lewis
Pilot:	Captain S.B. Horn
Observer:	
Date:	7th July, 1918
Time:	8-15 & 8-20 p.m.
Locality:	Doulieu & Steenwerck
Duty:	Offensive Patrol
Height:	16,000 feet
Result	{Destroyed 1
	{Driven down out of control 1
	{Driven down

Remarks on Hostile Aircraft: Pfalz. 4 Fokker Biplanes.

NARRATIVE

When leading the patrol I saw 7 E.A. at 18,000 feet above us. I climbed towards the Lines the E.A. following. The front two dived, I then turned into the E.A. formation, two of them were on Lieut. Longton's tail. I shot one off which went* down completely out of control and watched it down for about 4,000 feet. I then got on the tail of a second E.A. which I followed down to 6,000 feet, the planes eventually coming off and machine crashing near Steenwerck.
I then saw a fight going on West of me, I dive towards it and saw Lieut. Longton shoot an E.A. down which crashed at Sheet 36A. F.14.

*This EA is confirmed in Lt. Longton's report.

APPENDICES

Appendix XXI

Major E. Mannock's Combat Report, 7 July 1918

Squadron:	No. 85
Type and No. of Aeroplane:	S.E.5A E.1295
Armament:	1 Vickers & 1 Lewis
Pilot:	Major E. Mannock
Observer:	
Date:	7th July, 1918
Time:	8-20 p.m.
Locality:	Doulieu (L.5) Sheet 36A
Duty:	Offensive Patrol
Height:	7,000 feet
Result	{Destroyed 1 {Driven down out of control 1 {Driven down

Remarks on Hostile Aircraft: Fokker Biplanes. Black & White. (One with Red body destroyed).

NARRATIVE

Observed combat taking place over me at locality above mentioned. Fight descended to 7,000 feet and S.E. was attacked by red-bodied E.A. which dived and lost height. Followed the E.A. down, firing when opportunity presented itself. This E.A. went vertically into the ground at approximately a mile East of Doulieu. Height at termination of engagement 1,500 feet.

Climbed for about 1,000 feet and observed second S.E. being engaged by two E.A. Took one which was on S.E.'s tail and engaged same. Fired approximately 30 rounds from each gun when E.A. went into a spin at about 1,000 feet and I lost sight of it almost at once. I am sure that this E.A. crashed. Lieut. Longton saw the first E.A. go down.

Appendix XXII

Lieutenant W.H. Longton's Combat Report, 10 July 1918

Squadron:	No.85
Type and No. of Aeroplane:	S.E.5A D.6026
Armament:	1 Vickers & 1 Lewis
Pilot:	Lieut. W.H. Longton
Observer:	
Date:	10th July, 1918
Time:	6-50 a.m.
Locality:	Sheet 36A. K29.
Duty:	Offensive Patrol
Height:	7,000 feet
Result	{Destrozed 1 {Driven down out of control {Driven down

Remarks on Hostile Aircraft: Hannovraner [sic] & Escort

NARRATIVE

Two-seater observed at approximately 7,000 feet. Sheet 36 M.4. I attacked from N.E. and fired one burst of about 54 rounds at close range, the E.A. spiraled steeply. Lieut. Dymond attacked at close range and both S.E.'s still followed to approximately 5,000 feet off the ground. The petrol tank of the E.A. appeared to have been hit as I noticed that the pilot did not use his engine during the fight. This machine was observed by Lieut. Dymond to crash at approximately Sheet 36A L.7. I consider that both S.E.s were equally responsible for the destruction of this E.A.

1 brought down.

Appendix XXIII

Major E. Mannock's Combat Report, 14 July 1918

Squadron:	No.85
Type and No. of Aeroplane:	S.E.5A E.1295
Armament:	1 Vickers & 1 Lewis
Pilot:	Major E. Mannock
Observer:	
Date:	14-7-18
Time:	8-35 a.m. & 9-5 a.m.
Locality:	N. of Merville
Duty:	Offensive Patrol
Height:	7,000 feet
Result	{Destroyed 1 {Driven down out of control {Driven down
Remarks on Hostile Aircraft:	(A) Fokker biplane marked thus: [swastika] with white tail & black fuselage. Swastika in white. (B) Two-seater, green mottled. Type not definitely noted.

NARRATIVE

Dived with patrol from 10,000 feet over Merville on leader of two Scout E.A. Disengaged owing to observing a Fokker biplane (A) on tail of an S.E.5. Fought this machine down to 1,000 feet and observed it crash N.E. of Merville (1 mile approx.). This machine confirmed by Capt. Randall. Patrol of S.E.5's unfortunately split up at this juncture.

Attacked two-seater N.E. of Merville form the east – both machines firing. S.E.5 was hit by pilot's gun. The E.A. turned north after both machines had passed each other, side-slipping, and turned over about a mile east of Merville and slightly north. Height at termination of combat 2,000 feet. This two-seater did not appear to break up on landing but landed down wind in rough ground. Probably the engine was much damaged by gunfire.

Appendix XXIV

Captain A.C. Randall's Combat Report, 14 July 1918

Squadron:	No.85
Type and No. of Aeroplane:	S.E.5A C.1928
Armament:	1 Vickers & 1 Lewis
Pilot:	Capt. A.C. Randall
Observer:	
Date:	14-7-18
Time:	8-36 a.m.
Locality:	N. of Merville
Duty:	Offensive Patrol
Height:	7,000 feet
Result	{Destroyed 1 {Driven down out of control {Driven down

Remarks on Hostile Aircraft: (A) Pfalz Scout, yellow tail & fuselage.
(B) Albatross two-seater green mottled.

NARRATIVE

Dived with Major Mannock's patrol on E.A. over Merville & finding 1 E.A. making East I turned & got into favourable position on his tail and fired several bursts from both guns until just North of Armentières, he went down and crashed. I saw E.A. Scout with black & white tail plane ?? marking driven down and crashed N.E. of Merville by S.E.5. Making back to the lines I met a Hannovranner between Merville & Estaires and on opening fire on him he made off East. I then dived on E.A. two-seater (Albatross) with S.E.5 letter K (Lt. Longton), got good burst into this E.A. but had to turn off owing to both guns being jambed. S.E.5 "K" followed E.A. down and I saw him crash N.E. of Estaires.

APPENDICES

Appendix XXV

Lieutenant J.C. Rorison's Combat Report, 14 July 1918

Squadron:	No.85
Type and No. of Aeroplane:	S.E.5A B.7870
Armament:	1 Vickers & 1 Lewis
Pilot:	Lieut. J.C. Rorison
Observer:	
Date:	14-7-18
Time:	8-45 a.m.
Locality:	S.W. of Estaires
Duty:	Offensive Patrol
Height:	9,000 feet – 500 feet
Result	{Destroyed 1 {Driven down out of control {Driven down

Remarks on Hostile Aircraft: Fokker Scout. Planes and tail white.

NARRATIVE

Diving with Capt. Dixon's patrol on E.A. patrol, I got into position on the tail of one Pfalz Scout and fired several bursts. In the general combat which followed I lost sight of this E.A. meantime another E.A. dived on me from above, whereupon I turned and engaged this E.A. which was a Fokker Scout, getting in several good bursts at very close range at height of 1,000 feet, whereupon E.A. dived steeply away and I saw the debris on the ground in a field S.W. of Estaires, being then at 500 feet. Just before engaging this E.A. I observed Capt. Dixon firing at close range at a white tail Pfalz Scout which appeared to be completely out of control.

Lieut. Rorison landed later then the main body of the patrols hence the delay in the report, and which also accounts for this decisive result not having been advised to the Wing H.Q.s together with the originally submitted results.

APPENDICES

Appendix XXVI

Lieutenant W.H. Longton's Combat Report, 14 July 1918

Squadron: No.85
Type and No. of Aeroplane: S.E.5A D.6927
Armament: 1 Vickers & 1 Lewis
Pilot: Lieut. W.H. Longton
Observer:
Date: 14-7-18
Time: (A) 8-35 a.m. (B) 8-55 a.m.
Locality: N.E. Estaires
Duty: Offensive Patrol
Height: 5,000 feet

Result
{Destroyed   1
{Driven down out of control
{Driven down

Remarks on Hostile Aircraft: (A) Pfalz Scout, yellow tail and fuselage.
(B) Albatross two-seater, green mottled.

NARRATIVE

(A) Followed leader from 10,000 feet above Merville on two Scout E.A., leader zoomed away. Followed E.A. down getting in two bursts at close range, was on is tail at 200 feet when Vickers jambed. Lewis drum empty. E.A. last seen going east over Armentières with S.E.5 letter "H" on his tail (Capt. Randall on "H").

(B) After clearing jamb in Vickers and fitting new drum on Lewis, dived on to E.A. two-seater with S.E.5 letter "H", getting in several good bursts at close range. Got final burst at E.A. at 200 feet, this empties Lewis drum, so zoomed up to change same, this machine was seen to crash by Capt. Randall N.E. of Estaires. Height at termination of engagement 200 feet.

APPENDICES

Appendix XXVII

Major E. Mannock's Combat Report, 19 July 1918

Squadron: No.85
Type and No. of Aeroplane: S.E.5A E.1295
Armament: 1 Vickers & 1 Lewis
Pilot: Major E. Mannock
Observer:
Date: 19th July, 1918
Time: 8-23 a.m.
Locality: Merville
Duty: Offensive Patrol
Height: 3,000 feet

Result   {Destroyed   1
                                  {Driven down out of control
                                  {Driven down

Remarks on Hostile Aircraft: Albatross two-seater.

NARRATIVE

Observed this Machine flying well over by Estaires and steering west. Led Patrol north east, and engaged E.A. from the East, head on, over K.26 approx: Fired approximately 80 rounds from both guns at point blank range from front, and also from beneath E.A., the machine then dived and commenced to flame. The observer was killed or badly wounded at the first onset. The E.A. crashed, still burning at Sheet 36A. K.34b. All members of the Patrol confirming this.

Height at attack 3,000 feet - 2,000 feet.

Appendix XXVIII

Major E. Mannock's Combat Report, 20 July 1918

Squadron: No.85
Type and No. of Aeroplane: S.E.5. E1295
Armament: 1 Lewis & 1 Vickers
Pilot: Major E. Mannock
Observer:
Date: 20-7-18
Time: (A) 11-17 A.M. (B) 12-15 Noon
Locality: Salome (E of La Bassée)
Duty: Special Mission & Offensive Patrol
Height: 4,000 Ft.

Result: {Destroyed — One
{Driven down out of control — One
{Driven down

Remarks on Hostile Aircraft: (A) Two-seater (Type undefined) Camouflaged. (B) Fokker Biplane (Tail white and Check wings, Fuselage black).

NARRATIVE

(A). This E.A. was pointed out to me by A.A. fire. S.E.'s dived from 10,000 feet East and attacked E.A. from the front and on same level, E.A. went down almost vertically, pieces of fabric breaking away from machine. Followed the E.A. down to 4,000 feet E.A. flattened out, turned North, then vertically to the South again and crashed approximately at Illies N.E. of La Bassée. This machine floated about quite a long time before crashing. Lieut. Brown will be able to confirm this.

(B). Time 12-20 p.m. Locality S. of Steenwercke.
These three Fokker Biplanes were observed at 10,000 feet near Merville. Main Patrol of S.E.'s attacked from West and I attacked from East. After close combat at 8,000 feet my antagonist went down out of control and smoking. This was observed by Lieut. Callahan in same combat. I could not observe this machine crash, as other E.A. engaged my attention.

Appendix XXIX

Major E. Mannock's Combat Report, 22 July 1918

Squadron:	No.85
Type and No. of Aeroplane:	S.E.5AE.1295
Armament:	1 Lewis & 1 Vickers
Pilot:	Major E. Mannock
Observer:	
Date:	22-7-18
Time:	9-52 a.m.
Locality:	Armentières
Duty:	Offensive Patrol
Height:	14,500 feet
Result	{Destroyed　　1 {Driven down out of control {Driven down

Remarks on Hostile Aircraft: Triplane. Mottled brown, green etc.

NARRATIVE

Five E.A. Triplanes observed approximately over Steenwercke at 9-25 a.m. These E.A. attempted to attack us from behind, without success. Part of my patrol flew N.W. and the top three S.E.'s flew N.E. thus bringing the E.A. between. Climbed steadily towards Lille and intercepted the E.A. patrol over Armentières. Fired tentatively at several and followed one into the clouds and shot the tail off. This was observed by Lt. Dymond. Height at termination of combat 10,500 – 11,000 feet.

Appendix XXX

Captain M.C. McGregor's Combat Report, 24 July 1918

Squadron:	No.85
Type and No. of Aeroplane:	S.E.5A D.6923
Armament:	1 Lewis & 1 Vickers
Pilot:	Capt. M.C. McGregor
Observer:	
Date:	24-7-18
Time:	10-45 a.m.
Locality:	S.E. of Kemmel
Duty:	Offensive Patrol
Height:	11,000 feet
Result	{Destroyed — One {Driven down out of control — One {Driven down

Remarks on Hostile Aircraft: Fokker biplane

NARRATIVE

While leading the top layer patrol of four S.E.'s we got East of six E.A. which were being decoyed by our lower layer patrol led by Capt. Randall. Getting to point blank range, I fired a good burst into one E.A. As I zoomed away I observed E.A. going down in a wide spiral with the propeller stopped, apparently completely out of control. Seeing another E.A. on Lt. Inglis' tail I fired a good burst into him from close range. E.A. went down and I observed it crash at Sheet 28 S.6.0. This machine was confirmed by Lt. Longton. Height at termination of combat 4,000 feet.

APPENDICES

Appendix XXXI

Lieutenant W.H. Longton's Combat Report, 24 July 1918

Squadron: No.85
Type and No. of Aeroplane: S.E.5 C/1904
Armament: 1 Vickers & 1 Lewis
Pilot: Lieut. W.H. Longton
Observer:
Date: 24th July, 1918
Time: 10.45 a.m.
Locality: Sheet 28 S.6d
Duty: Offensive Patrol
Height: 10,000 feet

Result {Destroyed One
{Driven down out of control
{Driven down

Remarks on Hostile Aircraft: Pfalz Scout. Yellow Tail and Fuselage.

NARRATIVE

Followed leader towards our lines, E.A. followed on our tail; top patrol went round E.A. and attacked from East, waited until E.A. came below me, and dived onto one which half rolled under me and dived straight down, followed and got onto his tail, getting in several good bursts at close range E.A. went out of control, and watched him crash at Sheet 28 S.6d. Height at termination of combat 3,000 feet. I also saw E.A. crash at Sheet 28 S.6c which was being followed closely by an S.E. this proved to be Captain McGregor.

Appendix XXXII

Captain A.C. Randall's Combat Report, 24 July 1918

Squadron:	No.85
Type and No. of Aeroplane:	S.E.5A C.1931
Armament:	1 Lewis & 1 Vickers
Pilot:	Capt. A.C. Randall
Observer:	
Date:	24th July, 1918
Time:	10-45 a.m.
Locality:	Neuve Eglise
Duty:	Offensive Patrol
Height:	10,000-3,000 feet
Result	{Destroyed One {Driven down out of control {Driven down
Remarks on Hostile Aircraft:	Fokker biplane. Black fuselage with white on tail.

NARRATIVE

About 10-40 a.m. I noticed an E.A. patrol about 12,000 feet over Armentières. Being on lower layer; patrol went north towards Dickebusch, and then turned S.E. losing height. E.A. formation came down on patrol while top layer under Capt. McGregor got East and attacked E.A.

I noticed one of top patrol getting good bursts at a Fokker when the latter dived away with black smoke coming from fuselage. As E.A. came down he pulled out of dive and I got in a burst with both guns at very close range. E.A. then seemed to have some difficulty in getting control. Meantime I sat on his tail and got in several more bursts until about 3,000 feet, when I saw him crash at Sheet 36 B.12. This was confirmed by Capt. Brewster who came down with me.

APPENDICES

Appendix XXXIII

Lieutenant O.A. Ralston's Combat Report, 24 July 1918

Squadron:	No.85
Type and No. of Aeroplane:	S.E.5A E/1398
Armament:	1 Vickers & 1 Lewis
Pilot:	Lieut. O.A. Ralston, (U.S.A.S.)
Observer:	
Date:	24th July, 1918
Time:	10-35 a.m.
Locality:	N.W. Armentières
Duty:	Offensive Patrol
Height:	11,000 feet
Result	{Destroyed One {Driven down out of control {Driven down

Remarks on Hostile Aircraft: One Fokker Biplane. Colour Green & Black.

NARRATIVE

While on patrol in formation of four at about 12,000 feet we sighted six E.A. stating to dive on our lower formation. We circled quickly and apparently took the E.A. by complete surprise. I fired at close range on a Fokker from the side. This machine went into a spin. Then attacked another from the rear and to the side. After firing a long burst the E.A. (Fokker Biplane) went slowly to the side and dived past the vertical I dived after him firing my drum of Lewis. The E.A. stayed in the dive until it crashed. I followed to 4,000 feet before flattening out.

APPENDICES

Appendix XXXIV

Lieutenant D.C. Inglis's Combat Report, 24 July 1918

Squadron: No.85
Type and No. of Aeroplane: S.E.5A E/1294
Armament: 1 Vickers & 1 Lewis
Pilot: Lieut. D.C. Inglis
Observer:
Date: 26th July, 1918
Time: 5.30 a.m.
Locality: Lestrem
Duty: Special Mission
Height: 200 feet

Result   {Destroyed   One
                                    {Driven down out of control
                                    {Driven down

Remarks on Hostile Aircraft: Two-seater. Type unknown.

NARRATIVE

While following Major Mannock in search of two-seater E.A.'s we observed an E.A. two-seater coming towards the Line and turned away to gain height, and dived to get east of E.A. E.A. saw us just too soon and turned East, Major Mannock turned and got in a good burst when he pulled away. I got in a good burst at very close range after which E.A. went into a slow left hand spiral with flames coming out of his right side. I watched him go straight into the ground and go up in a large cloud of black smoke and flame.
I then turned and followed Major Mannock back at about 200 feet. About half way back I saw a flame come out of the right hand side of his machine after which he apparently went down out of control. I went into a spiral down to 50 feet and saw machine go straight into the ground and burn. I saw no one leave the machine and then started for the line climbing slightly; at about 150 feet there was a bang and I was smothered in petrol, my engine cut out so I switched off and made a landing 5 yards behind out front line.

Appendix XXXV

Captain A.C. Randall's Combat Report, 31 July 1918

Squadron:	No.85
Type and No. of Aeroplane:	S.E.5A C.6454
Armament:	1 Vickers & 1 Lewis
Pilot:	Capt. A.C. Randall
Observer:	
Date:	31st July, 1918
Time:	8.5 p.m.
Locality:	S.E. Estaires
Duty:	Offensive Patrol
Height:	6,000 feet
Result	{Destroyed 1 {Driven down out of control {Driven down

Remarks on Hostile Aircraft: Two-seater Albatross. Scarlet Fuselage. Green Planes.

NARRATIVE

At 8 p.m. saw two-seater E.A. making towards Line South of Estaires. Patrol cut E.A. off but another S.E. Patrol dived at E.A. from Lines and E.A. went East. Patrol climbed towards Merville and then East towards Armentières.

Getting East of E.A. Patrol dived and I got into firing position at very close range of first E.A. Fired good burst from both guns and seeing E.A. start to smoke drew away. E.A. then burst into flames and crashed into village of Vieille Chapelle causing large conflagration. Height at termination of fight 4,000 ft.

This was confirmed by Lieut. Rorison, U.S.A.S.

Appendix XXXVI

Captain M.C. McGregor's Combat Report, 3 August 1918

Squadron:	No.85
Type and No. of Aeroplane:	S.E.5A E.3922
Armament:	1 Vickers & 1 Lewis
Pilot:	Capt. M.C. McGregor
Observer:	
Date:	3rd August, 1918
Time:	8-10 a.m.
Locality:	East of Bailleul
Duty:	Offensive Patrol
Height:	13,000 feet

Result {Destroyed   One
        {Driven down out of control
        {Driven down

Remarks on Hostile Aircraft: Fokker Biplane.

NARRATIVE

While leading patrol of three S.E.s I obtained position in the sun, east of five E.A. which were being decoyed by patrol lead by Lieut. Longton. We attacked when E.A. dived on bottom patrol. Getting on one E.A.'s tail I fired a good burst from both guns. Pulling out because of my cowling coming loose. I observed E.A. going down completely out of control. This was confirmed by Capt. Canning, 79 Squadron and Capt. Carruthers of my patrol who saw it crash near Steenwerke.
Capt. Carruthers also got into good position on another E.A. which went out of control, but was afterwards seen flattening out. E.A. were driven East.

APPENDICES

Appendix XXXVII

Lieutenant W.H. Longton's Combat Report, 9 August 1918

Squadron:	No.85
Type and No. of Aeroplane:	S.E.5A D.6963
Armament:	1 Lewis & 1 Vickers
Pilot:	Lieut. W.H. Longton
Observer:	
Date:	9th August, 1918
Time:	7-40 a.m.
Locality:	Sheet 36 B.7a
Duty:	Offensive Patrol
Height:	4,000 feet
Result	{Destroyed One {Driven down out of control {Driven down

Remarks on Hostile Aircraft: Albatross 2-seater. White tail. Mottled green fuselage.

NARRATIVE

Diving with Capt. Randall on E.A. two-seater from the East, Capt. Randall attacked same at close range, and then pulled out, apparently with gun stoppage. I then got to very close range of E.A.'s tail, and got in good burst with both guns killing the observer who hung over the side, the E.A. started to smoke and then burst into flames, and crashed at Sheet 36 B.7a. This was confirmed by rest of patrol. Height at termination of combat 3,000 feet.

Appendix XXXVIII

Captain A.C. Randall's Combat Report, 9 August 1918

Squadron:	No.85
Type and No. of Aeroplane:	S.E.5A C.6454
Armament:	Lewis & 1 Vickers
Pilot:	Capt. A.C. Randall
Observer:	
Date:	9th August, 1918
Time:	7-55 a.m.
Locality:	Sheet 36 G 10c
Duty:	Offensive patrol
Height:	4,000 feet
Result	{Destroyed One {Driven down out of control {Driven down
Remarks on Hostile Aircraft:	Albatross two-seater. Camouflaged brown and green.

NARRATIVE

Seeing E.A. two-seater over Ploegsteert, Patrol went North to Ypres climbing through clouds. Turned South & dived through clouds East of E.A., which was now working towards Bailleul. I then got to very close range on E.A. & opened fire with both guns; on guns stopping pulled out & E.A. was then attacked by Lt. Longton & eventually took fire & crashed at Sheet 36 B.7a.

Patrol then worked South towards Merville and allowed another E.A. two-seater to come up to line by Steenwerke. Patrol then cut off this E.A. & getting to very close range I got in long burst from both guns when E.A. went down in very steep dive & crashed at Sheet 36 G 10c. This was confirmed by Lt. Longton & other Patrol. Height at termination 3,000 feet.

Appendix XXXIX

No.85 Squadron Combat Report, 22 August 1918

Squadron:	No.85
Type and No. of Aeroplane:	S.E.6A
	(a) D.6963
	(b) E.3922
	(c) E.3983
	(d) D.6955
	(e) D.6454
	(f) C.1904
Armament:	1 Vickers & 1 Lewis
Pilot:	(a) Lt. W.H. Longton
	(b) Lt. J.W. Warner
	(c) Lt. O.A. Ralston (U.S.A.S.)
	(d) Capt. M.C. McGregor
	(e) Capt. A.C. Randall
	(f) Capt. S.B. Horn
Observer:	
Date:	22nd August, 1918
Time:	(a) 4-50 p.m.
	(b) 4-50 p.m.
	(c) 4-50 p.m.
	(d) 4-50 p.m.
	(e) 4-50 p.m.
	(f) 4-50 p.m.
Locality:	(a) Haut-Allaines
	(b) Clery-sur-Somme
	(c) N.W. of Peronne
	(d) N.W. of Peronne
	(e) Maricourt
	(f) Suzanne
Duty:	Offensive Patrol
Height:	11,000 feet
Result	{Destroyed (a, b, c, d) Four
	{Driven down out of control (e, f) Two
	{Driven down

Remarks on Hostile Aircraft: (a) Fokker Biplane. Yellow bands round fuselage.
(b) Fokker Biplane. Black & white check tail.
(c) Fokker Biplane. Green & yellow bands round fuselage.
(d) Fokker Biplane. Not noticed.
(e) Fokker Biplane. Green & brown.
(f) Fokker Biplane. Orange nose. Green & black fuselage.

NARRATIVE

(A)   Followed patrol leader under formation of E.A., turned under them, E.A. attacked and saw E.A. on S.E.5's tail, so dived on to it getting in good burst. E.A. half rolled and dived away East, dived after E.A. and got onto his tail getting in good burst at close range. E.A. went over vertical on to his back, and crashed at N.W. of Haut-Allaines. This was also seen by Lt. Warner. Height at termination of combat 2,000 feet. I also saw an E.A. turn over, and crash on landing N. of Clery-sur-Somme followed closely by an S.E.5 marked with the letter "C" which is Lt. Warner.

(B) While on Offensive Patrol on the 22nd, the patrol attacked nine E.A. I dived on one, but had to pull away to avoid collision with other S.E.'s. After circling I saw one S.E. coming back to the line with E.A. on his tail. I dived at him and he half rolled, and doing the same I put a long burst from close range into him, then he dived vertically to within a few hundred feet of the ground. I followed him down to 1,500 feet and saw him pull out of his dive and try to land, but he crashed and turned over on his back on the ground. This was confirmed crashed by Lieut. Longton. I also saw E.A. slightly East of me come down out of control and crash, followed by S.E. with letter "L" on it, which is Lieut. Longton.

(C)   About 4-50 p.m. Squadron in three flights at different layers attacked 9 E.A. Fokker biplanes. Our flight of 5 machines, led by Capt. McGregor, attacked from the South. The Huns immediately dived on our lower formation a little lower and East of us. I fired a burst into one who spiralled away. I then attacked another and got a short burst into him with both guns. He dived and I followed until at 3,000 feet he flattened out, when I fired about 50 rounds into him. His right extension of his top plane flew into pieces, and he went into a spin and crashed a short distance N.W. of Peronne.

(D) Attacked one of nine Fokker Biplanes which were diving on lower formation. From point blank range fired 150 rounds. E.A. continued to fly straight until he slowly went into a wide torque spin. For a few seconds it looked as if he would go into flames, Lt. Baldwin & myself distinctly seeing a flash of flame in cockpit. I observed E.A. still out of control for three thousand feet losing sight of him when I started manoeuvring with a second E.A.
Lieut. Baldwin confirms this.

(E) About 4-45 p.m. saw E.A. formation coming South from Arras. Led bottom layer East & then under E.A. formation when our top layer dived on E.A. out of sun. Got to very close range on 1 E.A. & gave him large burst, when he turned on his back & went down completely out of control. Owing to elevator controls being shot away by another E.A. I had to leave formation. Lieut. Benzies also saw this machine going down completely out of control.

(F) While leading the top formation, the lower patrol was dived on by nine E.A. I dived on an E.A. which was an S.E.'s tail. I fired about 60 rounds into it and E.A. went down completely out of control. I could not see it down to the ground as I had to cure a stoppage. I watched it doing a spiral falling lock for 4,000 feet.

Confirmation.
I saw Capt. Horn fire at E.A. which went down completely out of control in broad spiral for 6,000 feet. Was unable to follow it further because of nearness of other E.A.

Appendix XL

Lieutenant J.W. Warner's Combat Report, 15 September 1918

Squadron:	No.85
Type and No. of Aeroplane:	S.E.5A E.3922
Armament:	1 Vickers & 1 Lewis
Pilot:	Lieut. J.W. Warner
Observer:	
Date:	15-9-18
Time:	6-5 p.m.
Locality:	Bourlon Wood
Duty:	Line Patrol
Height:	9,000 feet

Result {Destroyed   One
       {Driven down out of control
       {Driven down

Remarks on Hostile Aircraft: Fokker Biplane. Dark green & yellow camouflaged.

NARRATIVE

While on patrol on the evening of the 5th, the formation attacked 5 E.A. but had to pull away owing to a top formation diving down on A patrol of Camels coming up from the south drove off the top formation of E.A. thus allowing us to continue attack. I half rolled on to E.A. who had straggled slightly and owing to his not seeing me, I got to very close range before firing. After firing one long burst, E.A. dived vertically the tail falling off, this E.A. was last seen N.W. of Bourlon Wood at the height of 5,000 feet.

APPENDICES

Appendix XLI

Second Lieutenant R.A.H. Lloyd's Combat Report, 16 September 1918

Squadron:	No. 85
Type and No. of Aeroplane:	S.E.5A C/5978
Armament:	1 Vickers & 1 Lewis
Pilot:	2/Lieut. R.A.H. Lloyd
Observer:	
Date:	16th September, 1918
Time:	6-45 p.m.
Locality:	Biache
Duty:	Offensive Patrol
Height:	14,000 feet
Result	{Destroyed One {Driven down out of control {Driven down

Remarks on Hostile Aircraft: 4 Fokker Biplanes in V formation.

NARRATIVE

Whilst on patrol at 14,000 feet at 6.45 p.m. I observed 4 hostile aircraft (Fokker Biplanes) 1,000 feet below flying East above the River Scarpe. Being some distance [behind the] remainder of the flight, and unable to point out the E.A. to the latter, I approached to within 50 yards of the rear machine of the hostile formation and fired two short bursts with both guns. Flame was seen immediately to issue from side of E.A., which fell simultaneously over on its side and went down in flames. The remainder of the patrol confirmed this.

APPENDICES

Appendix XLII

Captain S.B. Horn's Combat Report, 17 September 1918

Squadron:	No.85
Type and No. of Aeroplane:	S.E.5A C/1904
Armament:	1 Vickers & 1 Lewis
Pilot:	Capt. S.B. Horn MC
Observer:	
Date:	17th September, 1918
Time:	2.10 p.m.
Locality:	Graincourt-lez-Havrincourt
Duty:	Offensive Patrol
Height:	5,000 feet

Result {Destroyed   One
       {Driven down out of control
       {Driven down

Remarks on Hostile Aircraft: Two-seater. Type unknown.

NARRATIVE

Whilst on Patrol I saw a two-seater working just North of Havrincourt Wood. I dived down on E.A. and fired a short burst at long range, the E.A. dived below the clouds, when I got below the clouds I saw E.A. burning on the ground slightly S.E. of Graincourt-les-Havrincourt.

Confirmation.
I saw this E.A. burning on the ground.
I saw the two-seater and later saw trail of smoke and machine burning on ground.

Appendix XLIII

Lieutenant J.W. Warner's Combat Report, 25 September 1918

Squadron:	No. 85
Type and No. of Aeroplane:	S.E.5A. E/3922
Armament:	1 Vickers & 1 Lewis
Pilot:	Lieut. J.W. Warner
Observer:	
Date:	25th September, 1918
Time:	5-55 p.m.
Locality:	Urvillers
Duty:	Offensive Patrol
Height:	2,000 feet
Result	{Destroyed One {Driven down out of control {Driven down
Remarks on Hostile Aircraft:	4 Fokker Biplanes. Camouflaged, with blue on fuselage.

NARRATIVE

While on Patrol on the 25th, the formation dived on 4 E.A. which were attacking a French two-seater. I dived on to one which was on two-seater's tail, he saw me before I got to close range and turned away, I half rolled and getting behind him put in a burst from close range with both guns. E.A. dived steeply with black smoke coming from machine, and on crashing burst into flames, and burnt on the ground.
This E.A. was confirmed by Capt. McGregor and the rest of the formation.

APPENDICES

Appendix XLIV

Captain M.C. McGregor's and Lieutenant P.D. d'Albenas' Combat Report, 8 October 1918

Squadron:	No.85
Type and No. of Aeroplane:	S.E.5A C.1143
	S.E.5A E.5695
Armament:	1 Vickers & 1 Lewis
Pilot:	Capt. M.C. McGregor
	Lieut. P.D. d'Albenas
Observer:	
Date:	8-10-18
Time:	1300
Locality:	E. of Maretz
Duty:	Balloon Attack
Height:	1,000 feet
Result	{Destroyed One
	{Driven down out of control
	{Driven down

Remarks on Hostile Aircraft: Balloon.

NARRATIVE

Attacked balloon north east of Maretz accompanied by Lieut. d'Albenas. Both fired from close range and balloon went down in flames. Machine gun fire from the ground intense, but not accurate. Observers escaped in parachutes.

APPENDICES

Appendix XLV

Lieutenant D.C. Inglis' Combat Report, 9 October 1918

Squadron:	No.85
Type and No. of Aeroplane:	S.E.5A E.3954
Armament:	1 Vickers & 1 Lewis
Pilot:	Lieut. D.C. Inglis
Observer:	
Date:	9th October, 1918
Time:	1635
Locality:	57B. W.10 b76
Duty:	Offensive Patrol
Height:	4,000 feet
Result	{Destroyed One {Driven down out of control {Driven down

Remarks on Hostile Aircraft: Fokker Biplane. White tail.

NARRATIVE

While leading "C" Flight on ground strafe, I dived down on transport and then noticed 5 E.A. below us, and dived on to the tail of a Fokker and got in a good burst on which his nose went down and he dived straight into the ground and burst into flames.
This was not observed by rest of patrol as we got separated chasing different Huns.

APPENDICES

Appendix XLVI

Captain C.B.R. MacDonald's Combat Report, 23 October 1918

Squadron: No.85
Type and No. of Aeroplane: S.E.5A E.5987
Armament: 1 Vickers & 1 Lewis
Pilot: Capt. C.B.R. MacDonald
Observer:
Date: 23-10-18
Time: 1005
Locality: Le Quesnoy
Duty: Offensive Patrol
Height: 4,000

Result   {Destroyed   One Balloon
                                {Driven down out of control
                                {Driven down

Remarks on Hostile Aircraft: 1 E.K.B. Black crosses on sides.

NARRATIVE

Saw a single balloon at 2,000 feet at Leuvignies lez Quesnoy left formation signalling Capt. McGregor, and attacked it. Fired on balloon with Vickers and followed with Lewis at close range. Both guns jammed, pulled out and dived on balloon again, getting in a good burst (?0 Rounds). Turned away to lines and saw balloon on fire being pulled towards ground. Termination of attack 500 feet.

Notes and References

Introduction to the New, Extended Edition
1. Middlebrook, Martin, *The Kaiser's Battle* (Pen and Sword, Barnsley, 2007).
2. Grinnell-Milne, Duncan, *Wind in the Wires* (Hurst and Blackett, Ltd, London, 1933), p.19.
3. Lewis, Cecil, *Sagittarius Rising* (Peter Davis, London, 1936), p.11.
4. The National Archives (TNA), AIR/11547/204/78/6.
5. TNA, AIR/680/21/13/2207; Report G9 'on accidents to Sopwith Camels with special reference to spinning' prepared by the Accidents Committee of the Advisory Committee for Aeronautics.
6. Winter, Denis, *First of the Few: Fighter Pilots of the First World War* (University of Georgia Press, 1983).
7. Hansard, Vol.107, cc1244-5W; House of Commons debate 27 June 1918.
8. MacLanachan, William 'McScotch', *Fighter Pilot* (Newnes, London, 1920).
9. TNA, AIR/11547/204/78/6.
10. Shores, Christopher, Franks, Norman, and Guest, Russell, *Above the Trenches, A Complete Record of the Fighter Aces and Units of the British Empire Air Forces 1915-1920* (Grub Street, London, 1990), p.348.
11. *The Yorkshire Post*, Wednesday, 3 August 1927.
12. Douglas, Sholto, *Years of Combat* (Collins, London, 1963), p.294.
13. Money, R.R., *Flying and Soldiering* (Ivor Nicholson and Watson, London, 1936), p.85.
14. Vaughan, David K., *Letters from a War Bird, The World War 1 Correspondence of Elliott White Springs* (The University of South Carolina Press, 2012), p.285.
15. TNA, AIR/76/173; Service record of Horace Frederick Fulford.
16. *Flight Magazine*, 15 June 1939.
17. Flying Officer David Fulford DFC, RAFVR, was serving with 611 Squadron when he was killed on 2 November 1942. He is commemorated on the Runnymede Memorial. Sergeant John Michael Fulford RAFVR, a pilot with 150 Squadron, was aged 22 when he was killed on 8 May 1941. He was buried in Nantes (Pont-du-Cens) Communal Cemetery.
18. Shores, Franks, and Guest, *op cit*, p.348.

NOTES AND REFERENCES

19. Oughton, Frederick, *The Personal Diary of 'Mick' Mannock VC, DSO (2 bars), MC (1 bar)* (Spearman, London, 1966), p.201.
20. Cunningham, G.H., *Mac's Memoirs: The Flying Life of Squadron Leader McGregor* (A.H. and A.W. Reed, New Zealand, 1937), p.59.

'The Flying Foxes': A Brief History of 85 Squadron
21. Hamer, A.C., *A Short History of No. 85 Squadron* (Services Publishing, Corby, undated).
22. Shores, Franks, and Guest, *op cit*, p.77.
23. Cunningham, G.H., *op cit*, p.54.
24. Shores, Franks, and Guest, *op cit*, p.275.
25. TNA, AIR 1/1227/204/5/2634.
26. Vaughan, David K., *op cit*, p.162.
27. Shores, Franks, and Guest, *op cit*, p.255.
28. MacLanachan, William 'McScotch', *op cit*.
29. TNA, AIR 1/1227/204/5/2634.
30. Shores, Franks, and Guest, *op cit*, p.199.
31. TNA, AIR 1/1227/204/5/2634.
32. Jones, James Ira Thomas 'Taffy', *King of Air Fighters* (Nicholson and Watson, London, 1934).
33. Cunningham, G.H., *op cit*.

Part I: The UK and Training, 20 September 1917 to 20 May 1918
34. RMS *Carmania* was a British ocean liner designed by Leonard Peskett and built by John Brown and Company for the Cunard Line. During the First World War *Carmania* was converted to an armed merchant cruiser.
35. Colonel Leslie MacDill. Learned to fly in 1915. Killed in a flying accident on 9 November 1938; the USAF named one if its bases after him.
36. Lieutenant Lawrence Kingsley Callahan DFC served with 85 Squadron and the US 148th Aero Squadron. He claimed four destroyed, one out of control. Re-joined the USAAF in the Second World War.
37. Captain Elliott White Springs DSC (US), DFC, the author of this book, served on 85 Squadron and US 148th Aero Squadron. Claimed ten and two shared destroyed, three and one shared out of control. Later a successful businessman.
38. Captain Fiorello Henry La Guardia is best known for being the 99th Mayor of New York City for three terms from 1934 to 1945. He joined up in 1916 and served in Italy, receiving the Italian War Cross and reaching the rank of Major.
39. Albert Spalding was a famous American concert violinist who toured Europe before the war and after the Armistice played for the New York Symphony Orchestra. He served in Italy in the First World War, becoming, at one point, aide-de-camp to Major Fiorello Le Guardia. Awarded the Cross of the Crown of Italy. During the Second World War, Assistant Secretary of State Adolf Berle successfully urged Spalding to accept an assignment with the Office of Strategic Services. He was posted to London, for six weeks, and then served in

North Africa until he was ordered to Naples where he was attached to the Psychological Warfare Division of SHAEF. In 1944, Spalding gave a legendary concert to thousands of terrified refugees stranded in a cave near Naples during an air raid.

40. William L. Deetjen. Commenced his air force training in Cambridge, Massachusetts, completing it in the UK. Serving in 104 Squadron RAF, he was shot down and killed whilst flying over the front near Nancy on 30 June 1918.
41. Paul Stewart Winslow. A member of the first contingent of fifty-two US cadets to arrive in the UK on 4 September 1917. He served with 56 Squadron from 29 June to 12 September 1918.
42. Alan Winslow served with *Escadrille* N152 and then the US 94th Aero Squadron. Became a prisoner of war on 31 July 1918.
43. Harrowby Camp near Grantham, Lincolnshire, was an army camp for machine-gun training and a gunnery ground school for the RFC.
44. The de Havilland 6 two-seat trainer.
45. Thetford in Suffolk was a busy RFC (and, in time, RAF) airfield with Nos. 35, 38 and 77 squadrons being formed there in 1917, followed by 80 Squadron in 1917 and 128 Squadron in 1918. It was also home to Nos. 51 and 119 squadrons.
46. The Henry Farman types used were the Longhorn and Shorthorn.
47. The Grafton Galleries in London were considered a fashionable venue during this period. They were renowned for exhibitions of photographs of the war as well as Red Cross fund raising events.
48. The airfield at London Colney was five miles south of Hatfield. As well as being the home to 74 Squadron at the time, the airfield was also the base for 56 Training Squadron.
49. Avro 504 series of training aircraft, which had its first flight in 1913.
50. Beatrice Gladys 'Bea' Lillie was a Canadian-born British actress and singer.
51. More specifically the Sopwith Pup, Spad VII and Avro 504.
52. The Curtiss JN-4.
53. Cadet Harold Ainsworth. Killed on 19 December 1917 whilst flying Curtiss JN-3 serial number A1259.
54. Cadet Joseph Sharpe. Killed flying a D.H.6, serial number A9761, at 48 Training Squadron, 7 January 1918.
55. Captain (later Squadron Leader) Alexander Augustus Norman Dudley Pentland, MC, DFC, AFC. He was credited with ten 'kills' prior to being injured by an artillery shell whilst flying his Spad and he was relegated to instructing where he met Grider. Pentland eventually went back to the front and flew with 87 Squadron. He was known as the 'Wild Australian' and ended the war with twenty-three claims, earning him a DFC and ranking him as the fifth highest scoring Australian. He also served with 56 Training Squadron at Hounslow.
56. Allen W. Bevin became a pilot with the 8th Aero Squadron and served in Italy.
57. Captain Roderick L. Keller MC and Bar. Killed while test flying a Sopwith Snipe, serial number E7998, at 41 TDS, 15 August 1918.

NOTES AND REFERENCES

58. Cadet Roy O Garver. Killed while flying a Sopwith Camel of 3 Training Squadron at Eastbourne Airfield, East Sussex, on 28 January 1918.
59. Captain (later Wing Commander) Alan Duncan Bell-Irving MC and Bar. A Canadian Ace who served with 60 Squadron, claiming five aircraft and one balloon, as well as one aircraft out of control. He was subsequently wounded and relegated to instructing.
60. Lieutenant Colonel Spencer Bertram Horn . Was credited by the end of the war with thirteen victories. Initially served on 60 Squadron, but was later posted to 85 Squadron as a founder member.
61. This accident actually occurred on 8 February. Lieutenant Douglas Quirk Ellis, a Canadian serving with 74 Squadron, was killed in the incident.
62. Cadet Lindley Haines De Garmo was killed whilst flying a Spad S7 of 56 Training Squadron on 16 February 1918.
63. Cadet Harold Kidder Bulkley was attached to 85 Squadron and was flying a Sopwith Pup when he was killed on 18 February 1918.
64. Cadet Donald E. Carlton was killed on 19 February 1918 whilst flying with 48 Training Squadron in an R.E.8. The accident occurred at Spittlegate, not Spiddlegate.
65. Cadet Joseph Frederick Stillman was badly wounded in the crash of an Avro 504, whilst serving with 74 Squadron, on 8 February 1918. He died of his injuries on 23 February 1918.
66. An Armstrong Whitworth FK3.
67. Lieutenant Frank G. Montgommery was killed whilst flying in an Armstrong Whitworth FK3 at 1 (Auxiliary) School of Air Gunnery. Second Lieutenant T.W. Manley RFC was also on board.
68. Cadet Clark Brockway Nicholl was killed whilst flying a B.E.2e on 18 February 1918.
69. Cadet W. Lloyd Ludwig was killed whilst flying an S.E.5a with 28 Training Squadron on 28 February 1918.
70. First Lieutenant Earl M. Hammer was later to be killed in action in France on 19 May 1918 whilst an 84 Squadron S.E.5a (serial number C6499).
71. Lieutenant Gustav Hermann Kissell was later killed in action, on 12 April 1918, whilst flying a Sopwith Camel from 43 Squadron.
72. Lieutenant Alexander Matthews. Killed in action during an air raid on Bertangles on 24 May 1918.
73. Lieutenant Richard Mortimer was killed whilst flying a Sopwith Camel with 73 Squadron on 22 May 1918.
74. The Hanriot HD.1 was a French single-seat fighter produced in 1916.
75. First Lieutenant Andrew Carl Ortmayer was killed whilst flying a Sopwith Camel at the school of aerial fighting on 7 March 1918.
76. Captain C.E. Foggin; later killed in a car crash in 1918.
77. First Lieutenant Thomas Cushman Nathan. Killed whilst flying a S.E.5a at the School of Aerial Fighting on 29 March 1918.
78. Lieutenant George Agustus Vaughn was posted to 84 Squadron RAF in May

NOTES AND REFERENCES

1918. This unit was based at Bertangles and was commanded by Sholto Douglas. Vaughn was attached to 'B' Flight, led by Hugh 'Dingbat' Saunders. Flying the S.E.5a, he claimed seven victories in his time with the squadron. In August 1918, Vaughn was transferred to the 17th Aero Squadron, United States Air Service, with which he flew the Sopwith Camel, claiming another six victories. He was awarded the US Distinguished Service Cross and British Distinguished Flying Cross.

79. Lieutenant Bonham Hagood Bostik. Travelled to the UK on *Carmania*. Attended ground school at Oxford; after training he was posted to 43 Squadron RAF. Wounded on 18 April 1918.
80. Later Air Marshal William Avery 'Billy' Bishop VC, CB, DSO and BAR, MV, DFC, ED (8 February 1894–11 September 1956). He took over command of 85 Squadron in March 1918.
81. In the book *Mac's Memoirs: The Flying Life of Squadron Leader McGregor* by G.H. Cunningham it states: 'Bishop was given practically a free hand in the selection of his pilots. Foremost among those chosen was Mac, whose previous war experience and marked flying ability made him a valuable acquisition. He was promoted to Flight Lieutenant and posted to C Flight, as deputy leader under Captain K.K Horn [Spencer B. Horn]. The squadron contained two other New Zealand pilots (Lieutenants J Canning and D.C. Inglis); the three Americans (Lieutenants E.W. Springs, L.K. Callahan and J. McG Grider) immortalised in the book *War Birds*; two Australians; one South African; two Scots; and six Englishmen.'
82. Lieutenant Garland 'Jake' Stahl was a player manager of the 1912 World Series Champion Boston Red Sox baseball team. On his return to the US he became, in 1919, President of the Washington Park Bank. He died in 1922 aged 43.
83. This is most likely to be Lieutenant Joseph R. Sandford. Sandford was killed in action on 12 April 1918 whilst flying Sopwith Camels with 54 Squadron.
84. Lieutenant Errol Zistel. Flew with 43 Squadron and then later with the 17th and 148th Aero Squadrons which were using the Sopwith Camel. Reached the rank of Major General, serving post-war in the Air National Guard.
85. Lieutenant George Whiting. With the RFC Certificate No.9696 he was posted to 43 Squadron in the spring of 1918, after which he joined the 148th Aero Squadron in July 1918.
86. Lieutenant William Dolley Tipton. First flew with 3 Squadro,n gaining two victories. He later served with the American 17th Aero Squadron. Awarded the British DFC. Seeing service in the Second World War, he gained the rank of Colonel but was killed in 1945 whilst flying a P-47 Thunderbolt.
87. Captain (later squadron leader) Malcolm Charles McGregor DFC and Bar. A New Zealand who served with Nos. 54, 91 and 85 squadrons. He scored one shared balloon, six destroyed aircraft and four out of control. He was killed in an air crash in New Zealand on 19 February 1936.
88. A Canadian with previous service in the Royal Engineers, Captain Charles Beverley MacDonald had served with Bishop at Royal Military College.

NOTES AND REFERENCES

89. Captain Edwin Louis 'Lobo' Benbow had seen service in France with the Royal Field Artillery since 1915. He became an Observer in the RFC in 1916, before undertaking pilot training. He served with 40 Squadron before joining 85 Squadron. He was credited with six, as well as one shared and one out of control. He was killed in action with 85 Squadron on 30 May 1918.
90. Captain G.B.A. Baker MC, previously of Nos. 19 and 23 squadrons.
91. Lieutenant Colonel Victor John Hastings MC, MID.
92. Everard Richard Calthrop was a British railway engineer and inventor who patented his first parachute in 1913.
93. Introduced into service in 1918, the Sopwith Dolphin Mk.I used the Hispano-Suiza 8B engine.
94. First Lieutenant George Orren Middleditch was killed while flying a D.H.4 at 44 Training Squadron with Cadet Pudrith on 12 March 1918.
95. Cadet Chester Pudrith died of on 30 April 1918 from injuries received during the crash with Middleditch.
96. Lord Leconsfield was probably Edward Scawen Wyndham, 5th Baron Leconfield.
97. Admiral William Sowden Sims, commander of all US naval forces operating in Europe during the First World War.
98. General John Biddle. In 1918 he was sent to the UK to take charge of American troops in the country.
99. Probably Lieutenant Lawrence Bennett Loughram who was killed in action flying a S.E.5a with 60 Squadron on 29 July 1918.
100. A Canadian, Lieutenant John Randolph Stacey was previously with 86 Squadron. He was killed whilst flying a Sopwith Dolphin on 8 April 1918. In his book *Indigenous Peoples of the British Dominions and the First World War* (Cambridge University Press, 2011), Timothy C. Winegard states that Stacey had served in the 114th Battalion Canadian Expeditionary Force prior to serving in the RFC/RAF, adding that he was 'a Mohawk from Kahnawake, Quebec'.

The Middlesex Chronicle of Saturday, 13 April 1918, provides the following account under the heading 'Fatality to Canadian Airman': 'The circumstances relative to the death of Lieut. John Randolph Stacey, aged 24, a Canadian belonging to the Royal Air Force, who was killed whilst flying on Monday evening [8 April 1918], formed the subject of an inquiry conducted by Mr. Reginald Kemp, J.P., (Coroner for West Middlesex), at the Church-room, Montague-road, on Wednesday afternoon. Mr. R. Sargeant was foreman of the jury; Insp. Harris represented the police; and P.C. Butcher was coroner's officer. 'According to the evidence of Captain Dyer, R.A.M.C., when admitted to the Military Hospital on Monday evening Lt. Stacey was suffering from a compound fracture of the right thigh and concussion of the brain, and died shortly afterwards.

'Lt. William Cushing, R.A.F., stated that deceased had done 20 hours solo flying. He possessed exceptional courage, and at the time of the accident was flying for the first time a new scout machine. He started on the flight at about 6.20 p.m.

and left the ground with the tail of the machine down, with the result that the aeroplane stalled. He made a flat turn to the left, the nose of the machine went down, and a side-slip ensued. – In answer to questions, witness said deceased asked to be allowed to take the machine up. He was quite a fit and proper pilot to be allowed to do this, having done 17 hours on the elementary type, when 15 hours was generally considered sufficient. The accident was due to an error of judgement on the part of an inexperienced pilot in a new machine. – Replying to a juror, who asked a question as to the dragging of the tail of the machine on the ground, witness said Lt. Stacey attempted to climb before attaining flying speed. This, however, would not affect the controls.

'First Air Mechanic Scattergood testified as to the machine being in perfect condition before the accident.

'P.C. Ireland stated that while on point duty in the vicinity he saw the aeroplane ascend, fly over the huts in the direction of Bedfont, and then side slip and fall into a field in Staines-road, the engine being on. Assistance soon arrived and the airman was conveyed to hospital.

'Summing up, the Coroner said no doubt this unfortunate officer, more or less inexperienced, met his death through an error of judgement when trying a new machine. Of course airmen had to try new machines at some time or another, and deceased's superior officer thought he was fit to fly this particular machine. Clearly no blame attached to anybody, and the fatality was one of those deplorable accidents which occurred from time to time.

'The jury returned a verdict of "Death from shock from a fractured thigh and concussion of the brain caused by his aeroplane accidentally side-slipping to the ground."

'The deceased officer was a personality of extraordinary interest, being a Chief of the Iroquois Indians and of five other North American tribes. As the inquest evidence showed, he was giving promise of becoming a most efficient and skilful airman.

'Full military honours were accorded at the funeral which took place at Heston Churchyard at noon yesterday. The cortege formed outside the mortuary in Montague-road shortly after eleven o'clock, and comprised the band of the Depot Royal Fusiliers, which played appropriate marches en route, the gun carriage bearing the coffin, and a contingent of the Royal Air Force. The Rev. J. Burrough (Chaplain to the Forces) officiated at the interment.'

101. The Royal Aircraft Factory S.E.5a was fitted with a 200hp Hispano Suiza 8b V8 or the 200hp Wolseley Viper engine.
102. First Lieutenant Earl M. Hammer was killed whilst flying a S.E.5a with 84 Squadron on 19 May 1918.
103. Cadet Elwood Stanberry was killed whilst flying a Sopwith Camel with 45 Training Squadron on 12 April 1918.
104. Opened in 1873, The Criterion restaurant faces Piccadilly Circus. Still open today, it is described by one source as 'in the Top 10 most historic and oldest restaurants in the world'.

NOTES AND REFERENCES

105. Lieutenant Tommy J. Herbert of the S.E.5a-equipped 56 Squadron.
106. Lieutenant Paul Winslow, also of 56 Squadron.
107. Lieutenant Thomas Frederick Mooney was killed whilst flying an R.E.8 at the Central Despatch Pool, 22 April 1918.
108. Probably Cadet George Atherton Braden, who was killed whilst flying a S.E.5a of 2 School of Aerial Fighting, 5 April 1918.
109. The formation of the RAF occurred on 1 April 1918.
110. Manfred Albrecht Freiherr von Richtofen, known as the 'Red Baron', was officially credited with eighty victories.
111. The Bristol Scout first flew in 1914. A total of 374 were built, many being fitted with the 80hp Le Rhone 9c rotary engine.
112. This may well be a reference to the big German Gotha raid on London on 19 May 1918, although there were still several smaller raids around this time.
113. Cadet William Winslow Wait was killed on 9 May 1918 whilst flying a Spad S7 with 56 Training Squadron.
114. Lieutenant Eugene Hoy Barksdale; served with 41 Squadron RFC.
115. Cadet Clarence Horn Fry was killed on 4 May 1918 whilst flying a Spad S7 with 56 Training Squadron.
116. Florence Leonora Stewart was an English musical comedy actress known as Billie Carleton.
117. Major James Thomas Byford McCudden VC, DSO & Bar, MC & Bar, MM was an English flying Ace and among the most highly decorated airmen in British military history. Interestingly, the S.E.5a that he flew on 56 Squadron, which had the serial number B4981, was later flown by Captain C.M. Crowe, who was to become the CO of 85 Squadron. McCudden achieved thirty-one victories with this machine.
118. Lieutenant Gustav Herman Kissel of 43 Squadron; see previous notes.
119. Lieutenant Hash H. Gile was missing officially on 13 June 1918. He became a prisoner of war.
120. Lieutenant Robert J. Griffith was killed whilst flying a D.H.4, not a D.H Nine, of 188 Aero Squadron on 9 May 1918.
121. *Fair and Warmer* was a 1915 comedy play by the American writer Avery Hopwood
122. Lieutenant Joseph Sandford, 54 Squadron; see previous notes.
123. Princess Marie Louise of Schleswig-Holstein (Franziska Josepha Louise Augusta Marie Christina Helena; 12 August 1872–8 December 1956) was a granddaughter of Queen Victoria. As Fuldord noted, she presented 85 Squadron with its silver fox mascot.
124. First Lieutenant Earl Hammer was killed in action on 19 May 1918 whilst flying an S.E.5a of 84 Squadron.

Part II: The Western Front – 25 May 1918 and Beyond

125. Springs's log book notes that his first leg to Lympne, in S.E.5a serial number 1885, took fifty minutes. It was followed by a thirty-five minute Channel

NOTES AND REFERENCES

crossing to Marquise in France. The final short hop to Dunkirk, on 22 May 1918, took a further thirty minutes. He notes four aircraft did not complete the journey. See, David K. Vaughan, *Letters From A Warbird*, p.131.

126. Major General William 'Billy' Mitchell.
127. Lympne in Kent was home to No.8 Aircraft Acceptance Park and some of the RFC's Home Defence squadrons.
128. Croydon was used as a landing ground by Nos. 141 and 29 squadrons.
129. Marquise, between Calais and Boulogne, housed No.1 Aeroplane Supply Depot, ex St Omer, from April 1918, following the retreat during the German Spring Offensive. Part of No.1 Aircraft Depot, it supplied aircraft to units on the northern part of the front. Other elements of 1 AD were also based on Marquise, including No.1 Aircraft Repair Park and the Reception Park which received machines flown in from the UK.
130. No.11 Squadron RNAS reformed on 10 March 1918 as a bomber squadron at Petite-Synthe, Dunkirk, operating the D.H.4 and D.H.9. Its operations were mainly directed against the ports of Bruges, Zeebrugge and Ostende, in an attempt to hamper the German U-boat campaign. On 1 April 1918, with the merging of the RNAS and the Royal Flying Corps, it was renamed No.211 Squadron RAF. It later flew operations in support of the Belgian Army in Flanders. From October 1918 it operated as a photographic reconnaissance unit.
131. Lieutenant Alan F. Bonnalie DSO.
132. No.88 Squadron was based at Cappelle and was a fighter reconnaissance unit equipped with the Bristol F.2b.
133. An extract from a letter Springs sent home to his mother at this time detailed an incident involving Grider that makes interesting reading: "Mac pulled a good one yesterday. He went up late to practice shooting and he was told there was a ground target in an aerodrome nearby so he went over and fired several hundred rounds at it. A few moments later a voice over the telephone made the air blue. Twas the CO of the other aerodrome and he said one of our pilots had been over shooting up his wind vane and chasing his mechanics into dugouts and he wanted it stopped because several other machines had seen him doing it and thought it was a grand target and now they are all firing at it." This is mentioned in *War Birds* in early June. See, David K. Vaughan, *Letters From A Warbird*, p.135.
134. Correctly spelt Fort Mardyck, this defensive site west of Dunkirk was constructed in 1622. It gave its name to the surrounding community, though development means that since 2010 the commune of Fort-Mardyck is now part of Dunkirk.
135. Major Bishops' first claim with 85 Squadron was on 27 May and he wrote about the combat in a letter to his wife: "This morning I had my guns sighted again and a lot of other things adjusted … this afternoon at 04:00 I went out … and crossed [over the lines] after a big fat two seater. There were ten scouts up higher, so I came back [over the lines] and got up to 17,500 feet, then went over

to worry them from above. Suddenly, 200 feet below me, coming towards me appeared a two-seater. He saw me at practically the same moment I saw him, and turned to allow his observer to fire and also to beetle off east. I then … slipped under his tail and he, seeing this, lost his head and put his nose down for all he was worth. So I closed up to 125 yards and let him have ten from each gun. I think the first burst killed both. He sort of went half out of control, skidding to the left, and I closed up to fifty yards and got in thirty five more [rounds] from each gun.' See Kilduff, Peter, *Billy Bishop VC: Lone Wolf Hunter – The RAF Ace Re-examined*, p.142.

136. Captain Spencer Horn claimed a Pfalz DIII on 30 May 1918.
137. Major Bishop claimed an Albatross DIII on 28 and 29 May. Captain McGregor claimed a two seater on 29 May and in the book written by Cunningham he claims that first blood went to McGregor! Captain Horn claimed a Pfalz DIII on the 30th. Bishop claimed three further aircraft on 30th May (for his combat report see Appendix I), and two on 31 May (see Appendices II and III). Bishop subsequently wrote of these actions in a letter home: "Tonight [29 May] Benbow, Carruthers, Canning, Horn and McGregor went out for a practice patrol and met a lot of Huns, which they attacked. A big fight followed and McGregor got one. So that makes four for the squadron in three days, not bad for a new squadron which hasn't officially crossed the lines yet is it." See Kilduff, *op cit*, p.144.
138. In Springs's letter home to his mother on 28 May 1918 he makes a comment about Benbow which unfortunately was a trait that lead to his downfall: "Captain Benbow decided he'd go up this morning and stalk one himself. So up he goes and proceeds to approach a nice fat Hun unseen. But just about that time six Hun scouts dove on him and chased him all the way back amid a hail of bullets. He was awfully fed up about it". See, David K. Vaughan, *op cit*, p.138.
139. It is worth pointing out that Lieutenant Elliott White Springs scored his first victory on 1 June 1918, the victim being a Pfalz DIII which fell near La Gorgue. In a letter to his mother dated 3 June he wrote: "Just over the lines we saw Major Bishop and went over and joined him and then we saw my six friends [the enemy aircraft] of the day before when we were miles in Hunland. They were in different layers again only this time their scheme did not work, as Captain Horn and I took on the top two ones, it developed into a dogfight and for several minutes the sky was full of lead and two Huns started for home. The Major got one, I got one, and MacGregor got two." See, David K. Vaughan, *op cit*, p.145.
140. Lieutenant Donald C. Inglis DCM. A New Zealander, Inglis initially enlisted in the Royal Artillery, going on to serve in the Dardanelles during 1915, before he transferred to the RFC.
141. McGregor claimed two Pfalzs on 1 June 1918; see Appendix IV.
142. Captain Edwin Louis Benbow MC was 85 Squadron's first loss on the Western Front; he was shot down on 30 May 1918 whilst out on a patrol on his own as

a 'lone wolf'. Bishop was upset by his death, writing the following in a letter home: "We learned today that poor old Lobo [Benbow's nickname], bless him, was killed last night, he fell just inside our lines. His funeral is tomorrow. I would like to go, but I don't think I shall, and I'm not allowing any of the flying officers to go, it's too upsetting." See Kilduff, *op cit*, p.145. Born in Abbotsbury, Dorset, and the son of Mr. and Mrs. J. Benbow, of La Mortola, Ventimigila, Italy, Benbow, who was 22 at the time of his death, is buried in Duhallow A.D.S. Cemetery near Ypres. An obituary notice published at the time of his death stated: "He went to France on February 2nd, 1915, and served with his battery for about twelve months. He afterwards served as Observer with the Royal Flying Corps for eight months, then, qualifying as a pilot, did work for which he was decorated with the M.C. by the King at the Investiture in Hyde Park on June 2nd, 1917."

143. In a letter home to his mother in early June 1918, Springs commented: "We came down from hunting and counted noses and compared notes and found captain Benbow was not back. After two hours it was evident that he was down somewhere but we all said 'engine trouble' and let it go at that. The next morning no news. Finally in the afternoon we got word from an Archie battery up close to the front. Of course we all feel pretty bad about it and nobody forgot about it for some time but there was no hullaballoo and the subject has not been mentioned since. No rotten sentimentality about it and yet you'd be surprised how deeply these Englishmen feel things and how much sentimentality they have in their nature." See, David K. Vaughan, *op cit*, p.147.

144. Bishop claimed one 'kill' on 2 June and a pair of Albatross DVs on 4 June. It is likely, therefore, that the diary is out by a day. However, the facts about Bishop's score are correct as these claims took his score to fifty-nine at that point; McCudden had fifty-seven. Appendices V and VI for details of Bishop's combats.

145. In *Macs Memoirs*, Cunningham noted how animals were a big part of squadron life: "Pilots of his squadron had become keen on collecting live stock. The nucleus of the collection was four chow pups, born at the aerodrome at Hounslow, and smuggled across to France. As each pilot aimed at possessing some sort of pet, it became obligatory for anyone visiting nearby towns to secure any beastie he was able to 'borrow'. As a result the squadron possessed, in the course of months, a motley collection of assorted dogs, goats and even poultry". See Cunningham, *op cit*, p.55.

146. This was S.E.5a serial number C6490, it being written off. Bishop then received C1904. See Shores, Franks, and Guest, p.78.

147. According to Springs's diary, Lieutenant H.G. Thompson claimed one enemy aircraft on 4 June, although this cannot be confirmed. However, in a letter home on 5 June he wrote: "Larry almost got a Hun yesterday. He and the Major and Thompson took on eight Huns and got two of them. Larry hit his alright, but didn't see it crash so does not claim it. The Major and Thompson saw theirs go down and crash." See, David K. Vaughan, *op cit*, pp.149-50.

NOTES AND REFERENCES

148. Bishop claimed two Albatross DVs on the 4th. His next kill was on 15 June, whilst McGregor's was not until 27 June. However, it is likely that there may have been a patrol and combat but no claims in this period.
149. Captain Arthur Clunie Randall DFC originally enlisted in the Border Regiment, before transferring to the RFC. He had previously served on 32 Squadron. His first claim on 85 Squadron was on 18 June 1918.
150. Lieutenant Richard Mortimer was killed whilst flying a 73 Squadron Sopwith Camel on 22 May 1918.
151. Enoch Arnold Bennet was an English writer. He is best known as a novelist, but he also worked in other fields such as journalism, propaganda and film.
152. Lieutenant Howard G. Thompson.
153. According to Springs's flight log, Grider shot down a German aircraft on 10 June 1918.
154. The gunnery officer was Lieutenant H. Fulford, whose annotated copy of *War Birds* led to the publication of this edition.
155. McGregor lost his teeth whilst flying with 54 Squadron on 29 June 1917 when his engine stopped at 200 feet in a Sopwith Scout.
156. As Bishop was desk bound around this period in June it is likely that this comment relates to general tasks prior to this date.
157. Springs mentions in his log book that they escorted bombers to Zeebrugge on 6 June, and to Nieuport on 7 June 1918.
158. Lieutenant C. Roy Hall, a Canadian who was one of the founder members of 85 Squadron, was shot down to become a prisoner of war on 13 June 1918. Springs mentions this incident in his log book.
159. Bishop's letters state that the moving date was 10 June. However, McGregor's book disagrees and gives it as 14 June as per *War Birds*. Springs's log book stated that they flew down to St Omer on 11 June.
160. St Omer had previously been home to 29 Squadron, which was equipped with S.E.5as, 210 Squadron with Sopwith Camels, and briefly 54 Squadron.
161. Bishop had flown on 15 June and claimed one Pfalz – his sixtieth victory. This extended his lead over McCudden's fifty-seven and Mannock's forty-nine, as their tallies stood at that time. For details on Bishop's combat on that date see Appendix VII.
162. McGregor did indeed experience combat with the enemy on this date, as noted in his biography, during which he shot one blade from his propeller; see Appendix VIII for his more information. Bishop (see Appendix IX), Callahan (Appendix X), and Cunningham-Reid (Appendix XI) all had combats that day with subsequent claims.
163. Captain Spencer Horn was another who had a combat on 16 June, though his combat report has not survived. He claimed a Pfalz DIII near Neuve-Eglise.
164. Lieutenant Howard Thompson became a prisoner of war on this date, which is noted in Springs's flying log book. This combat is also mentioned in one of Bishop's letters to his wife: "It has been a very exciting day. Horn got a Hun, as did Callahan and Cunningham-Reid a balloon … I got two Huns, one in

NOTES AND REFERENCES

flames and one crashed. Thompson is missing, he landed under control"; see Kilduff, Peter, *op cit*, p.149.
165. A goat according to *Mac's Memoirs: The Flying Life of Squadron Leader McGregor*.
166. Lieutenant J.C. Rorison, USAS.
167. Billy Bishop claimed three enemy aircraft as destroyed on 17 June (see Appendix XII).
168. Cunningham-Reid claimed one whilst Springs shared one with John McGavock Grider, who was flying S.E.5a C1883. The latter claim was for a Rumpler two seater north of Lille; Springs reported he saw the enemy aircraft go down on a vertical dive and crash near the Menin Road. En route back to base they flew into cloud and were being hounded by German anti-aircraft fire. When springs emerged, Grider was not to be seen. Grider was reported killed in action on 18 June 1918. He has no known grave.
169. Springs later wrote: "We had already lost Benbow and Thompson and I got hell for losing Mac from Captain Horn, though I wasn't leading". From this point on, Springs continues the diary as if it where Grider writing it when actually the events are recalled from his diary's and notes. Some of Springs's papers are now held at the University of South Carolina, and they reveal that Springs's own diary and letters were the basis for a large part of the writing for this book, as also explained in *Letters from a Warbird* by David Vaughan. Other papers, as well as images, are held by the Springs Close Family Archives, Fort Mill, SC.
170. Bishop claimed two on 18 June; see Appendix XIII.
171. Lieutenant H. Thomson was officially missing as of 16 June, so a few days previous to the date recalled by Springs in this book.
172. Lieutenant Donovan Joseph Trapp was killed in action on 19 July 1917, not 19 June. The son of Mr. T.J. and Mrs. N.K. Trapp of 407, Agnus Street, New Westminster, British Columbia, Canada, 23-year-old Trapp is commemorated on a special memorial in Anzac Cemetery, Sailly-sur-la-Lys.
173. As mentioned, Lieutenant Alec Stratford Cunningham-Reid had claimed a balloon on 16 June; see again Appendix XI.
174. Bishop claimed five victories on the 19th, all in combat in the area around Ploegsteert; see Appendix XIV. This is mentioned in Springs's log book.
175. No loss can be found on this date or close to it.
176. Lieutenant Joseph Graham Trees; killed whole flying with the Central Flying School in a Sopwith Dolphin on 13 June 1918. Lieutenant Richard Brumbach Reed was killed whilst flying a D.H.9 on 5 June 1918. Captain W.J. Cairns flew in 1917 with 19 Squadron before becoming an instructor. He was shot down and killed on 1 June 1918, whilst with 74 Squadron.
177. This was the series of combats that occurred on 19 June and which are outlined in Appendix XIV.
178. This meal occurred on 20 June 1918.
179. This action is mentioned in *Mac's Memoirs: The Flying Life of Squadron Leader McGregor*: "During the dawn patrol on June 23rd, Seventy Four and Eighty

NOTES AND REFERENCES

Five conjointly fought a large 'circus'. The sky became so filled with manoeuvring aeroplanes that collisions were inevitable. The commanding officer of seventy four, Major Caldwell collided at 16,000 feet with a member of his squadron, Lieutenant Carlin." The latter was Sydney Carlin MC, DCM. Note that some sources state that this collision occurred in September 1918.

180. As far as can be ascertained, Captain Horn did not claim on this day and Springs claimed one on 25 June.
181. Major James Thomas Byford McCudden VC, DSO & Bar, MC & Bar, MM.
182. Major (later Air Commodore) Keith Logan 'Grid' Caldwell CBE, MC, DFC & Bar.
183. Captain (later Wing Commander) James Ira Thomas 'Taffy' Jones DSO, MC, DFC & Bar, MM.
184. Captain G.B.A. Baker MC had first flown with 19 Squadron during 1916 and 1917, moving on to 23 Squadron before arriving on 85 Squadron at Hounslow.
185. Neither Captain George Clapham Dixon nor Randall submitted a claim on this date. S mentioned previously, Lieutenant C. Roy Hall was a PoW from 13 June.
186. It has not been possible to establish any further information or details on Captain Webster.
187. The 17th Aero Squadron moved to Petit-Synthe on 20 June 1918; it became operational on 15 July. Captain Samuel B. Eckert (USA) was the Commanding Officer. His first unit was No.84 Squadron RFC, followed by No.80 Squadron before a posting to the 17th Aero Squadron.
188. Lieutenant William D. Tipton (USA) was originally with the Oxford Cadets. He was posted to 3 Squadron and then the 17th Aero; shot down and captured on 26 August 1918.
189. Lloyd A. Hamilton (USA) trained at Oxford before being posted No.3 Squadron and the 17th Aero Squadron. He was killed in action on 24 August 1918.
190. Morton L. Newhall (USA) originally trained in the USA. He was posted to No.84 Squadron RFC before moving to the 17th Aero Squadron.
191. Lieutenant Parr Hooper of No.32 Squadron; killed in action on 10 June 1918 while flying a SE.5a.
192. Lieutenant Charles Douglas of No.73 Squadron was killed in action whilst flying a Sopwith Camel on 11 June 1918.
193. Lieutenant Cunningham-Reid made two claims on this day, although only one combat report survives – see Appendix XV. It is also worth noting that Springs made his last claim with No.85 Squadron prior to his crash and posting. The victim was an unidentified two-seater, which he wrote about in a letter home dated 26 June 1918: "I had rather a surprise yesterday. I was some distance back of the patrol and saw a Hun two-seater about three miles across the lines so went for him. I expected about 30 seconds close quarters under his tail and then watch him go down in flames. It looked like cold meat. So I started my final drive about 2000 feet above him. I picked the wrong Hun. It resulted in a duel lasting about five minutes and in the end the Hun only dove into the

ground from 1000 feet. I hope the pilot is still alive, he was certainly a stout fellow; if his observer had been a good shot I wouldn't be writing this now". See David K. Vaughan, *op cit*, p.167.
194. Springs was probably shot down and wounded by *Leutnant* Josef Raesch of Jasta 43 on 27 June 1918. On recovery from his wounds he was posted to the USAS's 148th Aero Squadron, which was operating the Sopwith Camel under the operational control of the RAF's 65th Wing. Springs did not return to fly with No.85 Squadron, so the diary/account from this point onwards is almost certainly complied through letters, hearsay and snippets of conversation picked up from other squadron members mixed in with extracts from his own diary and letters of his experiences whilst with the 148th.
195. In *Mac's Memoirs: The Flying Life of Squadron Leader McGregor* it states that "on June 26th the squadron suffered the loss of Lieutenant Springs, one of the two remaining Americans. He was shot down on the British side of the lines, and after he left hospital, he was transferred to No.148th American Aero Squadron." McGregor was leading the patrol that day and made a claim for one destroyed and one driven down (see Appendix XVI).
196. As well as Springs's return, the unit also no doubt celebrated the fact that Lieutenant John Warner had claimed a Pfalz DIII on 29 June 1918.
197. The engagement described here cannot be matched up with any of No.85 Squadron's surviving combat reports. It is known that Cunningham-Reid claimed one Pfalz DIII on 29 June (see Appendix XVII) and Lieutenant J. Dymond one on 30 June (Appendix XVIII).
198. Mathews is likely to be Alex Matthews, a No.84 Squadron pilot who was at Oxford with Springs.
199. In maintaining the narrative of No.85 Squadron, it is worth pointing out at this stage that Cunningham-Reid was in combat the following day, 3 July, following which he claimed one destroyed, a Pfalz DIII – see Appendix XIX.
200. Oliver Bennet (USA) trained in the UK and was posted to No.84 Squadron RFC before heading to the 148th Aero Squadron.
201. Henry R. Clay (USA) also trained in the UK and was posted to No.43 Squadron before the 148th.
202. Major Harold Fowler originally enlisted in the RFC in 1915 before transferring to the US Air Service in October 1917. He was the Air Service Liaison Officer to the BEF from May 1918, and therefore responsible for the co-ordination of postings of US personnel to RFC/RAF squadrons and to US aero squadrons under the command of the British.
203. Marvin Kent Curtiss (USA), trained at Oxford before being assigned to the 148th Aero Squadron. He was shot down on 24 August whilst flying with Springs and became a PoW.
204. John H. Fulford (USA) trained at Oxford before his posting to the 148th.
205. Linn H. Fortser (USA) also trained at Oxford before his posting to the 148th. He was killed in action on 2 September 1918.
206. George C. Whiting (USA) trained at Oxford before being posted to No.43

NOTES AND REFERENCES

Squadron RFC. From there he joined the 148th.
207. Eroll H. Zistell (USA) trained at Oxford, was posted to No.43 Squadron and the 148th. He was wounded in action on 3 October 1918.
208. Field Kindley (USA) trained at Oxford before joining No.65 Squadron RFC prior to the 148th.
209. William T. Clements (USA) trained at Oxford. After training he was assigned direct to the 148th.
210. Walter B. Knox (USA) was another Oxford trainee prior to his first posting to the 148th, with which he remained until the end of the war.
211. Merton L. Campbell (USA) trained at Oxford, after which he was posted to No.54 Squadron RFC. From this unit he joined the 17th Aero Squadron. Campbell was killed in action on 23 August 1918.
212. Having been trained at Oxford, George C. Dorsey (USA) was posted direct to the 148th. He was wounded in combat on 16 September 1918.
213. No.85 Squadron was in action against Fokker biplanes on 7 July, following which Longton, Horn and Mannock put in claims; no losses can be found for No.85 on this day – see Appendices XX and XXI for more detail. Lieutenant John Warner claimed a Fokker DVII although no combat report survives.
214. It is stated in some sources that Major Edward 'Mick' Mannock arrived on No.85 Squadron on 5 July 1918; see Shores, Franks, and Guest, *op cit*, p.376.
215. Lieutenant John M. Goad was killed in action whilst flying with No.48 Squadron in a Bristol F2b on 27 June 1918.
216. Having arrived on the squadron, Mannock was soon making an impression, as the following quote from *Mac's Memoirs: The Flying Life of Squadron Leader McGregor* shows: "His ability as a fighter and leader of patrols so appealed to Mac that Mannock and he became fast friends (and this is unusual as seldom was anyone mentioned by name in these). Mac's letters contained frequent references to this outstanding airmen."
217. William Ludwig Deetjen (USA) was posted to No.104 Squadron. He was killed in action flying a D.H.9 on 30 June 1918.
218. Lieutenant W.H. Longton and Lieutenant Dymond of No.85 Squadron were both in action on 10 July, sharing one aircraft destroyed, an Hannover two-seater; see Appendix XXII.
219. Although not mentioned in this account, with some dates not being detailed, a patrol from No.85 Squadron was in action on 13 July with Dixon as flight commander. The squadron's pilots shot down one Pfalz, as confirmed by Lieutenant Callahan (he also claimed one enemy aircraft which he witnessed crash). It was also on this date that Lieutenant William Robertson was shot down and killed.
220. Mannock's and Randall's flight was involved in a hectic combat on 14 July against a mixture of Fokker, Pfalz and Albatross types; some of the enemy aircraft were from Jasta 40. The other patrol was led by Captain Dixon. Claims were made by Mannock (Appendix XXIII), Randall (Appendix XXIV), Rorison (Appendix XXV) and Longton (Appendix XXVI). It is likely that Second

NOTES AND REFERENCES

Lieutenant H. Marshall was shot down by Carl Degelow of Jasta 40 and became a PoW.

221. Tiny Dixon was George Clapham Dixon, who was posted No.40 Squadron. Due to bad weather, there was little flying until 19 July. When it cleared, Mannock led a patrol during which he spotted an Albatross two-seater; this he shot down in the Merville area (see Appendix XXVII).

222. Mannock was involved in two combats on 20 July, claiming one camouflaged two-seater and a Fokker biplane; see Appendix XXVIII.

223. Springs wrote home on 30 July with news of Mannock's death: "Major Mannock has been killed – 85's new C.O who took Major Bishop's place. He has 65 Hun planes to his credit and a bullet from the ground got him. He and my old friend Inglis the New Zealander went down to 50 feet after a Hun and got him but on the way back he saw Mannock's machine burst into flames. Too bad. Next to Bishop he was the world's finest and his loss is a blow personally as well as officially." See David K. Vaughan, *op cit*, p.189.

224. On 22 July, Mannock's patrol was attacked by five triplanes. Mannock claimed one; see Appendix XXIX.

225. Though the date is not covered in the book, on 24 July McGregor was leading the top layer of a patrol at 11,000 feet with the remaining S.E.5s led by Randall acting as a decoy lower down. The result was McGregor, Longton, Randall and Ralston all making claims – combats which are detailed in Appendices XXX though to XXXIII. Of note is the fact that First Lieutenant Lawrence Callahan made his last claim with the squadron on this day, a Fokker DVII, before being posted to the 148th Aero Squadron.

226. Inglis Combat Report for 26 July 1918 can be seen at Appendix XXXIV.

227. On 9 July, Major James Thomas Byford McCudden VC, DSO and Bar, MC and Bar, had taken-off from Auxi-le-Château in a S.E.5a to fly to his new squadron. Just after take-off the aircraft plunged into the ground and caught fire. Although McCudden was pulled clear he had sustained a fractured skull and died that night at a casualty clearing station.

228. Extracts from Springs's log book note that he was on a patrol with the 148th Aero Squadron on 30 July when he was "chased home by two Fokkers". With reference to No.85 Squadron, on the same date he wrote: "I was talking to Larry [Callahan who was still on 85] on the phone and he was shot down the other day but succeeded in getting the Hun first". The latter was probably on 24 July when Callahan claimed a Fokker DVII.

229. Springs's next combat appears to be on 3 August 1918, when he claimed a Fokker DVII. Randall did make a claim for a two-seat Albatross on 31 July (see Appendix XXXV).

230. Captain M.C. McGregor was leading a patrol of three S.E.5s on 3 August; they were above a decoy being led by Lieutenant Longton. McGregor claimed one Fokker biplane (Appendix XXXVI).

231. Springs claimed a Fokker DV11 south-east of Ostend.

232. Captain Walter Hunt Longton was awarded the AFC in June 1918 for his

NOTES AND REFERENCES

valuable work as a test pilot before he joined No.85 Squadron. He survived the war but was killed in an air race at Bournemouth in June 1927.
233. Captain Alexander Augustus Norman Dudley Pentland was with No.87 Squadron.
234. Lieutenant W.H. Longton and Captain A.C. Randall made claims against Albatross two-seaters on 9 August – see Appendices XXXVII and XXXVIII respectively.
235. Springs was in combat on 13 August with the 148th Aero Squadron claiming one Fokker DVII.
236. This may be a reference to Lieutenant T.C. Martin who was killed in action whilst flying a S.E.5a of No.85 Squadron on 12 August 1918.
237. Lieutenant George Herbert Zellers (USA) was killed in action whilst flying a No.20 Squadron Bristol F2b on 30 July 1918.
238. Lieutenant Philip Dietz (USA) was killed in action whilst flying a D.H.9 of No.99 Squadron on 30 July 1918.
239. Lieutenant Rueben Lee Paskill (USA); killed in action whilst flying a S.E.5a with No.32 Squadron on 9 August 1918.
240. No.85 Squadron moved to Allonville on 13 August, then Bertangles later in the month.
241. Captain Spencer Horn was in action on 14 August and claimed a Fokker DVII near Guyencourt. First Lieutenant Walter Chalaire was previously a New York Herald reporter, who subsequently flew D.H.4s with 202 Squadron. He was shot down on this date flying D.H.4 D8402.
242. First Lieutenant Galloway Cheston was killed in action on 29 July 1918 while flying a D.H.9 with No.206 Squadron.
243. Lieutenant Clayton Knight (USA) was one of the Oxford Cadets and he flew on the Western Front with No.206 Squadron, only to become a prisoner of war. He went on to provide much of the original artwork used in early editions of *War Birds*.
244. From Springs's log book we can note that he was involved in a ground attack sortie with the 148th on 22 August 1918. His combat report states: "Dropped 8 bombs from a height of 1500 feet on a road just Southwest of Ecoust St. Menin. Fired 900 rounds at transport on road southwest of Queant." See David K. Vaughan, *op cit*, p.206.
245. No.85 Squadron was in the thick of the action against nine Fokker biplanes on this date, having set a trap by flying three patrols at differing heights as taught to them by Mannock. The result was four claimed destroyed and two driven down (See Appendix XXXIX). Longton claimed a Fokker DVII near Haut Allaines during this engagement – his last claim with No.85 before a posting to No.24 Squadron.
246. Lieutenant John Warner of No.85 Squadron claimed a Fokker DVII near Suzzanne/Péronne on 23 August 1918.
247. Two airmen of No.85 Squadron were killed on 24 August – Airmen II Class Adam Mann and Private Patrick Docherty. They were victims of an enemy

bombing raid on Bertangles airfield where No.85 was based at the end of August.
248. Lieutenant Richard Brumbach Reed (USA) was killed whilst training in a D.H.9 on 5 June 1918.
249. First Lieutenant Irvin David Shaw (USA) was killed in action whilst flying a Bristol F2B with No.48 Squadron on 9 July 1918.
250. Lieutenant Alexander Mathews (USA) of No.84 Squadron was killed in an air raid on Bertangles on 24 August 1918 – it is likely that it was the same raid that killed the two members of No.85 Squadron's groundcrew.
251. Lieutenant A.F. Bonnalie (USA) was awarded a DSO and American Distinguished Service Cross whilst flying with No.211 Squadron. See TNA AIR 696/21/20/211.
252. Lieutenant Paul Thayer Iaccaci (USA) was awarded a DFC whilst flying with No.20 Squadron. He was credited with seventeen victories.
253. First Lieutenant Henry Robinson Clay (USA) DFC, awarded the American DSC, flew with the 148th and claimed five and two shared destroyed with one out of control.
254. Captain Elliott White Springs (USA) DFC, DSC (US) claimed a total of sixteen flying with 85 Squadron RAF and the 148th Aero Squadron.
255. First Lieutenant George Augustus Vaughn Jnr (USA) DFC, DSC (US) flew with No.84 Squadron and the 17th Aero Squadron.
256. Lieutenant Merton L. Campbell served with No.54 Squadron and then the 17th Aero Squadron. He was killed in action on 23 August 1918 and was awarded a Silver Star to wear on his Victory Medal.
257. Lieutenant William D. Tipton (USA) was captured on 26 August 1918.
258. Lieutenant Marvin Kent Cutis (USA) was captured on 24 August 1918.
259. Lieutenant Fred T. Shoemaker (USA) trained at Oxford before being posted to the 11th Aero Squadron. He was shot down and captured on 14 September 1918.
260. Lieutenant Grady R. Touchstone (USA) was assigned to No.98 Squadron, followed by No.40 Squadron. He was shot down and became a prisoner of war on 8 August 1918.
261. First Lieutenant Roland H. Ritter (USA) was killed whilst flying with No.1 Squadron on 24 August 1918.
262. Private Charles Thomas Evans was killed whilst with No.209 Squadron in August 1918.
263. Private Ernest Adams was killed while flying as an Observer in a No.48 Squadron Bristol F2B on 26 June 1918.
264. For completeness, Appendix XL onwards are the remainder of the surviving combat reports for No.85 Squadron from the period of the end of the diary until the Armistice.

Select Bibliography

Cole, Christopher (Ed.), *Royal Air Force Communiques 1918* (Tom Donovan, London, 1990).

Cunningham, G.H., *Mac's Memoirs: The Flying Life of Squadron Leader McGregor* (A.H. and A.W. Reed, New Zealand, 1937).

Douglas, Sholto, *Years of Combat* (Collins, London, 1963).

Franks, Norman and Saunders, Andy, *Mannock: The Life and Death of Major Edward Mannock, VC, DSO, MC, RAF* (Grub Street, (London, 2008).

Grinnell-Milne, Duncan, *Wind in the Wires* (Hurst & Blackett, Ltd, London, 1933).

Hamer, A.C., *A Short History of No. 85 Squadron* (Services Publishing, Northants, undated).

Hobson, Chris, *Airmen Died in the Great War* (J.B. Hayward & Son, 1995).

Jones, James Ira Thomas 'Taffy', DSO, MC, DFC and Bar, MM, *King of Air Fighters* (Nicholson and Watson, London, 1934).

Jones, Wing Commander I., *Tiger Squadron: The Story of 74 Squadron RAF in Two World Wars* (W.H. Allen and Co. Ltd., London, 1955).

Kilduff, Peter, *Billy Bishop VC, Lone Wolf Hunter – The RAF Ace Re-examined* (Grub Street, London, 2014).

Lewis, Cecil, *Sagittarius Rising* (Peter Davis, London, 1936).

MacLanachan, William 'McScotch', *Fighter Pilot* (Newnes, London, 1920).

Middlebrook, Martin, *The Kaiser's Battle* (Pen and Sword, Barnsley, 2007).

Money, R.R., *Flying and Soldiering* (Ivor Nicholson & Watson, London, 1936).

Oughton, Frederick, *The Personal Diary of 'Mick' Mannock VC, DSO (2 Bars), MC (1 Bar)* (Spearman, London, 1966).

Philpott, Ian, *The Birth of the Royal Air Force* (Pen and Sword, Barnsley 2013).

Rawlings, John, *Fighter Squadrons of the RAF and Their Aircraft* (MacDonald, London, 1969).

Shores, Christopher, Franks, Norman, and Guest, Russell, *Above the Trenches, A Complete Record of the Fighter Aces and Units of the British Empire Air Forces 1915-1920* (Grub Street, London, 1990).

Vaughan, David K., *Letters from a War Bird, The World War 1 Correspondence of Elliott White Springs* (The University of South Carolina Press, 2012).

SELECT BIBLIOGRAPHY

Williamson, H.J., *The Roll of Honour RFC and RAF 1914-1918* (Naval and Military Press, Dallington, 1992).

Winter, Denis, *First of the Few: Fighter Pilots of the First World War* (University of Georgia Press, 1983).